The Killing of Gaza

The Killing of Gaza

Reports on a Catastrophe

Gideon Levy

VERSO

London • New York

First published by Verso 2024
Texts © Haaretz 2014–2024
Introduction and afterword © Gideon Levy 2024
Introduction and afterword translation © David B. Green 2024

1 3 5 7 9 10 8 6 4 2

Verso
UK: 6 Meard Street, London W1F 0EG
US: 388 Atlantic Avenue, Brooklyn, NY 11217
versobooks.com

Verso is the imprint of New Left Books

ISBN-13: 978-1-80429-750-6
ISBN-13: 978-1-80429-751-3 (UK EBK)
ISBN-13: 978-1-80429-752-0 (US EBK)

British Library Cataloguing in Publication Data
A catalogue record for this book is available from the British Library

Library of Congress Cataloging-in-Publication Data

Names: Löwy, Gideon, 1953- author.
Title: The killing of Gaza : reports on a catastrophe / Gideon Levy.
Description: London ; New York : Verso, 2024.
Identifiers: LCCN 2024021610 (print) | LCCN 2024021611 (ebook) | ISBN
   9781804297506 (trade paperback) | ISBN 9781804297520 (US EBK) | ISBN
   9781804297513 (UK EBK)
Subjects: LCSH: Palestinian Arabs—Gaza Strip. | Arab-Israeli
   conflict—1993- | Gaza Strip—History—21st century. | Israel—Politics
   and government--21st century.
Classification: LCC DS110.G3 L68 2024 (print) | LCC DS110.G3 (ebook) |
   DDC 956.05/3—dc23/eng/20240603
LC record available at https://lccn.loc.gov/2024021610
LC ebook record available at https://lccn.loc.gov/2024021611

Typeset in Sabon by MJ&N Gavan, Truro, Cornwall
Printed and bound by CPI Group (UK) Ltd, Croydon, CR0 4YY

To Catrin, whom I met in Gaza

Contents

Contents

Contents

Contents

Contents

2024

Contents

Contents

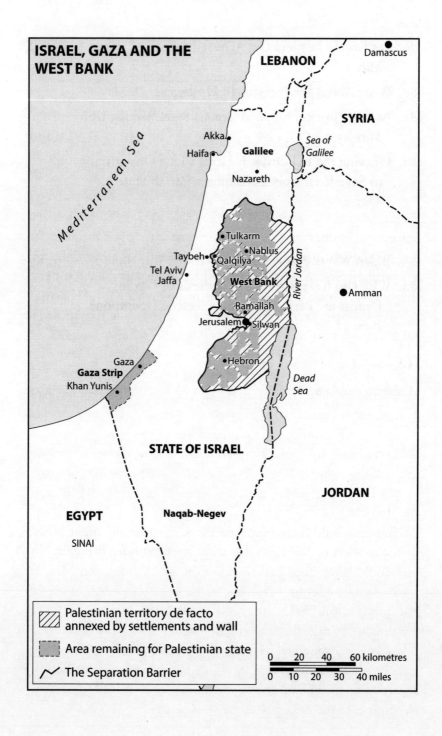

ISRAEL, GAZA AND THE WEST BANK

LEBANON

Damascus

SYRIA

Mediterranean Sea

Akka
Haifa
Galilee
Sea of Galilee
Nazareth

Tulkarm
Taybeh
Qalqilya
Nablus
River Jordan

Tel Aviv
Jaffa
West Bank

Amman

Ramallah
Jerusalem
Silwan

Gaza
Gaza Strip
Khan Yunis

Hebron

Dead Sea

STATE OF ISRAEL

JORDAN

EGYPT
Naqab-Negev

SINAI

Palestinian territory de facto annexed by settlements and wall

Area remaining for Palestinian state

The Separation Barrier

0   20   40   60 kilometres
0 10 20 30 40 miles

Introduction: Catastrophe Report

Saturday October 7, 2023, was a warm and pleasant autumn day in Israel. In addition to being Shabbat, it was also the day of a Jewish festival, Simhat Torah, which comes at the end of the three-week period of holidays that begins with Rosh Hashana, the Jewish new year. A little before 6 a.m., prior to sunrise, I headed out for my morning jog in Hayarkon Park, near my home in northern Tel Aviv.

It was the hour when the park begins to awaken on the weekend, and I recognized all of the morning sounds: the cries of the jackals beginning to subside; the call of a night bird, which also gives off its final cry just prior to sunrise. Now those voices were replaced by the chirpings of the morning birds and the grumblings of the wild geese, while at the same time the bicyclists began appearing, together with the walkers, the fishermen and the runners.

Nothing could have prepared the jackals or the night birds, or the runners or bicyclists, for what the next hour brought. No one could have imagined that within a half hour, the Middle East would undergo a tectonic shift, one whose full meaning and implications, even four months later, as I write these lines, are difficult to take in. When I left home that morning, I couldn't possibly have imagined that when I returned, earlier than usual, Israel would be a different place. In Gaza as well, no one was yet aware of what type of disaster was destined to befall them over the course of the next few days.

Somewhere around 6:30, the sound of air-raid sirens began to pierce the park, from one end to the other, rising and falling, drowning out all other sounds. The park came to a standstill. Not that we had never heard warning sirens here before; in May 2021, the same wail of a missile alert was sounded here, warning of incoming rockets from the Gaza Strip, some seventy kilometers away. This time, however, there was no advance inkling of approaching hostilities. Israelis were living their lives in tranquility, under a prime minister, Benjamin Netanyahu, who had succeeded in lulling the public into the belief that there was no need to deal with the Palestinian question, that we were "covered" by the Abraham Accords, the 2020 agreements that normalized relations between Israel and several Arab states.

In the exposed public park, with nowhere to take cover, the shriek of the missile alarm was especially frightening. A small group of people found themselves gathering next to the giant trunks of the park's ancient eucalyptus trees, in the dubious hope that these could protect them.

A moment later, the sound of an explosion was heard in the sky above the park. A thin trail of white smoke above our heads indicated that an incoming rocket had been intercepted by a defensive weapon. As I began running in the direction of home, another alert sounded, followed by the boom of a second explosion above, even more deafening than the first one. If after the first explosion it had been possible to believe that we were witnessing some sort of technical malfunction, it was now clear that something bigger was underway. Silence prevailed in the park, which quickly emptied of visitors, and I, too, hurried to make my way home.

That didn't stop me later from going out for my regular swim in the neighborhood pool, however. The usual swimmers were there, but on the gates of the center I was amazed to find signs directing people to the closest bomb shelter, signs that hadn't been necessary just a day earlier. This ratcheted up the war atmosphere a level, a feeling that reached its peak in the shower, following my swim, when the staff told me to finish up and leave. They were shutting the facility, after receiving reports that terrorists had penetrated Israel's south and taken control of entire communities there. I was the last swimmer in the Tel Aviv learner's pool before it closed down for a period of weeks.

Back home, the upstairs neighbor, with whom we normally shelter in the safe space of the apartment next door, informed us that 100 deaths had already been reported in the south.

A hundred dead? Not possible. In Israel, when you talk about "100 dead," the reference is to Israelis, and casualties of that magnitude in a single morning was not something we were accustomed to. That was what happened to Gazans. We were dumbfounded and shocked. Who could then have imagined that the number of dead that day would end up being 12 times higher?

The astonishment only intensified when a clip showed up on the social networks that seemed to belong to the world of fiction: A white pickup truck with Gaza license plates is seen tooling around the streets of an Israeli town, carrying some dozen men, Arabs by appearance, who are firing off machine guns in every direction. My initial reaction was that the video had to be a fake—maybe it was from Afghanistan. But the town in the clip whose streets were now controlled by local mujahideen was clearly Israeli, down to the yellow plates on the parked cars. Quickly enough it became clear: The town was Sderot, near the border with Gaza, and the truck was far from being the only Gazan vehicle that had invaded Israel. Our jaws dropped.

Thus began my war of October 7, with a sense of disbelief. Within hours, I would have to begin writing my regular column for the Sunday edition of *Haaretz*. For a brief period, I continued to see the violation, by a band of barefooted young people seated on the backs of motorcycles and bicycles, of the sophisticated and intimidating border barrier that separated Gaza from Israel—a feat of construction that had cost the country billions of shekels—as a hopeful sign. My first associations were to the images from the toppling of the Berlin Wall, and the joy that greeted them worldwide. The Berlin Wall was breached on

November 9, 1989, and now, on October 7, 2023, the fence surrounding the world's largest ghetto was falling before our very eyes. In the opinion column I wrote, I gave expression to this hope. But in short time, the editorial-page editor called me with the news of horrifying actions being reported from the south, including mass murder and the abduction of hundreds of Israeli citizens to Gaza. The comparison to the fall of the Berlin Wall itself crumbled.

In its place I instead wrote the following:

Behind all this lies Israeli arrogance; the idea that we can do whatever we like, that we'll never pay the price and be punished for it. We'll carry on undisturbed.

We'll arrest, kill, harass, dispossess, and we'll protect the settlers busy with their pogroms. We'll visit Joseph's Tomb, Othniel's Tomb and Joshua's Altar in the Palestinian territories, and of course the Temple Mount—over 5,000 Jews on Sukkot alone.

We'll fire at innocent people, take out people's eyes and smash their faces, expel, confiscate, rob, grab people from their beds, carry out ethnic cleansing and of course continue with the unbelievable siege of the Gaza Strip, and everything will be all right.

. . .

On Saturday, Israel saw pictures it has never seen before. Palestinian vehicles patrolling its cities, bike riders entering through the Gaza gates. These pictures tear away at that arrogance. The Gaza Palestinians have decided they're willing to pay any price for a moment of freedom. Is there any hope in that? No. Will Israel learn its lesson? No.

On Saturday they were already talking about wiping out entire neighborhoods in Gaza, about occupying the Strip and punishing Gaza "as it has never been punished before." But Israel hasn't stopped punishing Gaza since 1948, not for a moment.

After 75 years of abuse, the worst possible scenario awaits it once again. The threats of "flattening Gaza" prove only one thing: We haven't learned a thing. The arrogance is here to stay, even though Israel is paying a high price once again.

. . . We now have to cry bitterly for the Israeli victims, but we should also cry for Gaza.

Gaza, most of whose residents are refugees created by Israel. Gaza, which has never known a single day of freedom.

In the days that followed, I began traveling around the devastated Israeli south—Gaza was off-limits to me, just as it had been for the preceding 16 years—and I was shocked by the sights I encountered. Bodies were still laid out outside the kibbutz homes, and the smell of fire and death was present everywhere. Endless lines of burnt-out cars and houses told just a fraction of the story. I entered a handful of homes on Kibbutz Be'eri, and later in Nir Oz, and the story they told was a difficult one. Streams of blood everywhere, destruction, ashes and devastation, all interspersed with reminders of the lives that were being lived here until Saturday morning. A bottle of wine remained on a Sabbath dinner table, a half-empty coffee cup from breakfast that morning, a note posted to a refrigerator reminding of an upcoming dentist's appointment, a copy of the October 6 edition of *Haaretz* open to an article with the headline: "The limits of capitulation." The sights were not easy to take in.

Beyond the breached fence, inside Gaza, the Israel Defense Forces began aerial bombing, sowing death and destruction. I hoped that it might end with that. I hoped that Israel might punish the perpetrators of the massacre in the south by exacting its revenge from the air, and that that would conclude this round of hostilities. But, of course, this was only the beginning of what would become the most difficult period in Gaza's history since the Nakba, in 1948—and the most turbulent in Israel's history since the state's founding, that same year. I found myself more isolated than ever.

The months that followed presented Israel with a jolt unlike any it had known to date. The initial reaction of shock and stupefaction, combined with a sense of humiliation from the attack, was quickly replaced by trauma and with it a desire to punish and wreak revenge on everyone responsible for that trauma—and those who weren't as well. And as the extent of the death and destruction in the communities in the south became clearer, nearly all Israelis united around the aspiration to punish Gaza in its entirety.

In every past war, and there have been many, public support has initially been broad. But as each war dragged on, doubts began to appear, followed by criticism and even opposition from certain parts of the public. Not this time. Four months into the war, and Israel is almost unanimous in its wholehearted support for the war and its continuation. There is sharp opposition to the government of Benjamin Netanyahu, expressions of protest against the policy that to date has not brought about the release of all of Israel's captives in Gaza, but there is almost a complete lack of opposition to carrying on with the war, even as it exacts a heavy toll not only on the people of Gaza, but also from Israel, which only grows more distant from achieving its declared military goals, as if it were marching in place toward a receding target.

This then is a very special war, a war that faces no opposition or criticism within Israel. There have, for example, been nearly no public draft refusers. Nor have there been examples of pilots or army officers sending letters expressing their unwillingness to serve, to shell or to bomb, phenomena that have characterized previous rounds of fighting in Gaza. Israel's cruelest war has also turned out to be a war based on almost complete consensus. There are several reasons for this.

First, of course, is what happened on October 7. There is no one in Israel who wasn't shocked by the events of that day. The shock quickly turned into a license to kill anyone in Gaza and to leave no stone unturned. To most Israelis, everything became permissible and legitimate, even morally acceptable. "After what they did to us, there's nothing forbidden to us," became the raison d'être of this war. We wrapped ourselves in such self-justifications as "Every state has the right to defend itself"; "Any country would have responded the way Israel has"; "There are no innocents in Gaza, everyone is Hamas"; "If there is no opposition to

Hamas in Gaza, it's evidence that everyone supports the organization"; "Israel stands at the front line of world civilization
against Islamic fundamentalism"; up through "This is Israel's
second War of Independence—if we don't succeed in deterring
them this time, our very existence is at stake." Such slogans were
adopted by almost the entire public. They were accompanied by
a sick and violent rhetoric from the radical right, a movement
that now became politically acceptable. In Europe, some of the
things that were being said here would have led to the outlawing
of any party or organization whose representatives expressed
themselves that way.

Not only the extremist and settler right wing gave free rein to
racist sentiments. A retired general, a respected and mainstream
former head of Israel's National Security Council, proposed
dealing with the problem of Gaza by way of spreading diseases
there; another general, someone who sees himself assuming the
leadership in the near future of one of the left-wing, Zionist
parties, suggested starving the population of Gaza to death.
The commentator on Arab affairs of one of Israel's popular TV
channels suggested that Israel had erred in its management of
the hostilities. What it should have done was to kill 100,000
residents of Gaza in a single, initial blow.

The problem was less the very fact that such things were
being said than the widespread legitimacy that such ideas were
afforded. Israel was taking on the positions of the radical right
wing to an extent even greater than it had prior to October 7. At
the same time, any expression of solidarity with the Palestinians
in their suffering led to police investigations, to arrests and, at
times, to the people expressing them being put on trial, even as
the fascistic statements from the right incurred no such sanctions.
Incitement to genocide could be heard coming from the mouths
of senior government ministers, and even from the country's
president, as was stipulated several months later, at the end of
January 2024, by the judges of the International Criminal Court
in The Hague.

The second reason for the legitimizing of the nationalist right was provided by Israel's media, which at the time of the war's outbreak was already at a low point.

A few words on that subject: Israel has quite a free media landscape, with most media outlets in private hands. We still have a military censor, but it is focused on guarding military secrets and in that sense has a marginal impact. It is, then, a free and independent press—and for that reason its betrayal of its own mission and duty is so grave.

When the world mocks the Putinist Russian media for their coverage of the war in Ukraine, it does so with good reason. Consumers of the media in Russia have never received a full picture of reality, as the media serve the state. But there is a type of media that is even more pathetic and dangerous than that: one that voluntarily relinquishes its objectivity. It does this without pressure or threats from the legal system, the army, the government or the secret services. Israel's media have for the most part volunteered to serve the cause of national propaganda.

On October 7, 2023, the media ceased to be journalists and instead became an agent of nationalistic and militant emotions, stirring up and inciting, a ministry of propaganda, a public relations agency for the army, responsible for elevating the morale of a public at war. It's not even the "Quiet, there's shooting going on" approach of the past; this is "There's shooting going on, we need to hide the whole truth." The Israeli media donned fatigues, saluted the army and began to toe the line.

Gaza is hidden from the eyes of the Israeli public. Anybody watching television in Omaha, Nebraska, and any newspaper reader in Inverness, Scotland, has been witness to more of what is happening in the Gaza Strip than the average Israeli viewer, despite the fact that the lattermost probably lives within an hour's drive from the border with Gaza. The local TV stations turned into nonstop news studios, as happens during war, and began broadcasting the war 24/7. And what it broadcast was and remains to this day propagandistic: Israelis are being fed an exclusive diet of stories of soldiers' heroism and about their fall on the fields of battle; of tales of the Israeli captives in Hamas's hands and their families; about a rear that has suffered greater losses in this war than in its predecessors; of tales of sacrifice and personal stories, kitsch and death.

Only one specific reality is being concealed from Israelis: the reality of Gaza. Life and death in this stricken land is not covered in the newspapers, and it's not on TV. There's almost no coverage of Gaza, except in the pages of *Haaretz* and on some dissident websites. The children dying on the muddied, bloodstained floors of the hospitals of Gaza; the hundreds of thousands of uprooted individuals who must run for their lives from one place to another, with nowhere to hide; the tens of thousands of dead and wounded; the complete obliteration of entire sections of the Strip; the indiscriminate killing, the blind shelling and bombing as well as the shooting by snipers of innocent people who are waving white flags; and also, the hungry, the thirsty and the sick. The forlorn tent cities as winter approached. The children who barely survived on contaminated water and a lone piece of bread each day. The elderly who were driven from place to place, riding on the backs of halting donkey-drawn wagons from the north of the Strip to the south. The dead bodies left abandoned in the streets. This is a humanitarian disaster of enormous proportions, and it is not covered in Israel. Almost at all. Occasionally there will be a laconic report, mainly of statistics, little more than lip service offered out of obligation, without any professional sense of proportion indicating that in Gaza there is a human disaster transpiring that is almost beyond description, and that the people living there are in fact human beings.

Israel's media have acted this way for years. They conceal the occupation and whitewash its crimes. No one orders them to do this; it is done willingly, out of the understanding that this is what their consumers want to hear. For the commercial media, that is the top and foremost consideration. In this way Israel's media have become the most important agent for dehumanization of the Palestinians, without the need for censorship or a government directing it to do so. The media take on this role in the knowledge that this is what their customers want and expect of it. They don't want to know anything about what their state and army are carrying out, because the best way to be at peace with the reality of occupation, apartheid and war is with denial, suppression and dehumanization.

There is no more effective and tried means to keep alive an occupation so brutal and cruel as dehumanization via the media. Colonialist powers have always known this. Without the systematic concealment, over dozens of years, and the dehumanization, it may well be that public opinion would have reflected greater opposition to the situation among Israelis. But, if you don't say anything, don't show anything, don't know anything and have no desire to know anything, either, if the Palestinians are not truly human—not like us, the Israelis—then the crime being committed against them goes down easier, can be tolerated.

The October 7 war brought all of this to new heights. Israel's media showed almost nothing of what was happening in Gaza, and Israelis saw only their own suffering, over and over, as if it was the only suffering taking place. When Gazans counted 25,000 fatalities in less than four months, most of them innocent noncombatants, in Israel there was no shock. In fact, shock was not permitted, because it was seen as a type of disloyalty. While in Gaza 10,000 children were killed, Israelis continued to occupy themselves exclusively with their captives and their own dead. Israelis told themselves that all Gazans were Hamas, children included, even the infants, and that after October 7, everyone was getting just what they deserved, and there was no need to report on it. Israelis sank into their own disaster, just theirs.

The absence of reporting on what was happening in Gaza constituted the Israeli media's first sin. The second was only slightly less egregious: the tendency to bring only one voice into the TV studios and the pages of the printed press. This was a voice that supported, justified and refused to question the war. Any identification with the suffering in Gaza, or worse, any call to end the war because of its accumulating crimes, was not viewed as legitimate in the press, and certainly not by public opinion. This passed quietly, even calmly, in Israel.

In Israel, people were fine with not having to see Gaza. The Jewish left only declined in size, great numbers of people said they had the scales removed from their eyes—that is, October 7 led to their awakening from the illusions, the lies, the preconceptions they had previously held. It was sufficient for a single cruel attack for many on the left to have their entire value system overturned. A single cruel attack was sufficient to unite Israelis around a desire for revenge and a hatred not only of those who had carried out that attack, but of everyone around them. No one considered what might be taking place in the hearts and minds of the millions of Palestinians who have been living with the occupation's horrors for all these dozens of years.

What kind of hatred must exist there, if here in Israel such hatred and mistrust could sprout up after a single attack, horrific as it may have been. This "waking up" among the left has to raise serious questions about its seriousness and resilience. This wasn't the first time that the left crumbled in the face of the first challenge it encountered.

The second wave of potential opposition to the war should have arisen among Israel's Palestinians, the "Israeli Arabs," as they are referred to here. But the Israeli Arabs have been in a state of paralysis since October 7, paralysis caused by fear and near-existential terror. Not since 1948 have they been so fearful. They were scared to come into contact with Jews, they were scared to leave their homes or go to work, they were scared to speak Arabic among the Jewish public. They were scared to breathe, sensing that they were en masse suspected of supporting the Nukhba—the name of the Hamas commando force that invaded Israel that day.

Many Arabs were called in for questioning by the police because of a tweet or other social media post in which they had expressed human concern regarding their own relatives in Gaza, or solidarity with them. Many were fired or laid off from their work, as an Israeli McCarthyism took hold of the public arena, and with it a witch hunt. Under such circumstances, one couldn't expect the Arabs to express opposition to the war or to head to the streets to demonstrate against it. They were silenced and silent.

This is the state Israel was in when it entered the war: bloodied, grieving, fearful and wounded; surprised, shocked, astounded, insulted, humiliated and desirous of revenge; united and of one mind regarding the justice of the war and any means it employed. Democracy, for which so many Israelis had struggled over a period of many months in the face of the Netanyahu government's judicial coup, suffered far greater damage during the war than it would ever have undergone as a result of the coup. The democratic camp, the opponents to Netanyahu, and those who battled against his legal "reforms" were themselves complicit in their silence regarding the blow to that democracy.

It was made clear, and not for the first time, that on the basic questions, Israelis aren't genuinely divided into left and right, that the gaps between those two camps are far smaller than generally described, if they exist at all. And it is all the more disturbing to recognize that this is the case, in light of the impressive wave of protest during the months leading up to the war. When it comes to the fundamental issues that shape the state, there is nearly wall-to-wall agreement. Occupation and apartheid, which characterize the essence of the Israeli regime more than anything else, are accepted and agreed upon by the vast majority of Israelis—on the right, the center and among the Zionist left—and in that regard there is no real opposition.

In times of war, the absence of opposition, or even of alternative voices, is especially striking. Zionism, which today means a belief in Jewish superiority between the (Jordan) river and the (Mediterranean) sea, is accepted by all, and anyone who does question it is perceived to be a traitor. Thus, it has been the case that over the nearly 17 years during which Gaza has been under siege, there have never been any real opponents to the policy, neither on the right nor among the Zionist left. There was a consensus that a blockade of 2 or 3 million people is something normal and legitimate, and therefore something that could continue indefinitely.

On October 7, Israelis learned that this wasn't the case. Not that they will now internalize that truth or draw the proper conclusions from the heavy price they paid on that day. The price paid by the Palestinians is in any event far heavier.

Since June 2007, the Gaza Strip has been under a blockade imposed by Israel, with the collaboration of Egypt. Prior to the blockade, too, Israel controlled the sea and air space of Gaza, and also imposed a policy of separation of the West Bank and Gaza. When Hamas came to power in the Strip, the closure took on a new form, tighter and crueler.

As early as March 2008, several international NGOs published a report in which they characterized the humanitarian situation in Gaza as being at its worst since the beginning of the occupation, in 1967. From there, matters only deteriorated.

I don't recall the first time I visited Gaza, but my last visit I remember well. It was some eighteen years ago. I went to the nursery school run by Indira Gandhi, as the Palestinian teacher who ran it had been named by her parents. We arrived just in time for the funeral of her colleague Najawa Halif, a 20-year-old who had been killed in the nursery school's minibus, as witnessed by 20 children in the class whom she had been accompanying on their way to school. When we arrived, we were given a description of what had happened. One of the kids drew a picture of a woman lying in the street, bleeding, the children standing dazed behind her, and an Israeli tank shelling them all. At the time, I had no idea that this picture might become my last image from Gaza.

A few days after our visit, Israel tightened the closure, and Israeli journalists were now prohibited from entering the Strip. Since then, I have not been inside. I had loved my visits to Gaza, demanding and draining as they had been. I loved the people of Gaza, on the coast of the Mediterranean, who together with their parents and their children had endured an indescribable measure of suffering in their lives, and who nonetheless always retained a sense of humor, warmth, candor, solidarity and humanity. I have no idea to what extent these attributes survived those endless years of ghetto life, which surely took their toll on both the personal and societal levels.

Sometimes I wonder about the fate of the children from Indira Gandhi's nursery, about what happened to them. Nearly 18 years have passed. How many of those innocent children are still alive? How many have survived the war? How many survived the years of siege? How many ever even ventured beyond the borders of Gaza, the world's largest open-air prison? Some of the children born during the winter of 2006 might have been among the Hamas commandos who invaded Israel's south on October 7.

One thing is for sure: None of them forgets that terrible day in November 2006 when they rode together with their young teacher, Najawa, and an Israeli missile hit the vehicle carrying them, and killed her before their very eyes. What scar did that leave on their hearts? It's not hard to guess. Statistically speaking, it's hard to imagine that all the children who were in nursery school in 2006 survived to the present. One can only hope that some of them did. Perhaps they are today refugees of this war, just as their grandparents were refugees in 1948, and they are living in a tent in Rafah, or perhaps lie wounded on a hospital floor in Khan Yunis. Maybe some of them had the luck to have left Gaza in the interim.

Thoughts about these hundreds of victims of the occupation whom I met during the years I was able to visit Gaza will not leave me in peace. They have only multiplied since the outbreak of war. From 1987 until Gaza became off-limits to Israeli journalists, at the end of 2006—nearly 20 years—I would visit Gaza regularly to document life and death under Israeli occupation. The occupation changed its nature over time, but it always left Gaza as occupied territory, deprived of freedom and basic human rights.

When I look today at my reporter's notes from Gaza, I get goosebumps. Room No. 602, Shifa Hospital, June 24, 1994. An elderly father. Missing one hand and both of his legs, he attempts with his lone surviving hand to adjust the position of his paralyzed 13-year-old son, so as to help prevent the development of pressure sores. After that, he injects a syringe of pulverized food he himself prepared into a tube that is inserted directly into the child's stomach. An Israeli sniper shot the boy, Ala Nimr, in the head. By his side lay another child who had been badly wounded after being shot in the head, and next to the two of them was Abed el Nabi Abu Arman, 32, who had also been shot in the head. Two children and one adult in Room 602, and all three had been reduced to a vegetative state. Who remains today from their families?

I think about Iman Haju. In May 2001, she was killed when an Israeli artillery shell hit her grandparents' home, in Khan Yunis. She was 3½ months old at the time of her death, apparently making her the youngest *shahid* whose demise I ever covered. Today, Iman would have been 23. Maybe she would have survived the latest war, maybe not. And what would her life under siege have been like?

Nothing has changed: the same policy, the same twitchy finger on the trigger, the same dehumanization, the same occupation and the same evil. In 2024 as in 2001.

My inability to enter Gaza is painful to me. It's not possible to forget Gaza, and it's not possible to cover the occupation without being there, for it is there that it exists in its cruelest form and where the worst victims reside. There's no place I would more like to visit, at least once more, than Gaza, and it's doubtful that that will happen, unless I enter on the back of an IDF tank.

I wouldn't recognize Gaza today—or what remains of it. It's doubtful that any of my friends or acquaintances there are still alive. But I think about them. About Munir and Sa'id, two cab drivers who served as my regular and dedicated fixers in the Strip, with whom I covered hundreds of kilometers over the years traveling from Beit Lahia to Rafah and back. Munir grew up working as a laborer in the Hatikvah shuk in Tel Aviv. He worked at a butcher's and he still remembered the prayers said by observant Jews on the eve of Yom Kippur, the holiest of Jewish holy days, as they perform the Kapparot ritual—of swinging over the head, and then sacrificing, a chicken. The last time I spoke with him was a year ago, when Israel allowed several tens of thousands of Gazans to enter the country to work. Munir, who had already suffered a stroke that left him half paralyzed, asked me whether I could arrange a work permit for him here. He said that he understood that he could no longer do physical work, but wondered if he might not be able to work as an interpreter for Israeli employers and their Gazan workers.

That broke my heart. Since then, I haven't heard from him, and during the war I have been afraid to call him. I was afraid that the phone would not be answered, or that someone else would pick up in his place. And if he did answer, just what would I tell him? That he should hang in there? That maybe we would yet again be able to tool around Gaza in his old-model Mercedes, which had already driven more than a million kilometers, driving on vegetable oil already used to fry falafel, which spewed out smelly black exhaust, in place of regular gasoline, unavailable under the siege. Once Hamas came to power, I used to smuggle in cans of beer for Munir, as it was contraband in Gaza. He didn't know what to do with the used cans, because Hamas had informers everywhere who would have snooped into his garbage bin to look for evidence of alcohol consumption.

And how could I forget Sa'id, he of the mournful face, who would wait for days at the Erez checkpoint, hoping desperately for the appearance of a foreign journalist who might require his services so that he could earn a few shekels. But the foreign press had lost interest in Gaza; Israeli journalists had done so even prior to that, and Sa'id would wait for entire days in vain with his car that had been damaged by an Israeli missile, waiting for the reporters who didn't come.

I had countless unforgettable moments in Gaza. Sailing on the fishing boat in the dark of night in the sea that had also been closed to Palestinians by the Israeli siege, and a final fish meal at the home of one of the fishermen. The beautiful young Gaza girl who was struck with brain cancer, and who had to wait for months for an entry permit to Israel for medical treatment—and who, by the time the permit was forthcoming, was mortally ill. In her final days, I took her from the hospital where she had finally been admitted for a quick tour of Tel Aviv. At the Ramat Gan Safari Park, she saw a green lawn for the first time in her life. She died a few days later.

And the people who were left disabled after being shot and wounded. And the bereaved parents who had lost the most valuable thing in their lives, and the refugees who had lost everything, and who despite the impossible conditions, managed to hold onto a modicum of dignity and even some joie de vivre. I will remember them all.

But all are overtaken by the current war, the hardest and cruelest of Israel's wars on Gaza. It broke out because of the October 7 attack on the settlements in Israel's south, a vicious assault that killed without distinction civilians and soldiers, women, men, old people and babies; but since then, the war has lost all reasonable proportion required for punishment, revenge or future deterrence. Everything has already been said about this war, which as I write these words, still rages, but I have no doubt that, by any criterion, it should have come to its conclusion a long time ago.

Israel went to war without an endgame, without any strategy for "the day after." Assume that all of its goals are attained—the captives are released and Hamas is destroyed—what happens then? Who is supposed to lead Gaza? Who will oversee its reconstruction, after the vast devastation it has suffered? I am writing these words on a cold winter day in Tel Aviv, in a home with heating. What is supposed to happen now in the tents in which 2 million Gazans have taken shelter? The mind is boggled by the thought.

The mind is boggled because the majority of Israelis believe that the horrors of October 7 gave their army license to carry out killing and destruction of such terrifying proportions in Gaza. As if this mass killing in some way advances the cause of Israel's security. After all, in every family in Gaza that has lost someone, and there are tens of thousands of these, the next generation of Gazans will grow up, a generation that will never forget and never forgive: the children who made their way through the bodies in hope of identifying their parents, and the parents who rummaged through the bodies in search of their children; the families that made their way southward, dragging with them their elderly, their sick, their disabled, on foot and in worn-out wheelchairs or in wagons drawn by donkeys, journeying into the unknown and the impossible in search of a safe place in Gaza; the orphans in the hospitals who have no family members left, families that were erased. How will it be possible for them to forget or to forgive the people who carried out all that destruction?

Hamas cannot be absolved of criminal responsibility toward its own people, after it embarked on this war before making provisions to protect the civilian population. Hamas abandoned the people of Gaza, leaving them without bomb shelters, without a decent medical infrastructure, and without appropriate stores of food. Those who knew how to accomplish the construction of such a complex and ingenious network of tunnels even while the Strip was under siege could and should have gone to the trouble of building hospitals and defenses for its people in advance. Hamas did not do that, and for that it cannot be forgiven.

Where does all of this leave us? The international awakening, following the start of the war, concerning the issue of a two-state solution is a cause of simultaneous despair and hope. Despair, because it is critically late in coming, and hope, because at least it seems there is awareness in the world of the urgency of finding a solution to the Palestinian issue. Over and over, it has seemed as if both Israel and the world had forgotten the problem, and then, just when it seems as if the world is preoccupied with other issues, it emerges and again seizes its attention. Perhaps the profound concern that the October 7 war has evoked globally will be sufficient to instill the recognition that, so long as no solution is found, one that will be implemented by way of international involvement, the Palestinian question will continue to threaten world peace.

One thing needs to be clear: Without international involvement, there will never be a solution. Israel is not going to wake up one morning and say to itself or to anyone else, *The occupation, the siege, and the apartheid are not good—let's bring them to an end.* What has not taken place during 56 years of occupation, and during the hundred years of the Zionist movement, is not going to happen of its own volition.

But the two-state solution is dead. Seven hundred thousand Jewish settlers in the West Bank and East Jerusalem killed it. That was their intention, and it was also the intention of successive governments, which did not stand in the way when settlers expropriated stolen lands. Today, there's no place for a Palestinian state to come into existence, unless it's going to be a Bantustan. The world may well know this, but, if so, it's pretending that it doesn't. It's nice that Great Britain's foreign secretary, Lord Cameron, announced that soon his country would recognize Palestine, but how does that change the fate of a single refugee in the Jenin refugee camp? What is the significance of a recognition that can't actually be implemented on a practical level?

I would be happy to be proven wrong. I would be the first to celebrate that, because the two-state solution was once, indeed, the logical and implementable choice.

What remains, however, is the possibility of a single state. In fact, we have had a single state since 1967. Two peoples equal in population live between the Jordan River and the sea. The problem is that the one-state regime in place now is one of apartheid, in which the Jews have all the rights and the Palestinians none. What remains is to change the regime. Two options remain: democracy between the Jordan and the Mediterranean, or apartheid between the Jordan and the Mediterranean. I am not aware of any other practical possibility.

The path forward is long, but we must begin—the one-state solution at least offers a vision to aspire to, a dream to dream of. Continuing to make declarations about two states, knowing that such a solution is no longer feasible—that there is no place for the Palestinian state to establish itself—is tantamount to making the occupation eternal.

It's still too early to know if the current war has brought the solution closer or rather distanced it. The two peoples are today more distant from each other than they have been any time since the dawn of Zionism. Emotions are running high, the hatred, the fear and the mistrust have reached terrifying levels. There are those in Israel who are discussing Nazi-like solutions, ranging from expulsion up to physical annihilation. In the Palestinian territories, and also in growing circles around the world, there is talk of a free Palestine between the Jordan and the sea. One that has no place for Jews.

It is said that it's always darkest before the dawn.

Four months into the war, and the scenes are horrifying. The northern part of Gaza is almost empty of residents and empty of houses that remain intact. The south is a place of unthinkable crowding, hunger and thirst, and the twin threats of epidemics and of bombing that doesn't spare any part of the Strip. Both the south and the north of Israel also have seen many of their residents turned into refugees, with tens of thousands at least temporarily forced to leave their homes. As opposed to Gazans, however, those in Israel should have someplace to return to. Most of their homes are still standing. That's not the case for most Gazans. Their homes are now flattened lots, piles of ruins and ashes.

As an Israeli who is connected by every thread of his soul to his land, from which he has never emigrated and never considered emigrating from; as the son of parents who escaped from Europe in 1939, leaving behind their entire lives, and the grandson of a grandfather and grandmother who didn't survive; and as a man who believes in the universal values and has spent an entire professional career covering the betrayal of those values by our state—I cannot not help but feel a profound shame over what my country is doing to Gaza.

It's worth mentioning just what Gaza is: a haven for refugees who have been beaten down by Israel over and over, from 1948 to the present day. Uprooted and refugees once, twice and a third time, and today refugees yet again. The same policy and the same morality that led to their expulsion from their villages in 1948 has now led to their being forced from their homes into exile for a second or third time. Along the length of the coast, from Jaffa to Gaza City, not a single Palestinian village or town remains intact. All were wiped off the earth, and today it is the descendants of their residents who make up the current wave of refugees, who have had to pile into tents or into ruins of buildings, or in hospitals or even cemeteries, just like their parents did in 1948.

There's no absolving Israel of responsibility, even if Hamas shares in the guilt. Similarly, the international community cannot be absolved of responsibility for what is happening, for its generous and unconditional support for Israel, on the one hand, and for its apathy and lack of action. There are now 2.3 million people, among the most miserable humans living today on the face of the earth, one of the only communities in existence that lacks citizenship in any state, or basic rights or freedom. Now they are also without homes or property, and at times also without family, after their relations were killed, crowded into the southern end of their already bursting land, without any present or future, and without any reason for hope.

But maybe an opportunity is germinating now, without our even being aware of it. Maybe, against all odds, and despite all reason or realistic thought, a different reality can rise out of the ashes. Now, though, the key will not be in the hands of either Israelis or Palestinians. They are no longer capable of the task. The challenge is now at the world's doorstep.

Hayarkon Park has returned to a modicum of routine. The jackals are howling, the night bird whistles at dawn, the runners and bicyclists appear before the first light, and one could think that things are like they were before. But as I write these lines, the discomfiture that descended on Israelis in October has not yet dissipated; something very heavy hangs in the air, even if the conversation in the park has reverted to what it was before.

Once again, the conversations are about mortgages and the high cost of living, the next vacation and the next purchase of a jeep, at a time when only an hour's drive from here people continue to be the target of bombs, through no fault of their own.

But everything here is fragile, liable to change at any moment, on both sides of the Erez crossing, the barrier that separates two different worlds, Gaza and Israel, which have grown so much more distant from each other during the past cursed year.

PART I

2014

What Were We Thinking?

July 10

Following the kidnapping of three teenage Israelis in the territories and their murder, Israel wildly arrested some 500 Palestinians, including members of parliament and dozens of freed prisoners who had no connection to the kidnapping. The army terrorized the entire West Bank with a dragnet and mass arrests, whose declared aim was "to crush Hamas." A racist campaign raged on the internet and led to a Palestinian teenager being burned alive. All this followed Israel's punitive campaign against the effort to establish a Palestinian unity government the world was prepared to recognize, its violation of its commitment to release prisoners, a halt to the diplomatic process and a refusal to propose any alternate plan or vision.

Did we really think the Palestinians would accept all this submissively, obediently and calmly, and that peace and quiet would continue to prevail in Israel's cities?

What exactly were we thinking? That Gaza would live forever in the shadow of Israeli (and Egyptian) caprice, with the restraints sometimes loosened a bit, or sometimes painfully tightened? That the biggest prison in the world would carry on as such? That hundreds of thousands of its residents would remain cut off forever? That exports would be blocked and fishing restricted? What exactly are 1.5 million people supposed to live on? Is there anyone who can explain why the blockade of Gaza,

THE KILLING OF GAZA

even if partial, continues? Can anyone explain why its future is never discussed? Did we think that all this would continue, and Gaza would accept it submissively? Anyone who thought so was a victim of dangerous delusions, and now we are all paying the price.

But please, just don't act surprised. Just don't raise hell about the Palestinians raining rockets on Israeli cities for nothing—such luxuries are no longer acceptable. The dread Israeli citizens are feeling is no greater than the dread felt by hundreds of thousands of Palestinians who in recent weeks waited in terror for soldiers to break down their doors and invade their homes in the middle of the night, to search, trash, destroy, humiliate and then snatch a member of their household. The fear we're experiencing is no greater than the fear felt by Palestinian children, several of whom were killed needlessly by Israeli Defense Forces fire in recent weeks. The trepidation Israelis feel is certainly less than that felt by Gaza residents, who have no Color Red warnings, no "secure spaces" and no Iron Dome to save them, only hundreds of scary sorties by the Israeli Air Force that end in destruction and the death of innocents, including the elderly, women and children who have already been killed during this operation, as during all its predecessors.

The operation already has a childish name, "Protective Edge." But Operation Protective Edge started and will end like all previous operations—giving us no protection and no edge. The media and public opinion want Palestinian blood and destruction, with the center-left supporting this, of course, as it always has at the beginning. But what comes next has already long been written in the chronicles of all the senseless and bloody Gaza operations through the ages. What's amazing is that from operation to operation, nobody seems to learn anything, and nothing changes except the weapons.

Prime Minister Benjamin Netanyahu indeed acted with restraint at first and was duly praised for it, but it was impossible for him to hold back in the face of the rocket fire from Gaza. Everyone knows—Netanyahu wasn't interested in this confrontation. Is that so? If he really wasn't interested in it, then he should have seriously pursued diplomatic negotiations. But he didn't, so it's clear he really *was* interested in confrontation. The headline of his newspaper, *Israel Hayom*, declared, "Take it all the way." But Israel will never achieve the insane end desired by *Israel Hayom*, certainly not by force.

"There's no way to evade punishment for what's been happening here for almost 50 years," the writer David Grossman told the Israel Conference on Peace this week. That was only a few hours before the next in the series of crimes and punishments landed on Israeli civilians, who are so innocent and blameless.

Death to Arabs

July 13

The goal of Operation Protective Edge is to restore calm; the means: killing civilians. The slogan of the Mafia has become official Israeli policy; Israel sincerely believes that if it kills hundreds of Palestinians in the Gaza Strip, quiet will reign. It is pointless to destroy the weapons stores of Hamas, which has already proved capable of rearmament. Bringing down the Hamas government is an unrealistic (and illegitimate) goal, one that Israel does not want: It is aware that the alternative could be much worse. That leaves only one possible purpose for the military operation: death to Arabs, accompanied by the cheering of the masses. The Israel Defense Forces already has a "map of pain," a diabolical invention that has replaced the no less diabolical "bank of targets," and that map is spreading at a sickening pace. Watch Al Jazeera English, a balanced and professional television channel (unlike its Arabic sister station), and see the extent of its success. You won't see it in Israel's "open" broadcast studios, which as usual are open only to the Israeli victim, but on Al Jazeera you will see the whole truth, and perhaps you will even be shocked. The bodies in Gaza are piling up, the desperate, constantly updated tabulation of mass killing that Israel boasts of, which already numbers dozens of civilians, including 24 children as of noon on Saturday; hundreds of people injured, in addition to horror and destruction. One school and one hospital have already been bombed. The aim is to strike homes, and no amount of justification can help: It's a war crime, even if the IDF calls them "command-and-control centers" or "conference rooms." Granted, there are strikes that are much more brutal than Israel's, but in this war, which is nothing other than mutual attacks on civilians—the elephant against the fly—there aren't even any refugees. In contrast to Syria and Iraq, in the Gaza Strip the inhabitants do not have the luxury of fleeing for their lives. In a cage, there's nowhere to run.

Since the first Lebanon war, more than 30 years ago, the killing of Arabs has become Israel's primary strategic instrument. The IDF doesn't wage war against armies, and its main target is civilian populations. Arabs are born only to kill and to be killed, as everyone knows. They have no other goal in life, and Israel kills them. One must, of course, be outraged by the modus operandi of Hamas: Not only does it aim its rockets at civilian population centers in Israel, not only does it position itself within population centers—it may not have an alternative, given the crowded conditions in the Strip—but it also leaves the Gazan civilian population vulnerable to Israel's brutal attacks, without seeing to a single siren, shelter or protected space. That is criminal. But the barrages of the Israeli Air Force are no less criminal, on account of both the result and the intent: There isn't a single residential building in the Gaza Strip that is not home to dozens of women and children; the IDF cannot, therefore, claim that it does not mean to hurt innocent civilians. If the recent demolition of the home of a terrorist in the West Bank still stirred a weak protest, now dozens of homes are being destroyed, together with their occupants. Retired generals and commentators on active duty compete to make the most monstrous proposal: "If we kill their families, that will frighten them," explained retired Maj. Gen. Oren Shachor, without batting an eyelid. "We must create a situation such that when they come out of their burrows, they won't recognize Gaza," others said. Shamelessly, without question—until the next Goldstone investigation finds that the IDF targets civilians.

A war with no goal is among the most despicable of wars; the deliberate targeting of civilians is among the most atrocious of means. Terror now reigns in Israel as well, but it's unlikely there is a single Israeli who can imagine what it's like for Gaza's 1.8 million inhabitants, whose already miserable lives are now totally horrific. The Gaza Strip is not a "hornet's nest"; it is a province of human desperation. Hamas is not an army, far from it, despite all the fear tactics; if it really did build such a sophisticated network of tunnels there, as is claimed, then why doesn't it build Tel Aviv's light rail network, already.

The 1,000-sortie and 1,000 tons-of-explosives marks have almost been reached, and Israel is waiting for the "victory picture" that has already been achieved: Death to Arabs.

What Does Hamas Want?

July 20

After we've said everything there is to say about Hamas: that it's fundamentalist; that it's undemocratic; that it's cruel; that it does not recognize Israel; that it fires on civilians; that it's hiding ammunition in schools and hospitals; that it did not act to protect the population of Gaza—after all that has been said, and rightly so, we should stop for a moment and listen to Hamas; we may even be permitted to put ourselves in its shoes, perhaps even to appreciate the daring and resilience of this, our bitter enemy, under harsh conditions.

But Israel prefers to shut its ears to the demands of the other side, even when those demands are right and conform to Israel's own interests in the long run.

Israel prefers to strike Hamas without mercy and with no purpose other than revenge. This time it is particularly clear: Israel says it does not want to topple Hamas—even Israel understands that instead it will have Somalia at its gates—but it is also unwilling to listen to Hamas's demands. Are they all "animals"? Let's say that's true. But they are there to stay. Even Israel believes that's the case, so why not listen?

Last week 10 conditions were published, in the name of Hamas and Islamic Jihad, for a 10-year cease-fire. We may doubt whether these were in fact the demands of those organizations, but they can serve as a fair basis for an agreement. There is not one unfounded condition among them.

Hamas and Islamic Jihad demand freedom for Gaza. Is there a more understandable and just demand? There is no way to end the current cycle of killing, and not have another round in a few months, without accepting this. No military operation by air, ground or sea will bring a solution; only a basic change of attitude toward Gaza can ensure what everyone wants: quiet.

Read the list of demands and judge honestly whether there is one unjust demand among them: withdrawal of Israel Defense Forces troops and allowing farmers to work their land up to the fence; release of all prisoners from the Gilad Shalit swap who have been rearrested; an end to the siege and opening of the crossings; opening of a port and airport under UN management; expansion of the fishing zone; international supervision of the Rafah crossing; an Israeli pledge to a 10-year cease-fire and closure of Gaza's air space to Israeli aircraft; permits to Gaza residents to visit Jerusalem and pray at the Al-Aqsa mosque; an Israeli pledge not to interfere in internal Palestinian politics such as the unity government; and opening Gaza's industrial zone.

These conditions are civilian; the means of achieving them are military, violent and criminal. But the (bitter) truth is that when Gaza is not firing rockets at Israel, nobody cares about it. Look at the fate of the Palestinian leader who had had enough of violence. Israel did everything it could to destroy Mahmoud Abbas. The depressing conclusion? Only force works.

The current war is a war of choice, a choice that we had. True, after Hamas started firing rockets, Israel had to respond. But as opposed to what Israeli propaganda tries to sell, the rockets didn't fall out of the sky from nowhere.

Go back a few months: the breakdown of negotiations by Israel; the war on Hamas in the West Bank following the murder of the three yeshiva students, which it is doubtful Hamas planned, including the false arrest of 500 of its activists; stopping payment of salaries to Hamas workers in Gaza; and Israeli opposition to the unity government, which might have brought the organization into the political sphere. Anyone who thinks all this would simply be taken in stride must be suffering from arrogance, complacence and blindness.

Terrifying amounts of blood are being spilled in Gaza—and in Israel to a lesser extent. It is being spilled in vain. Hamas is beaten down by Israel and humiliated by Egypt.

The only chance for a real solution is exactly the opposite of the way Israel is going. A port in Gaza to export its excellent strawberries? To Israelis this sounds like heresy. Here once again, the preference is for (Palestinian) blood over (Palestinian) strawberries.

Go to Gaza, See for Yourself

August 10

Can we possibly conduct a discussion, however brief, that is not saturated with venomous hatred? Can we let go for a moment of the dehumanization and demonization of the Palestinians and speak dispassionately of justice, leaving racism aside? It's crucial that we give it a try.

In the absence of hatred, one can understand the Palestinians. Without it, even some of Hamas's demands might sound reasonable and justified. Such a rational discourse would lead any decent person to clear-cut conclusions. Such a revolutionary dialogue might even advance the cause of peace, if one may still dare say such things. What are we facing? A people without rights that in 1948 was dispossessed of its land and its territory, in part by its own fault. In 1967 it was again stripped of its rights and lands. Ever since it has lived under conditions experienced by few nations. The West Bank is occupied and the Gaza Strip is besieged. This nation tries to resist, with its meager powers and with methods that are sometimes murderous, as every conquered nation throughout history, including Israel, has done. It has a right to resist, it must be said.

Let's talk about Gaza. The Gaza Strip is not a nest of murderers; it's not even a nest of wasps. It is not home to incessant rampage and murder. Most of its children were not born to kill, nor do most of its mothers raise martyrs—what they want for their children is exactly what most Israeli mothers want for their own children. Its leaders are not so different from Israel's, not in the extent of their corruption, their penchant for "luxury hotels" nor even in their allocating most of the budget to defense.

Gaza is a stricken enclave, a permanent disaster zone, from 1948 to 2014, and most of its inhabitants are third- and fourth-time refugees. Most of the people who revile and who destroy the Gaza Strip have never been there, certainly not as civilians. For 8 years I have been prevented from going there; during the preceding 20 years I visited often. I liked the Gaza Strip, as much as one can like an afflicted region. I liked its people, if I may be permitted to make a generalization. There was a spirit of almost unimaginable determination, along with an admirable resignation to its woes. In recent years Gaza has become a cage, a roofless prison surrounded by fences. Before that it was also bisected. Whether or not they are responsible for their situation, these are ill-fated people, a great many people and a great deal of misery.

Despairing of the Palestinian Authority, Gazans chose Hamas in a democratic election. It's their right to err. Afterward, when the Palestine Liberation Organization refused to hand over the reins of power, Hamas took control by force.

Hamas is a national-religious movement. Anyone who champions hatred-free dialogue will notice that Hamas has changed. Anyone who manages to ignore all the adjectives that have been applied will also discern its reasonable aspirations, such as having a seaport and an airport. We must also listen to scholars who are free of hatred, such as Bar-Ilan University Mideast expert

Prof. Menachem Klein, whose reading of Hamas goes against the conventional wisdom in Israel. In an interview with the business daily *Calcalist* last week, Klein said Hamas was founded not as a terror organization but rather as a social movement and should be viewed as such even now. It has long since "betrayed" its charter and conducts a lively political debate, but in the dialogue of hatred there is no one to hear it.

From the perspective of the dialogue of hate, Gaza and Hamas, Palestinians and Arabs, are all the same: They all live on the shore of the same sea and share the single goal of throwing the Jews into it. A less primitive, less brainwashed discussion would lead to different conclusions. For example, that an internationally supervised port is a legitimate and reasonable goal; that lifting the blockade on the Strip would also serve Israel; that there is no other way to stop the violent resistance; that bringing Hamas into the peace process could result in a surprising change; that the Gaza Strip is populated by human beings, who want to live as human beings.

But in Hebrew, "Gaza," pronounced 'Aza, is short for Azazel, which is associated with hell. Of the multitude of curses hurled at me these days from every street corner, "Go to hell/Gaza" is among the gentler ones. Sometimes I want to say in response, "I wish I could go to Gaza, in order to fulfill my journalistic mission." And sometimes I even want to say: "I wish you could all go to Gaza. If only you knew what Gaza is, and what is really there."

War, What War?

September 18

Sometime this summer, between the singer Ninet's getting pregnant and getting married, a war went on here. It ended and was forgotten.

That's how it is in a bipolar society that fluctuates between mania and depression, between scandal and festivities, between commemoration and suppression. One moment the entire nation is an army at war, the next it's as if nothing had happened. Even the Israeli sacrifice has been forgotten—not to mention the killing and destruction in Gaza, which were never really mentioned in the first place. Except for the direct victims, nobody seems to remember that a war went on.

It goes without saying that nobody is drawing conclusions or learning lessons (except for defense officials and their extortion of the state budget). Israel is jubilant again. It has returned to its nonsense as if there hadn't been a war, as if another will never break out, as if an hour's drive from Tel Aviv there was no devastated swath of land, smashed by Israel's hands, where the inhabitants are suffering horribly while Israel is exultant.

Gaza hasn't forgotten. There's a whole list of people who can never forget: the 1,500 orphaned children; the 3,000 wounded children; the 1,000 crippled children; the 110,000 residents still crowded in UNRWA shelters in inhumane conditions; the tenants of the 18,000 buildings destroyed or badly damaged, leaving 2.5 million tons of debris nobody knows what to do with; the 450,000 people without water and the 360,000 who, according to the World Health Organization, are suffering from PTSD after our bombardments. None of these people can be expected to forgive, and this isn't the first time this has happened.

Not only has Israel forgotten they exist, the world might be about to abandon them. Apart from Norwegian foreign minister Børge Brende, no foreign statesman has bothered to visit Gaza to see the scope of the disaster. That's because of Hamas; you know, those guys the Quartet [the UN, EU, US and Russia] once decided, in one of its most idiotic decisions, not to talk to. Then there's Israeli propaganda, which compares Hamas to the Islamic State.

Israel's suppression and the international abandonment of Gaza are intolerable. Even if we put aside the crassness and moral blindness in Israel, which wasn't shocked by a single event during the war, it's impossible to comprehend the complacency afterward.

There was a war here—Israel paid, too, and already it's forgotten? No soul-searching? No cost-benefit analysis, at least? The public debate hasn't found time for questions that should disturb every Israeli, like, uh, was it worth it? What did Israel get out of this war? What's it doing to prevent the next one? Do not disturb, Israel is busy with zero-VAT on apartment purchases.

Nothing has been learned. The negotiations with Hamas should be resumed soon, but there are no signs that Israel plans to find the time. Far-reaching proposals to solve Gaza's problems are a pipe dream. The "victor" will continue to push the "defeated" into a corner, leaving it in ruin and misery, which will lead to another round of violence sooner or later. And the world isn't lifting a finger—either in the form of pressure on Israel (and Egypt) to stop the blockade, or for the urgent rebuilding of Gaza.

Winter is coming, so what will happen to the tens of thousands of homeless people? The negotiations' resumption date is approaching, so what will happen if the talks aren't resumed, or if they flame out? Is anybody thinking about it?

When the rockets return to Israel's skies—and they will if the blockade isn't lifted—Israel will again pretend to be surprised, offended and angry. How dare they! Then the planes will bomb and the big guns will fire shells—another inevitable round of fighting that will lead nowhere.

For such is Israel's arrogance and complacency. There was a war, it was forced on us, of course, and we won. Maybe there will be another one soon, though it also won't be Israel's fault, and Israel will win again. In the meantime, we have Ninet.

2015

A Futile Report

June 25

The United Nations Human Rights Council's report did not tell us anything new. We did not need to wait a year to know that Israel (and Hamas) committed war crimes; there was no need to impanel a committee to know that Israel went wild in Gaza; there was no need to bother Judge Mary McGowan Davis in order for her to tell us that it is unacceptable to drop a one-ton bomb in the middle of a neighborhood. We have known that for a long time.

The UN report also did not tell us anything new about Israel's response. There was no need to publish it to know the scope of unreceptiveness and denial within Israeli society, the low level to which the Israeli media stooped in finally allowing itself to become an agent of propaganda, and the lack of interest that all this killing and destruction in Gaza arouse in Israel. We have known all that for a long time.

The world knows the fundamental truths, and every commission repeats them like a parrot, and nothing changes: Israel ignores international law. It is convinced that it applies to all countries, except for itself. According to its combat theory, when the life of one Israeli soldier is at stake it is all right to wreak havoc with everything, and when Israel says everything, it means everything. There is no chance Israel will change its doctrine of death and destruction, unless it is punished severely. Therefore this report, like all its predecessors, has no value at all.

If the Goldstone Report, which described in harsher colors a less brutal attack, did not prevent Operation Protective Edge, then why do we need all these reports? If the international community, which knew in real time what the Israel Defense Forces was doing in Gaza, did not respond immediately with actions that would stop it, then there is no reason for these commissions of inquiry after the fact.

If in the wake of this commission, too, the international community does not take practical steps against war criminals, then there is no further reason for commissions. The next war, the next commission, the next Israeli attack on Gaza will certainly come, and it will be more vicious than the previous one, with McGowan Davis or without her. Yesterday the American judge already mumbled: If Israel had only cooperated with her, then the conclusions would have been different. Your honor, are you hinting that your commission did not present the full truth? Would the testimony of a few of those injured by Qassam rockets in Sderot have changed the picture? And is it even right to draw a comparison between a non–state organization, whose weapons are primitive and inaccurate, and the most sophisticated arsenal of weapons in the world which could have hit, or in principle not hit, to its heart's desire?

But these pro-Israeli murmurings of the commission did not change, of course, the depth of the Israeli denial: IDF soldiers killed 500 children—and we are having a tea party. They killed 1,500 civilians—and here they are competing to see who will ignore it more.

Is the headline "hypocrisy report" stronger than the "report for terror rights," in the media that does not have any information on what happened, not even false information, only false adjectives? And the height of it is: "Report with blood on its hands," according to Naftali Bennett, a person who knows a thing or two about blood on the hands. True, these spasms point to the loss of the way, but they also won't prevent the next Shujaiyeh [a neighborhood in Gaza City that was especially battered during last summer's war].

The report will be quickly forgotten. Gaza will once again remind us of its existence and its distress in the only way it has left, with the only weapon at its disposal, the weapons of war crimes. Israel will once again act in the only way it knows how, a way which causes much more terrifying war crimes.

An Australian judge, a South African professor and a Belgian prosecutor will establish a commission of inquiry, Israel will once again boycott it and in Gaza thousands of bereaved families will once again sit under the ruins of their homes and wail helplessly at the international community, which was supposed to protect them—and instead it establishes commissions.

No Picnic, No Tragedy

July 2

Defense Minister Moshe Ya'alon said there is no humanitarian distress in Gaza. The defense minister also said that the situation in Gaza "isn't pleasant." If that's his definition of the situation in Gaza, then it's not pleasant to live in a country in which Ya'alon is defense minister.

Ever since Dov Weissglas, an adviser to then prime minister Ehud Olmert, spoke in 2006 of tightening the blockade on Gaza and putting its residents "on a diet," we haven't heard such inhumane remarks about everything that's going on only an hour's drive from Tel Aviv. Ya'alon, the newest (and strangest) friend of the lesbian, gay, bisexual and transgender community, said that there is no siege on Gaza, and in the same breath said he would not allow the recently launched flotilla to enter the (unbesieged) Strip. But his remarks about the lack of humanitarian distress reveal the true world of this Dr. Strangelove from the cowshed of Kibbutz Grofit.

Ya'alon is right; no one is dying of starvation in Gaza. Cattle feed is indeed being supplied to the biggest pen in the world. There is no humanitarian disaster. But something else is happening in Gaza, something apparently unique to its residents; they aren't satisfied with just food. These are strange people who have needs other than just a pita with onion and tomato. For example, sometimes they need water, which is becoming increasingly polluted at a shocking pace; it's no longer possible to drink the salty water coming out of the taps. Ya'alon would surely be willing to send bottles of mineral water through the transit points, but it's not certain that everyone in Gaza can afford to live off bottled mineral water.

Gaza's sewage is flowing directly into the sea—the same sea as Israel's—and its groundwater is becoming filthy at an alarming rate. Gaza's residents also need electricity—can you believe such a thing? In the upscale community of Maccabim-Reut [in central Israel] they've never heard of such people, but that's Gaza's spoiled population for you. And they only get electricity for a few hours a day, in this heat. Ya'alon surely remembers that Israel bombed the only power plant in Gaza and destroyed it, but even this is not a (humanitarian) disaster.

Even before the horrors of Operation Protective Edge, a report by the United Nations Relief and Works Agency stated that by 2020 Gaza would be unfit for human habitation. But who knows what could happen by 2020—God is great, and so is Ya'alon. Meanwhile, the residents of Gaza, some 2 million people, if we are permitted to call them that, have a few other needs. Some 100,000 survivors of the warrior Ya'alon's last campaign have yet to return to their destroyed homes, not one of which has been rebuilt. They are homeless, crowding into the homes of relatives, taking shelter in the rubble or in UNRWA shelters (which house around 10,000 of them). But what are they complaining about? They're not on the street.

Around a thousand of their children have been left disabled for life from that war, but that's not a tragedy, either. One can, of course, live with the poverty and unemployment data that have no parallel: 43 percent unemployment among the adults and 60 percent among young people, with 80 percent receiving welfare and 40 percent beneath Gaza's poverty line, which is not the same poverty line as in Maccabim-Reut. A disaster? No.

Nor is it a disaster that all the university and college graduates there have no chance of ever finding work in their fields. Another lost Gaza generation—no picnic, but no tragedy, either.

Neither is the siege a picnic. Eight years without anyone but the privileged few able to leave Gaza—not to study, not to work, not to visit anyone, not to attend funerals or family celebrations. Not even to just take a break from the inferno. This isn't considered a disaster, or even a siege.

Ya'alon has a solution: Let them export strawberries instead of Qassam rockets. That's an idea. Earlier this year, Israel for the first time allowed Gaza to export a certain amount of agricultural produce. The number of trucks that left the Strip was less than 5 percent of the number that used to leave before the non-blockade. Unpleasant, but no disaster.

2016

**It's Never Israel's Fault: Two Gazan Children
Are Dead and Their Story Goes Untold**

March 17

She was 6, he was 10, blood siblings. Did they die in their sleep?
Did they wake up right before the missile struck their home?

Did they hear the plane and take fright before they died,
perhaps attempt to flee? Was there anyplace to go? What did they
do before going to bed on their last night alive? Did they dream
of anything on their last night? Did they have any dreams? Israa
and Yassin, girl and boy, sister and brother, between Friday and
Saturday in the Gaza Strip. Between Friday and Saturday in the
Gaza Strip, 2:30 a.m., long-suffering and bombardment-weary.

Beit Lahia woke up in terror to the ill-boding sounds of a
plane. My friend M. told me his children jumped from their beds
in fright. Israel was avenging the firing of four Qassam rockets
into Israel hours earlier. The rockets landed in open areas and
caused no damage. Between Friday and Saturday in the Gaza
Strip, Israeli Air Force planes struck four targets, "Hamas terror
installations."

The plane flew over Beit Lahia, and the pilot released the
bombs. The hits were good. The screen in the plane did not show
Yassin, dead, or Israa, dying.

One of the "terror installations" was the house of Israa and
Yassin Abu Khoussa. "House" is an exaggeration; a ragged asbes-
tos roof, ragged clothes on the windowsill, thin mattresses on

the floor covered by cheap blankets, some of them now soaked in blood. Here Israa and Yassin were born, here they lived and here they died. On the floor of the room that was hit slept the family's seven children, from 2 years old to 15, and their mother. They are all in shock.

The Israel Defense Forces knows this hut in Beit Lahia well; it has wrecked it a few times already. But the family continued to live in it; where would they go? Now Suleiman Abu Khoussa, 45, a farmer, sits there, stunned by the death of two of his children in front of their mother, their sisters and their brothers. The mother hides herself away; it's not possible to talk with her.

Their home is about 300 meters from a Hamas training camp, a distance made much smaller by the IAF's skilled pilots. Yassin died at the scene. Israa was taken to Beit Lahia's Indonesia Hospital in critical condition and then to Shifa Hospital in Gaza City, where she died. They were buried side by side in the al-Salatin cemetery, a brother and sister with no present and no future.

The incident was barely reported in Israel. It's hard to think of a baser dehumanization than the disgraceful coverage by the majority of Israeli media outlets of the killing of these two Palestinian children. *Israel Hayom* mentioned the killing in a tiny subheading that took a contemptible, dismissive tone: "Hamas claims: As a result of the attack, two children were killed." It's not hard to imagine what would have happened had Hamas killed two children, brother and sister, with a Qassam rocket. One can imagine not only a ruthless military retaliation but also the emotional reporting: *Beasts*, the headlines would surely have shouted, *Hamas child-killers*.

But our child-killers are pure—after all it wasn't intentional. It never is. Israel was not asked to issue a condemnation, no one even thought to express regret, much less to offer compensation.

I would very much like to visit the Abu Khoussa home in order to tell Israelis what their air force did there. But Israel doesn't let Israeli journalists into Gaza. Britain's the *Independent* was there this week to report to its readers. *Yedioth Ahronoth* reported on the guitar that Aviv Geffen gave to a guy whose own guitar broke when he hit a terrorist in the head with it, together with our hearts.

If Gazans Don't Fire, No One Listens

June 1

We have to say it simply and honestly: They're right. They have no choice but to fight for their freedom with their bodies, their property, their weapons and their blood. They have no choice, except for the Qassam and the mortar. There is no way open to them except for violence or surrender. They have no way of breaching the fences that pen them in without using force, and their force is primitive and pathetic, almost touching.

A people that is fighting for its freedom with kites, tunnels, mirrors, tires, scissors, incendiary devices, mortar shells and Qassam pipes, against one of the most sophisticated war machines in the world, is a people without hope. But the only way they can change their situation is with their pathetic weapons.

When they're quiet, Israel and the world take no interest in their fate. Only the Qassam restores awareness of their disaster. When do we hear in Israel about Gaza? Only when Gaza is shooting. That's why they have no choice but to shoot. That's why their shooting is justified, even if it criminally harms innocent civilians, instills fear and terror in the residents of the south and is intolerable to Israel, and rightly so.

They have no weapons that are more precise, and therefore it's also impossible to blame them for harming civilians: Most of their mortars fall in open areas, although that is not their intention, either. It's hard to blame them for hitting an empty kindergarten: They would certainly prefer precise weapons that aim at military targets, like those that Israel has, which incidentally harm far more children.

It's clear that their violence is cruel, like any violence. But what choice do they have? Every hesitant attempt they make to take a different path—a truce, a change in leadership or in their political positions—immediately encounters automatic Israeli dismissal and rejection. Israel believes them only when they shoot. After all, there's a clear control group: the West Bank. There's no Hamas there and no Qassams, there are barely any vestiges of terror, and what good did that do Mahmoud Abbas and his people?

They're right, because after all the diversions and deceptions and lies of Israeli propaganda, nothing can blur the fact that they have been thrown into a huge cage for the rest of their lives. An unbelievable siege, 11 years without respite, which is the greatest war crime in this arena. No propaganda can conceal their identity—their past, their present and their future. Most of them live in the Gaza Strip because Israel made them refugees. Israel expelled their forefathers from their villages and their land. Others fled for fear of Israel, and afterwards were not allowed to return—a crime no less serious than the expulsion.

All their villages were destroyed. They lived for 20 years under Egyptian rule, and another 50 years under Israeli occupation, which never stopped treating them cruelly in so many ways. When Israel left Gaza for its own purposes, it imposed a siege on them, and their fate became even worse. They haven't been free for a single day in their lives. Nor is there any sign of hope that they will be. Not even the children. They live on one of the most crowded pieces of land in the world, which the United Nations has declared will be unfit for human habitation in another year and a half. Isn't that enough for them to deserve support?

They are the last fighters against the Israeli occupation. While most of the occupied West Bank behaves like it's given up, Gaza is not giving up. They were always more determined and daring than their brothers in the West Bank, maybe because of their greater suffering. There isn't a single Israeli who can imagine his or her life in Gaza, the meaning of growing up into their reality. Everything has already been said about that, and nobody gets upset. They have a harsh, undemocratic government, but Israel cannot cast the blame on Hamas. In the West Bank there's a far more moderate government, and Israel is doing nothing to end the occupation there.

In recent weeks they buried 118 people—which, relative to the size of the population, is like 500 dead for us—and they will never stop fighting. They're right, too.

Broken Families in Limbo

July 8

Khaled Dawabsheh snuggles on his uncle's lap. If the uncle leaves him, even for a minute, little Khaled runs to the front door, opens it wide and rushes into the street, as though trying to escape from the house, which is not his home.

Khaled hardly speaks: Communication with him has been almost nonexistent since he became convinced that his mother has abandoned him. In fact, she calls every day, but Khaled refuses to speak to her. He hasn't seen her for three months, since they were separated. It's not clear when he will see her again. He hasn't seen his father for three months, either, other than on one occasion, in a military court, when his father was in handcuffs. It's not clear when the little boy will see his father again.

Explaining to Khaled why his parents are not with him is no easy task. It's also hard to make a promise that they will be reunited anytime soon. Dad is in prison, Mom is in the Gaza Strip. Total uncertainty exists in Khaled's limbo; the only sure thing is that the mental scars will cut deep.

Khaled is not alone. His little brother shares his fate. Khaled is 3½, Jud is not yet 2. At present, Jud is sleeping in his bassinet. He actually sometimes speaks to his mother on the phone, as much as an almost-2-year-old can speak; he was still being breast-fed when he was separated from her.

Jud and Khaled are too young to understand what's going on. But even an adult is hard-pressed to comprehend the occupation's brutal sundering of families—a mother separated hard-heartedly from her husband and their children.

In the situation of an almost-total disconnect between the West Bank and the Gaza Strip, the number of these human tragedies is increasing. In 2013, according to Gisha, the Legal Center for Freedom of Movement, an Israeli nonprofit, 26 percent of the residents of besieged Gaza had relatives in the West Bank—and 7 percent of all Gazans had first-degree relatives there. These are people who are almost totally cut off from one another: parents separated from children, husbands from wives, for years. The only communication is by phone or Skype. For the past few years, Israel has forbidden them to meet, or even to visit each other. "There is no siege of Gaza"? "The occupation of Gaza has ended"? These families are split apart precisely because of the "nonexistent" siege and occupation.

Duma. The Dawabsheh family. The end of this month will mark the first anniversary of the murderous terrorist attack, in which the family's house was apparently torched by Jews, resulting in the death of a toddler and his two parents. Khaled and Jud are distant relatives of those who were burned to death. The way to their uncle's home passes by the burned house, which stands scorched and barren, like a monument, an olive tree in the front.

Amar Dawabsheh, a 38-year-old art teacher, has three children of his own. Now his two nephews are also under his care. His brother, Urawa, the father of the toddlers, is 25. He lived with his parents in Jordan until 1994, when the family returned to Duma. Some years later, he went back to Jordan to attend school, where he met the brother of Islam, his future wife. They corresponded via Facebook and decided to get married. Islam's father is Egyptian; her mother, a Gaza Palestinian. She grew up in Gaza's Zeitoun neighborhood and has a Palestinian ID card. They were married in Jordan, and she is 24 years old now.

When Khaled was born, the couple tried to move to Duma, but Islam was turned back at the Allenby Bridge border crossing by the Israeli authorities because she is registered as a resident of the Strip. Israel does not allow Gaza residents to visit the West Bank or to be united with family members there. Last summer, the couple tried again, and were denied entry again.

Urawa longed to return to his village—where his parents and siblings live—together with his wife and children. Finally, he decided that he would cross into the West Bank first, with the two children, and then try to find a way to have his wife join him. On April 10, the father and his two children arrived at the Allenby Bridge again, accompanied by Urawa's sister, Alaa, who had traveled to Jordan from Duma with their mother in order to help with the move and the crossing.

At the bridge, the Israeli authorities delayed them for three hours, before informing them that Urawa was under arrest. Of course, no one told them why. The children were taken to Duma by their aunt. Almost two months would pass before the toddlers' father would see his children again—on June 3, when he was brought for remand to the Salem military court. He is incarcerated in Megiddo Prison.

The Israel Defense Forces spokesman's office told *Haaretz* this week: "On June 9, 2016, Urawa Dawabsheh was indicted in Samaria military court for years-long involvement in Hamas organizational and military activity. This included, among other offenses, transferring funds from Jordan to the Judea and Samaria Region to finance terrorist activity. With the agreement of the defense, the military court ordered Dawabsheh to be held in custody until the conclusion of the legal proceedings against him."

Khaled and Jud are listed on their father's Jordanian passport. As long as he is in jail, they cannot go to Jordan to rejoin their mother, who is waiting for them there. Moreover, it's likely that, if Urawa is convicted—and maybe even if he is not—Israeli security forces will not allow him to leave the West Bank anytime soon. It's a vicious trap.

The rest of the family in Duma has tried various means, including appeals to the International Red Cross and other human rights organizations, to get Islam a permit to enter the West Bank and be reunited with her children.

Meanwhile, on Sunday, Islam took advantage of the last days of the month of Ramadan, when the Rafah border crossing was open (for just five days) and returned from Jordan via Egypt to her home in Gaza's Zeitoun neighborhood. The family hopes that Israel will allow her to get to the West Bank from there, via the Erez checkpoint. "She is going out of her mind," Amar Dawabsheh, the children's uncle, says.

A spokesperson for the Coordinator of Government Activities in the Territories informed *Haaretz* that the Shin Bet security service is responsible for preventing Islam's entry into the West Bank. The Shin Bet does not usually explain its considerations, but its policy is to prevent any passage of residents from the Gaza Strip into the West Bank, including for brief visits.

The case of the Dawabsheh family is not unique. There's a similar case in the village of Azoun Atama, near Qalqilyah. Sahar Basath, 37, a native of the village, is married and the father of three. In 2000, he went to Jordan, flew to Cairo and from the Egyptian capital traveled to visit relatives in the Gaza Strip. There he met Nabila al-Hawani, from the Al-Magazi refugee camp, and married her. Nabila is a nurse in Gaza City's Shifa Hospital. The couple's three children are 1, 4 and 6.

Sahar worked in a biscuit factory in the Strip, but the ordeals of the blockade and the hardscrabble life there, coupled with his desire to spend time with his ailing and elderly father in his waning years, prompted efforts to get Sahar and his family home, to Azoun Atama. It doesn't sound so far-fetched—a return home or a relocation—but not under the conditions of the Israeli occupation.

The family applied for an entry permit to the West Bank, which they received on March 9. But at the Erez checkpoint, they discovered that the permit was valid only for the father and the three children; Nabila was not allowed to leave Gaza. The family was stunned, Sahar told B'Tselem human rights organization field researcher Abed al-Karim a-Saadi. Nevertheless, they decided that Sahar and the children would go through and leave Nabila behind, in the hope that in time she would be allowed to join her family. Nabila wept bitterly at the checkpoint, Sahar related. She phones her husband and children several times a day. Geographically, they are a two-hour drive apart, but in practice they are separated by the hills of darkness.

A spokesperson for the Coordinator of Activities told *Haaretz* this week that responsibility for this decision, too—not to allow a nurse from Gaza to enter the West Bank—rests with the Shin Bet. That organization, as already pointed out, isn't in the habit of revealing the reasons behind its decisions.

About a month ago, Nabila launched a hunger strike in Gaza, to protest her separation from her family, and she was subsequently hospitalized. This week, when we wanted to meet with Sahar, he told us that he is feeling depressed and would rather not see us. Totally despondent, he decided this week to leave his village, and his ailing father, and move to Gaza with the children in order to reunite them with their mother. He has already submitted a request to the occupation authorities.

2017

The Wall of Insanity

August 13

The next time a cap gun is fired or a toy balloon is launched at Israel from the Gaza Strip, the army will start building a steel dome over the Strip to prevent it. The ceiling will also cut off the territory from the sky. After all, we're talking about national security. When the first crack forms, and another balloon is launched or cap gun fired, the defense establishment will proceed to the next phase: flooding the Gaza Strip with water until it is completely submerged. After all, we're talking about Israeli security.

Until that happens—the plans have already been drawn up—the modest, hard-up Israeli army is making do with smaller measures: It's building a new "barrier" around the Strip, the father of all the fences and the mother of all the walls with which Israel is surrounding itself, six meters high and reaching tens of meters underground. Israel is becoming a state with a wall at its heart. There's nothing it likes more than to surround itself.

History is replete with megalomaniacal rulers who built palaces. For now, Israeli megalomania settles for walls. The separation barrier and the border fence, the Good Fence on the Lebanese border and the bad fence, the entire country is fences. Just give defense officials an excuse and they will surround us with a fence costing billions. For that, money can always be found.

The fence of horrors on the Egyptian border to keep out African refugees and the separation wall facing barefoot residents of the Deheisheh refugee camp in the West Bank. Now it's the turn of the Gaza border fence to stop tunnels from being dug under the fence that it is replacing. Next thing you know, there will be an electronic fence around the Israeli-Arab city of Umm al-Fahm, in response to the terrorism emanating from there as well.

The chief of the Southern Command made the announcement, the military correspondents quoted him slavishly and Israel responded with either a yawn or a "Yes!" The method is tried and true: First you create a demon (the tunnels); then you find it a megalomaniacal solution. And there you have it, another $800 million Zionist project, to be built by workers from Moldova and asylum seekers from Africa. There we have it: another wall.

The details range from the fantastic to the grotesque, including the use of bentonite, a clay that becomes viscous on contact with water; a "see and shoot" security network that can kill with the flick of a joystick, operated by daring women soldiers who will be praised in the media for every kill; and enormous iron cages with waterproof pipes and warning sensors. Only one kind of warning is missing from the system: a warning when the system goes crazy.

Donald Trump on the Mexican border, Israel on the Gaza border—and the insanity is remarkably similar.

Israel has traffic accidents. They claim many more lives than all of the terrorism from the Gaza Strip, but no one has thought about spending on the roads the amounts being spent on the defense establishment's new toy.

There are hospital patients who are dying, housed in corridors because there aren't enough rooms for them all. The budget for the Gaza barrier could turn that situation around. That, too, would save lives, but hospitals are not part of the security cult, and it therefore wouldn't occur to anyone to redirect the money from the Gaza border to the Hadassah Medical Center.

Gaza is a cage, the doors of which are now being shut that much more tightly, in a strong-armed, arrogant and unilateral move, as with all of the measures Israel takes vis-à-vis the Palestinians, from building the separation barrier on their land to the settlements. It's not hard to guess what Gazans will feel in the face of this intensifying closure. It's also not hard to guess what kind of state is being built here, a state that surrounds itself with walls to the point of insanity.

As with past measures, this latest strong-armed step will solve nothing. The only way to deal with the threat from Gaza is to give Gaza its freedom. There never was and never will be any other way. And when this wall is built, the contractors may get rich, and Israelis living near the border may celebrate, but soon enough breaches in the wall will be found and the residents' joy will again be dashed.

Israelis deserve what's happening, if such excessive spending is carried out here without any public debate, because then we won't be getting better medical care or roads. Israel has opted for another wall, and Israel will pay for it.

Sacred Sovereignty

November 2

Breaking yet another record for chutzpah, Israel justified its strike on the Islamic Jihad tunnel by calling the tunnel a "violation of sovereignty," and threatened to hit anyone who tries to infringe on its sacred sovereignty. The prime minister, defense minister and chief of staff recited it as one. Funny. A state that has violated almost every sovereignty around it and respected none, that forcibly rules territories in which it lacks sovereignty, sanctifies the idea of sovereignty when expedient. It gives hypocrisy a bad name.

The tunnel from Gaza was absolutely a danger to Israeli lives. Islamic Jihad said it was intended for the purpose of abducting soldiers. Snatching people from their beds is, of course, a privilege reserved for Israeli soldiers. They do it nightly. Israelis said the tunnel would be used to murder women and children. In any case, Israel had a right, a duty even, to foil the threat to its citizens and residents' safety and hit the tunnel. But the timing was suspicious: just as the Palestinians are trying to unite in Gaza, just before the transfer of responsibility for the border terminals between the Gaza Strip and Egypt.

One needn't be overly suspicious to realize that Israel would do anything to sabotage Palestinian reconciliation; it jeopardizes Israel's intransigence and threatens to call its bluff. Just imagine a unified Palestinian partner for peace suddenly appearing, God forbid. In the absence of evidence, Israel can enjoy the benefit of the doubt. It can be assumed that the timing was random; Israel found a tunnel and bombed it.

It's harder to believe Israel didn't know Islamic Jihad commanders were in the tunnel. Perhaps Israel didn't plan to kill them in advance—highly doubtful—but it certainly did nothing to prevent it. The army and the Shin Bet security service, which know the color of every Islamic Jihad fighter's briefs at any given moment, didn't know these figures were in the tunnel? There's a limit to disingenuousness.

Israel almost always prefers bombing to any other option, especially when Palestinian unity lurks in the background. Moreover, had Israel truly wanted to prevent the near–mass killing, it could have done what it always boasts of doing in Gaza: a "roof knocking" warning strike a few minutes in advance, to prevent unnecessary deaths. Since this was not done, it must be assumed that killing the Islamic Jihad heads was a goal, or at the very least a welcome bonus.

It isn't hard to imagine what would have happened if a Palestinian organization had wiped out eight Israeli generals. Gaza's skies would have gone red, its buildings would tremble. And note the characteristic debate over whether the army spokesman apologized for the deaths—he didn't—as though it's forbidden to apologize for killing Arabs, in any circumstance; only rejoicing is permitted. Is it permissible to remember that senior figures in Islamic Jihad, a violent extremist organization that is not merely a charity, are also human beings and that in a period of quiet there's no reason to eliminate them?

But the claim of sovereignty infringement was just too much. Israel has no right to preach about respecting sovereignty. When its troops invade Area A West Bank cities (under Palestinian control) nightly to abuse residents, to make a show of force, to keep the soldiers alert, to make arrests or confiscate cash, separately or together, it cannot demand that its sovereignty be respected. When it treats Lebanon's skies as its own and bombs Syria as if it owned it; when it bars Gazan fishermen from going to sea and shells them, and prevents farmers from approaching the border fence and shoots them, how can it complain about a tunnel in the name of sovereignty?

When Israeli soldiers shot dead an innocent driver and wounded his sister at Halamish junction on Tuesday, simply because they didn't obey the soldiers' orders, in the name of what sovereignty did they act, in a piece of land that has no sovereignty?

But Israel sees itself as the sovereign of the universe. That's why it's allowed to do so.

2018

Strangling Gaza

April 5

The fence separated them. On each side stood the children of
the late 1990s, young people of the same age, Israeli soldiers
and Gaza demonstrators. They stood opposite each other, the
armed and protected soldiers with their jeeps, bulldozers, dirt
barriers, barbed wire and watchtowers, and opposite them the
exposed demonstrators, a parasol and an ambulance. Several
dozen Gaza residents came to the fence at midweek, too, to stand
and silently defy the fence and soldiers, while behind them 18
families mourned their loved ones and hundreds nursed their
wounds—victims of the mass shooting last Friday.

It was afternoon. The earth-moving equipment that's building the huge underground barrier and putting up dirt barriers
all along the fence raised dust that sometimes blocked visibility.
The drilling machines, watchtowers and jeeps—overloaded with
intelligence and protective gear on their roofs—lent the place the
appearance of a science fiction film.

Nothing makes sense here, at the fence of the huge concentration camp called Gaza: the residents who helplessly watch the
bulldozers closing in on them, intensifying the siege and the stran-
gulation. The drivers of the heavy engineering equipment, some
of whom are Israeli Arabs who use a phosphorescent bulletproof
vest as a prayer rug, while on the other side they're kneeling for
that same afternoon prayer toward the same Mecca and to the

same God. The huge quantities of concrete being poured into the bloody earth to achieve even more imaginary security for Israel, opposite the group of barefoot men whose most sophisticated weapons this week were large mirrors with which they tried to blind the snipers firing at them.

How sad it is to travel along the Burma Road, the military's nickname for the patrol road next to the fence that locks in Gaza; how sad to see the houses on the other side up close, like stretching out an arm and touching it, and think about the fate of the inhabitants. How sad it is to see the huge sums being poured into the earth in this imaginary underground barrier, at the edge of which cement factories have been built to satisfy its appetite for concrete, and think about how much good could be done with this money. How sad it is to observe the Gaza prison from outside.

The Erez crossing is empty. The terminal that was built to let through tens of thousands of people, which is almost empty even on ordinary days, emptied out completely this week. A wheelchair that was rushed to the entrance heralded the passage of one patient; a pair of cats burrowing in a dumpster was a reminder that there is life here. An intelligence balloon was sent aloft once again to keep track of the people.

The family of Emil Fugato donated money from his estate to develop the security highway surrounding Gaza, as inscribed on the stone slab standing on the hill between Sderot and Gaza and overlooking Beit Hanun. During the Gaza wars, curiosity seekers gathered here to watch the shelling, but now it's quiet even on this hill, which has a tree planted at its highest point.

At the Arele Campsite people are picnicking. They're celebrating Passover, the festival of freedom, opposite the largest prison in the world. The Cease-fire House has been renovated, a "national heritage site" in a place where the word "cease-fire" is no longer familiar. At the foot of the campsite are the fields of wheat and stubble of Kibbutz Nir Am that reach right up to Gaza, the sight of which you can't escape. "We're here," people shout from inside a Kia Picanto car that has arrived at the campsite.

The Black Arrow Memorial is also here, and also overlooks Gaza—a marble block for each of the reprisal acts undertaken by Israel's Paratroopers Brigade in the 1950s, which were called retaliatory acts. Several of them took place in Gaza, others in Jordan. Operations in Khan Yunis, Kissufim (Operation An Eye for an Eye), Qalqilyah, Kuntilla (Operation Egged)—all acts of revenge. Terror for terror. Quotations from Genesis, Natan Alterman, Hannah Szenes, Yitzhak Shalev, and, of course, Ariel Sharon, the leader of the reprisal campaign.

The sign says the Black Arrow booklet is available from "Erol," and provides a phone number. Tourists from the city of Yavneh arrive for an organized visit among the commemorative stones of the reprisal operations. Yavneh was once the Arab town of Yibneh—and the descendants of its 1948 refugees live in the besieged enclave opposite us. It's doubtful whether any of the vacationers here is thinking about their fate.

"Why did the Sinai Campaign begin?" asks the guide, and someone asks what the Sinai Campaign was. "Have you heard of the attack against Moshav Patish? There was a wedding. Terrorists came."

The Jabalya refugee camp is opposite us. "Dan shall be a serpent by the road, a viper by the path" (Genesis 49:17), it says on the memorial. Shujaiyeh, where dozens of Gazans were killed during 2014's Operation Protective Edge, isn't far away, either.

A crocheted kippa, a head scarf and a guitar on the stone bench beneath the eucalyptus tree. A couple from Moshav Bnei Netzarim, evacuees from the Gaza Strip. He's singing a love song to her. And from here, too, Gaza is on the horizon. It doesn't let go.

Next to the tank-parking area from the days of Operation Protective Edge, opposite the entrance to Kibbutz Nahal Oz, there is a cement factory for the barrier now under construction. The cement trucks are waiting in line. "We shall clothe you in a dress of concrete and cement," 2018 version, which even Alterman, who wrote these words in a poem about the building of Tel Aviv, never dreamed of.

The Faiz Road and the Roman Road. War names. In a large watermelon patch that ends almost at the border fence, Israeli Bedouin women are collecting huge plastic sheets that covered the watermelons. Spring has arrived. From here you can already see Gaza's houses clearly. Kibbutz Nahal Oz's fields of potatoes, cabbage and kohlrabi reach almost to the border.

Here the watchtowers are surrounded with a dome that gives them a strange appearance. Nobody stops us and we're on the Burma Road. Maybe they think we're also with the contractors who are building the largest subterranean barrier in history. Meanwhile, to be on the safe side, they've added innumerable barbed-wire fences at the edge of the fields as a second line of defense against the demonstrators who might break through the big fence.

There's a garbage dump on the other side of the fence, white birds are burrowing in it, and not far away there's a small tent city of the demonstrators. White tents and a few motorcyclists move among them. A yellow Caterpillar earth mover belonging to Morad Yehezkel Ltd. is eating into the earth, building another dirt barrier. Who knows how much more Israel will entrench itself, surround itself with walls, fences and barriers, and imprison its neighbors even more.

Some of the construction workers and supervisors work here wearing flak jackets and steel helmets. Others, like the operator of the Volvo engineering equipment who's praying on the phosphorescent vest that he spread out, are completely exposed. The sight of the demonstrators, opposite all these steel machines, is even more heartrending. Suddenly the soldiers start running toward the fence. There's tension in the air. The soldiers take shelter behind the concrete blocks. One of them tosses a tear gas grenade at the other side. There are no casualties.

And returning from an English lesson at the Islamic University of Gaza where he studies, to his home in the center of Gaza City on the other side of the site where we were standing, is student Hasan Farhat. He's 20 and he returned home to Gaza in 2011, after spending six years with his parents in Australia, while his father completed a doctorate in linguistics. Farhat was happy to return. He likes life in Gaza, even under siege, and prefers it to life in Australia.

We speak via Skype. Farhat didn't take part in the demonstration last Friday, although he supports them. He has two younger sisters at home, and they were worried about him and asked him not to go to the demonstration, fearing he'd be hurt.

"I believe that demonstrations are the last nonviolent means. The situation here is constantly deteriorating, and people know that the violent struggle has no chance. We only want to make our voices heard. We want them to know that there are human beings living here, just like everywhere else, with dreams, just like everywhere else."

Farhat, who is active on the social networks, says 62 percent of the young people and 45 percent of the adults in Gaza are unemployed, and his fellow students are very worried about will happen when they finish their studies and receive their degrees. "As long as we're studying, there's at least somewhere to go," he says. "And so many students are prevented from continuing to study abroad. So many people in the world can enjoy freedom."

Farhat says the idea of a nonviolent march toward the border was thought up as early as 2011 by Ahmed Abu Rteima, a Palestinian journalist and writer, author of the Arabic-language book *Organized Chaos*, and now a spokesperson for the "Great March of Return." At the time people thought the idea was crazy, because they were afraid Israel would fire at the marchers.

This demonstration doesn't belong to any organization. People here are tired of politics. People in Gaza have nothing more to lose. "There are people in Gaza who prefer getting killed quickly at the border to dying slowly in Gaza," he says. "I remember that when I was in Australia we were once asked if we would prefer to die slowly in a cage full of ants or to die quickly in a cage of lions.

"Almost everyone said in a cage of lions, to die quickly." On Sunday, he says, there was a wedding near the fence. People sang songs and even danced. "But we, those born in the '90s, we're a lost generation," he says. Still, he's glad he returned to Gaza.

Bleeding in the Sand

April 24

His left leg was amputated in Shifa Hospital in the Gaza Strip, and now efforts are underway, in Istishari Arab Hospital in the West Bank, to ensure that his right leg doesn't suffer the same fate. More than two weeks passed between the amputation of the first leg—which itself could have been prevented—and the time the action required to save the other one was undertaken. Precious time in which Israel refused to allow Yousef Kronz, the first Palestinian seriously wounded during the recent weekly protests in the Gaza Strip, to be moved to the hospital outside Ramallah. The High Court of Justice finally forced the Defense Ministry to bring this disgraceful conduct to an end and allow the transfer of the 19-year-old student and journalist from Bureij refugee camp to that more sophisticated facility.

On Friday, March 30, Kronz was shot, first in the left leg, by an Israel Defense Forces sniper, and then, seconds later, when he tried to get up, in the right leg, by a second sniper. According to Kronz, the rounds that slammed into his legs and shattered his life came from two different directions. In other words, he was shot by two different marksmen as he stood 750 meters away from the Gaza border fence, armed with no more than his camera, wearing a vest with "Press" emblazoned on it, trying to document the incessant firing by IDF snipers at unarmed Palestinian demonstrators. After he was hit, he tells us now, he saw more and more people falling to the sand, bleeding, "like birds."

The incident occurred on Land Day, the first day of the Marches of Return opposite the Gaza fence.

Istishari Hospital is situated high in the village of Surda, north of Ramallah. It's a large, new, sophisticated private facility, luxurious and glistening. Kronz has a private room, spacious and well-lit with an adjustable bed, a television, wood-paneled walls and a breathtaking view. Israel did not allow anyone from his family to accompany Kronz to the West Bank or tend to him, other than his aged grandfather, Mohammed Kronz, who's 85, and who, after a few days, was compelled to go to the home of relatives in the distant Aroub refugee camp, near Bethlehem, to rest. Now Yousef, who is suffering from serious pain in his stump and in his remaining leg, is being looked after with infinite devotion by a cousin, Ghassan Karnaz, who is also from Aroub. The two cousins had never met before. Like all the young people in Gaza, Kronz had never been outside the Strip. Now he's breached the siege on it—without his leg.

A first-year communications student at Al-Azhar University in Gaza, he is from a family that hails from Faluja, in the Negev. His father receives his salary as a Gaza-based police officer from the Palestinian Authority. Kronz was active in the social networks, reporting on the situation in the Strip. A few months ago, he purchased a Canon 5D stills camera for $5,000, half of it from savings, the rest from his father, and started to work for the local Bureij news agency.

Kronz was the first journalist shot during the month of demonstrations, though not the last. He was well acquainted with Yaser Murtaja, a journalist killed in cold blood by IDF snipers on April 6. Like Kronz, Murtaja, too, was from a Gaza refugee camp—Jabalya.

On March 30, Kronz walked about 1.5 kilometers from his home to the site of the demonstrations to photograph them for his news agency. He recited the midday prayers in the journalists' tent set up there. The 25 local reporters then discussed how they would divide up the area of the protests they were documenting. The atmosphere was tense, he recalls now; everyone expected large numbers of casualties.

Did he think the IDF would use live ammunition? "The IDF always fires live ammunition." His face is contorted with pain, but Kronz is well groomed, despite his condition. He constantly glances at the mirror or at the camera in his cell phone, to be sure his designer haircut looks okay.

After the prayers, he continues, the young people started to set fire to tires. Signs set up by the organizers showed the way to the toilets and various tents, and also the distance from the border fence at each point. Thus Kronz knew he was 750 meters away from the barrier. The day before, the IDF had dropped leaflets in nearby Jabalya warning that anyone who came closer than 300 meters from the fence would be risking his life. With plenty of experience under their belts, Gazans take those warnings seriously. The organizers marked a permitted green zone and a forbidden, and dangerous, red zone. Karnaz says he was hundreds of meters outside the boundary of the red zone.

At 2 p.m., the situation reached a boiling point. IDF troops started to hurl tear gas grenades as young people approached to within 100 meters of the fence. They used slingshots to hurl stones at the soldiers but were too far away to hit them. Karnaz says he saw a few dozen soldiers opposite him on the other side of the barrier; three jeeps and the barrel of a tank were peeking out from behind an embankment. He, too, found a small dirt mound and perched behind it, placing the tripod with his camera on it to one side and his backpack on the other. He knelt on the sand, his legs crossed before him. The barrage of tear gas grew more intense, the soldiers fired the grenades in volleys, and the skies became covered with thick, burning gas. The wind carried the gas in his direction; demonstrators used onions to protect themselves from it. Kronz took about 950 photos.

He remembers looking at his watch at 3 p.m. Later that afternoon, a friend, Bilal Azara, was getting married in Bureij, so he thought he should head home, shower and change. Kronz picked up his camera and backpack and stood up. At that precise moment, the first bullet struck him. He didn't hear anything but felt a searing pain. The camera was thrown from his hands and he collapsed, then immediately tried to get up. That's when the second bullet ripped into his other leg. The first entered five centimeters below the knee, the second seven centimeters above the other knee. Paralyzed, he tried to shout for help but his voice betrayed him. He says he felt as if he'd been electrocuted. His camera was left behind in the sands of Gaza.

A few meters away was a young man of the same age, Ahmed al-Bahar, an assistant to one of the other photographers. Bahar ran to Kronz and tried to lift him up—but just then he, too, was shot in the leg and fell to the ground, bleeding.

At this point in our conversation, distant relatives of 11-year-old Abed al-Rahman Nufal, who also lost a leg in Gaza and is hospitalized here at Istishari, enter the room to say hello. Nufal is one of only three other wounded Gazans, out of 1,500 wounded in the demonstrations to date, whom Israel has allowed to be moved here. The family, former Gazans now living in the West Bank, have come to see how the boy is doing.

Young people carried Kronz and Bahar to the only ambulance in the area. In short order the vehicle was crammed with six wounded people lying next to each other; Kronz was the most badly injured. The soldiers went on hurling tear gas; Kronz felt as if he was suffocating in the ambulance. A paramedic placed an oxygen mask on his face, but the crowding inside prevented him from stanching the bleeding from Kronz's legs. Drifting in and out of consciousness, Kronz was taken to Al-Aqsa Hospital in Dir al-Balah.

At the hospital he saw his left leg for the first time; it was shattered, the bone protruding, the flesh lacerated. At the sight of it, he passed out. He was anesthetized and taken immediately to the larger Shifa Hospital in Gaza City, because of the severity of the wounds. At Shifa he underwent six hours of surgery to stanch the bleeding.

After four days in Shifa the condition of Kronz's left leg deteriorated, and the physicians were compelled to amputate it above the knee. He received 24 transfusions of blood. The request to transfer him to Ramallah for treatment was submitted to Israel just hours after he was wounded but was rejected by the authorities. The situation of the right leg looked dire as well.

Nine days after Kronz was wounded, on April 8, two rights groups—Adalah, the Legal Center for Arab Minority Rights in Israel, and the Gaza-based Al-Mezan Center for Human Rights— petitioned the Israeli High Court to allow Kronz and another wounded Gazan, Mohammed Alajuri, to be transferred urgently to Ramallah for treatment. The court apparently saw no real urgency in dealing with the case and waited four days before deliberating on the petition, whereupon the justices demanded a response from the state within four days.

The amputations of the limbs of both young men could have been prevented if the state had "fulfilled its obligation under humanitarian international law," Sawsan Zahar, an attorney for Adalah, told the justices.

The state's attorneys, for their part, told the court, "On the surface, the petitioners' condition appears to fulfil the medical criterion for receiving a permit [for transfer to Ramallah], but the authorized officials decided not to grant their requests. The main consideration for the refusal stems from the fact that their medical condition is a function of their participation in the disturbances."

On April 16, Justices Uri Shoham, George Karra and Yael Willner said they were not persuaded that the government had fully considered whether the circumstances in Kronz's case justified its deviation from normal procedure. "There's no dispute over the fact that the medical treatment the petitioner needs to prevent the amputation of his leg is unavailable in the Gaza Strip," they wrote. Therefore, the petitioner is included among the cases in which entry to Israel is to be permitted for "the purpose of passage to Ramallah."

The justices also deigned to declare that Kronz does not represent a security risk to Israel. That same day, he was moved to Istishari Hospital. (As for Alajuri, before the court got around to issuing a ruling on his case, the doctors in Gaza had had no choice but to amputate his leg. He remains in Gaza.)

Yousef Kronz is now undergoing a rough patch, finding it difficult to adjust to being an amputee. Four days after being brought to the Ramallah hospital he underwent surgery on his right leg, whose condition appears to have been stabilized. Now, however, he faces lengthy rehabilitation, which will last at least four months, in a hospital in Beit Jala, adjacent to Bethlehem. Before we take our leave, he asks us whether we think he'll ever be able to walk on one leg.

In the Fields of Philistia

May 18

On Tuesday, the tires burned on both sides of the fence that imprisons the residents of the Gaza Strip. Thick black columns of smoke rose into the air a few hundred meters apart, dispersing with the shifting winds, blackening the skies of the Strip and of what's called the Gaza "envelope"—the Israeli communities along the border—blotting out the landscape.

Fires raged in the fields of Philistia, on both sides of the border fence. In both cases, it was Palestinians who lit them. On their side they burned tires, elevating their protest skyward in the form of dense smoke. Toward the Israeli side they sent their burning "foxtails," the fire kites, no less primitive than the fire started by Samson in the Bible story (in Judges 15).

One of the kites set a field ablaze and also ignited a few terrifyingly large truck tires which for some reason were stacked next to the entrance of an Iron Dome missile-intercept battery somewhere in the fields of a kibbutz near the Gaza border, sending dark, acrid smoke wafting up. A soldier from the Israel Defense Forces Spokesperson's Unit strode, distraught, through the black plumes of smoke, trying to stop us from photographing the flames that were almost licking the launcher's base. "It will be Hamas's victory photo," he cried out. "Iron Dome burning."

The fire was finally extinguished right next to the fence of the launch zone. A few hours earlier, when we had first passed by the site, a female soldier was ensconced in the guard post, dozing in the warm sun, a cap draped over her face. Now the fire reached the edge of her position. Firefighters and soldiers worked hard to douse it, but shortly afterward it flared up again, on the surrounding sand mounds. It was a late fire—a revenge fire, if you will—of black smoke that evoked Black Monday, a day earlier, when some 60 people were massacred and about 1,200 wounded by live fire at the hands of IDF soldiers. We reached the fire at the same time as a yellow army fire engine.

The flames spread rapidly, consuming fields of thistles. The fields of the Gaza envelope were stained with black splotches, carpets of soot that a short time earlier were fields of wheat and grassy stubble, now completely burned. But the disaster is, of course, immeasurably more terrible on the other side of the fence. The "kite terror" is as nothing in the face of the siege, the sniper fire and the bombs.

Tuesday, Nakba Day, was intended to be the peak of the March of Return, which had begun six weeks earlier and had already taken the lives of more than 100 demonstrators and left thousands wounded. But the shock of what happened in these fields the previous day apparently had its effect.

The area abutting the fence on this day, Tuesday, was fairly quiet. Gaza was burying and grieving for its dozens of dead. Perhaps the demonstrators were afraid to return to the barrier; perhaps they were prevented from doing so, or they may have been too occupied with mourning. A photograph taken by Agence France-Presse shows a mother hunched over the body of her infant son, wrapped in shrouds, on her way to the grave. That image spoke louder than words, and likely shocked many people around the world. In Israel, people were still busy celebrating the US Embassy ceremony in Jerusalem and the Eurovision contest.

A field of sunflowers lies at the edge of the Nahal Oz farmlands. The yellow flowers all point eastward, as though turning their back and diverting their vision from the events to the west, in the Gaza Strip. The sunflowers don't want to see what's going on in Gaza, just like the Israelis who tend them. The field of sunflowers extends almost to the fence, with its host of protective devices and the earth ramparts on which the snipers are perched. The pomegranate grove of another kibbutz, Nir Oz, far to the south, also reaches not far from the barrier. The pomegranate trees are now giving off their scent and above all displaying their flowers and first fruits.

Late morning. Behind the fence two fairly small bonfires of tires are already visible, a demonstration of presence. A large Palestinian flag flaps in the breeze, and a few people can be seen in the sandy area that runs down to the fence. The view of the

Gaza prison always stirs grim thoughts, which are made even grimmer on a day when so many are being laid to rest. The smoke hides the houses of the Strip, behind the area of the demonstrations. From afar the Gaza Strip looks normal; up close, nothing is normal there.

In the pine grove next to the Black Arrow monument, commemorating a 1955 revenge operation against the Egyptian army in Gaza by the Paratroopers Brigade, are the war correspondents of the world—both those who are fearful of entering the Strip and those who are not allowed in. It's a long way to the border fence from here, but this is the only place that the IDF allows media people to be, not including those who can find their way to the fence through the many paths in the fields here. Female soldiers from the Caracal Battalion, armed with knee protectors, are something of an attraction for the foreign reporters. A Knesset member, Haim Jelin (Yesh Atid), who lives in the area, hardly misses a camera; these are his 15 minutes of fame.

The weirdest place in the sector is the Kerem Shalom crossing, at the southern edge of the Strip, near Rafah. It's here, in days long gone by, that we would pass on the daily bus to Cairo that departed from Tel Aviv and crossed the Suez Canal, believe it or not. It's also the last crossing point for merchandise between Israel and Gaza that's still open: Karni passage was closed in 2007, Sufa in 2008, Nahal Oz in 2010 and the Karni conveyor in 2011; and Kerem Shalom, too, was closed last week for a few days after the Palestinians set fire to the Gaza side.

The place is desolate. On Tuesday, Israel decided to renew the passage of goods through Kerem Shalom, so it was reported, but only about half a dozen idle trucks were in the large parking area: a few fuel and gas tankers of Ephraim Burstein, and two trucks bearing signs, "Gan Eden [Paradise] Ltd.," and "Pandoor doors: A sign that you didn't cut corners."

Paradise or not, corners cut or not, the passage to Gaza is deserted. Far more abandoned than the crossing to Egypt. Ruined buildings, torn signs, run-down facilities, and only a dense barbed-wire fence and Egyptian flags on the other side.

An Egyptian armored vehicle passes across the way, and the soldiers look at us. This is a trilateral crossing point—Israel, Egypt, Gaza—and a double point of evil, of Israel and of Egypt: one the source of Gaza's troubles and the other, the one that cuts it off from the world.

At the exit from this surrealistic site, where not a soul is to be found—certainly not one is visible, plus there's no one to stop us from wandering around freely—a tattered road sign still lists the traffic symbols that are in use in Israel.

Welcome to Israel. This was once the southern gateway into the country for those coming from Egypt. The letter "S" in the word "Shalom," on the large sign above the concrete wall, "Kerem Shalom Crossing," tilts forward, wrenched from its place.

An equally forgotten reality is projected by signs along the way here that direct one to the "safe passage" between Gaza and Hebron, created in the wake of the 1993 Oslo Accords. How many discussions were held about the traffic arrangements and how few vehicles ever traveled the route, before Israel canceled the arrangement and severed the Strip completely from the West Bank, long before Hamas took over Gaza.

An object in the sky, opposite the Black Arrow monument. Is it a terror kite or a bird of freedom? Only birds and the planes of the Israeli Air Force can move here without being shot at, between Gaza and Israel, between prison and liberty. A flock of birds with snow-white wings flies directly over the fields, moving from side to side, birds without borders. We are following the black smoke and the IDF's yellow fire engine to the fire that's liable to damage the Iron Dome battery and give Hamas its "victory photo." On the other side, the first fatal casualty of the day is counted.

We Should Be Saluting the Gaza Strip

July 15

Were it not for the Gaza Strip, the occupation would have been long forgotten. Were it not for the Gaza Strip, Israel would have erased the Palestinian issue from its agenda and continued on blithely with its crimes and annexations, with its routine, as if 4 million people were not living under its heel. Were it not for the Gaza Strip, the world would also have forgotten. Most of it already has. This is why we must now salute the Gaza Strip— mainly the spirit of the Gaza Strip, the only one that is still breathing life into the desperate and lost cause of the Palestinian struggle for liberty.

The resolute struggle of the Gaza Strip should also spark admiration in Israel. The handful of people with a conscience who still remain here should give thanks to the unbroken spirit of the Gaza Strip. The spirit of the West Bank crumpled after the failure of the second intifada, as did the spirit of the Israeli peace camp—most of which shattered long ago. Only the spirit of the Gaza Strip stands steadfast in its struggle.

And so, anyone who does not want to forever live in an evil country must respect the embers that the young people of the Gaza Strip are still trying to stoke. Were it not for the kites, the fires, the Qassam rockets, the Palestinians would have entirely exited the awareness of everyone in Israel. Only the World Cup and the Eurovision Song Contest would hold any interest. Were it not for the blackened fields in the south, there would be a huge white flag fluttering not only over the Gaza Strip but over the entire Palestinian people. Seekers of justice, including in Israel, cannot wish for this kind of submission.

It's difficult, even insolent, to write these words from tranquil and secure Tel Aviv, following one more sleepless and nightmarish night in the south, but all days and nights in the Gaza Strip are much more difficult due to Israel's inhumane policy, supported by most of its citizens, including people who live in the south. They don't deserve to shoulder the burden, but every struggle exacts a price from innocent victims, who we wish do not become casualties. One should remember that only Palestinians are being killed. On Saturday, the 139th victim of Israeli fire along the border died. He was 20. On Friday a 15-year-old boy was killed. The Gaza Strip is paying the full price in blood. This doesn't cause it to desist. That is its spirit. One cannot but admire it.

The spirit of the Gaza Strip is unbroken by any siege. The evil ones in Jerusalem shut down the Kerem Shalom border crossing, and Gaza shoots. The malicious ones in the Kirya government complex in Tel Aviv prevent young people from receiving medical treatment in the West Bank in order to save their legs from being amputated.

For years they have been preventing cancer patients, including women and children, from receiving lifesaving treatment. Only 54 percent of requests to leave the Gaza Strip for medical reasons were approved last year, compared to 93 percent in 2012. That is wicked. One should read the letter written in June by 31 Israeli oncologists who called for a cessation of the abuse of Gaza women with cancer whose applications for exit permits take months to process, sealing their fates.

The 31 rockets fired into Israel from the Gaza Strip Friday night are a restrained response to this malice. They are no more than a muted reminder of the fate of the Gaza Strip, addressed to those who think that 2 million people can be treated like this for over 10 years while continuing as if nothing was happening.

The Gaza Strip has no choice. Nor does Hamas. Any attempt to pin the blame on the organization—which I only wish was more secular, more feminist and more democratic—is an evasion of responsibility. It wasn't Hamas that closed the Gaza Strip. Nor did the Gaza Strip's inhabitants close themselves off. Israel (and Egypt) did it. Every hesitant attempt by Hamas to make some progress with Israel is immediately answered by automatic Israeli refusal. Nor is the world willing to talk with them; who knows why.

All that's left are the kites, which might lead to another round of merciless bombing and shelling by Israel, that Israel, of course, does not want. But what choice does the Gaza Strip have? A white flag of surrender over its fences, like the one the Palestinians in the West Bank raised? A dream of a green island off the coast of the Mediterranean, which Israeli Transportation Minister Yisrael Katz will build for them? The struggle is the only path remaining, a path that should be respected, even if you are an Israeli who might be its victim.

2019

"It Would Be More Convenient If We'd Died"

June 7

At 4:40 p.m. on Sunday, May 5, the ringing of a cell phone woke Hamis Ziada from his nap. It was an unidentified number. A voice on the other end said, "Am I speaking with Hamis Ziada? You're talking to the Israeli Shin Bet. There's a school opposite your house. Are there people in it at this time of the day?" Ziada replied that there was no one in the school in the late afternoon on that particular day, the first day of the Ramadan fast, and in any case school had been canceled because of the Israeli bombing raids. The security service agent continued, "Are you sure there are no women and children in the school? Are you positive there's no one?" And then, "I'm giving you five minutes to tell your family and everyone in the residence you live in to go outside. We have to blow up the building in another five minutes."

Dumbstruck, Ziada tried to protest. He explained to the mysterious caller that it was impossible to evacuate a seven-story building—where 15 families, including some with children and elderly people, lived—within five minutes. The Shin Bet man replied: "That's of no interest to me. I already told you: You have five minutes."

Thus began the most nightmarish five minutes in the life of Hamis Ziada, 54. After they ended, his home was destroyed, his world fell apart and his life was ruined. In the month since then, he has lived in a lean-to, together with his two wives and 12 children, the youngest of whom is 4.

The Israeli Air Force attack left a heap of rubble; the apartment building imploded in seconds, raising a thick dark cloud of dust. It was the last day of the most recent round of fighting in the Gaza Strip and in the Israeli communities around it. As usual, the Israel Defense Forces wanted to end it with the resounding crescendo of the toppling of a multistory residence.

Ziada wasn't able to save a thing—neither his belongings nor his apartment, which he was able to purchase only after working for years as an electrician in the garage of the Egged bus company in Holon. Nothing survived, not so much as a shirt.

Ziada, who now does annual car inspections for the Palestinian Authority, dredges up the Hebrew he learned in Holon years ago. He used to read bus repair manuals in Hebrew, he says. He worked for Egged from 1987 until 1993—those were good times, he says.

His second wife, Donya Daher, 42, joined the extended Skype conversation I had with Ziada last week. His first wife, Fat'hiya, who's 45 and a relative of senior Palestinian negotiator Saeb Erekat, also lives with him along with their children. "Everyone lives in the building that the planes finished off," he tells me.

Their apartment, which Ziada bought 10 years ago, was in a building in Gaza's Tel al-Halwa neighborhood. He finished paying off the mortgage two years ago. During the past three years he's earned only 1,000 shekels (about $280) a month, because the salaries of PA employees in the Strip have been cut in half. As the son of refugees who had to leave Jaffa in 1948, he receives food aid from UNRWA, the United Nations refugee agency.

Ziada's first-floor apartment had five rooms. The office of Islamic Jihad's welfare agency was on the floor above it—which is why the air force demolished the entire building. Every morning between 9 a.m. and noon, he says, needy families would come to the office to receive assistance. For the rest of the day the office was empty; no other activity took place there. There was no one there when the building was bombed, either. All the other apartments in the building were private residences.

The first time Ziada's building was damaged was five years ago, in Operation Protective Edge, when a drone fired a warning missile at it; as the occupants rushed out, an Israeli helicopter sprayed it with machine-gun fire. Two or three days later, the occupants returned home. It took until a year ago to finish repairing the damage. But on May 5 of this year, their luck ran out. "Until about 4:30 that afternoon everything was fine," says Ziada. "And then it was all over."

In the morning he had gone shopping with Daher. When they returned at 3:30 p.m., he went to sleep. After the Shin Bet called to warn about the impending strike, Ziada shouted to his wives and children to go downstairs fast. His son Amar, 24, rushed to the top floor of the building, making his way down after knocking on the door of every apartment and shouting to everyone to vacate the premises immediately. Donya Daher wrings her hands as her husband continues to describe the horrors of the evacuation.

Ziada: "Everyone in my home started to shout and cry, and in the middle of it all I was on the stairs yelling at everyone to leave, that in another five minutes they're going to bomb the building. One woman, who's 30, became stiff as a board and couldn't budge, out of fear. My son put her on his back and carried her all the way downstairs. Women who need to cover their heads before leaving the house went outside without a head covering. We were barefoot; none of us managed to find our shoes.

"Old people and children ran around and cried—that's what happened in the five minutes we were given by the Israeli authorities. There was hysteria. We're still in hysteria. During those five minutes, we became hysterical. Up until this very moment, a month later, all the people who were in the building are living with the fear of what happened to us during those five minutes. Do you know what it's like to evacuate a multistory building in five minutes?

"Finally, I went downstairs, too," Ziada continues. "We had Amar's wedding a month before the bombing, so I took with me the new suit I had bought. Other than that, I didn't manage to take anything. Neither documents nor money. Nothing. The children didn't take anything, either. Do you know what they did to us in those five minutes? Created madness in the brain. Up until this moment, as I'm speaking with you, I'm afraid.

"I worked in Israel for many years to buy that home. On the days of the work strikes during the first intifada, I walked to the Erez checkpoint so I wouldn't lose a day of work. I left home at 3 a.m. and got back at 6 in the evening. I burned up years of my life in Israel so I could buy that apartment. And now I have lost not only my home, I've lost my life. I've lost my daughters' lives. How will I buy another house at my age? I'm naked.

"The pants and shirt I'm wearing I got from other people. Someone gave me underwear. Someone gave me shoes. I'm like nothing. And what they did to my mind, to the minds of my wives, my children. The children wake up in the middle of the night and say, 'We want to go back home. Back to our books.' And I say, 'Where do you think we will go? We have no home.'

"Your government and your army—how can they do something like that? Don't they know we are civilians? Don't they know? I'm not just talking about myself. There are people who didn't finish paying off their mortgage. If we'd been bombed and had stayed inside the building, it would have been easier for us than those five minutes. It would be more convenient if we had died."

His voice breaks. The Skype connection also breaks off for a few minutes. Our conversation was made possible thanks to the devoted work of Gaza Strip field researchers Olfat al-Kurd and Khaled al-Azayzeh, from the Israel human rights organization B'Tselem. They had heard about the story and arranged for us to speak, since we Israeli journalists are not allowed into the Strip.

Once the building's residents were on the street, they all ran as far and as fast as they could from the building. The Shin Bet agent called again, to ascertain that the building was empty. The people stood down the street, appalled, and watched as their homes were bombed by pilots of the "moral" Israeli Air Force. Neighbors gathered with them. "We watched as our house was bombed. As it came down. We all waited to see how the planes fired missiles at the building. How it came down."

A drone fired three or four warning missiles at the roof—a tactic called "roof knocking"—and then, at 5 p.m. precisely, on the fifth day of the fifth month, the warplane fired the missile that caused the building to collapse instantly. The noise was ear-splitting. Clouds of smoke and dust columned into the air and lingered there for a long time. The former occupants scattered in every direction, unable to bear the scene of destruction, spending their first homeless night with neighbors and relatives.

The Ziada family spent the night in a shack near the home of relatives. People donated mattresses, clothing, blankets.

It was very, very hard for us," Ziada explains. "We slept like dogs, like animals. I couldn't fall asleep: The next day was [still] Ramadan, I had to fast and I needed to live with this day. We drank tea. We drank water. Neighbors brought us halvah and we got through the night." They stayed in the lean-to for a month. "We had nowhere to go. We were like beggars. We begged people to help us. One person brought us pita, another one brought rice."

It was only this week that the family succeeded in renting a three-room apartment, for $200 a month. The Palestinian Employment Ministry will help to pay the rent for six months. What happens after that? Ziada has no idea. No one has spoken to him, either from the PA or from Hamas: "They didn't even come to offer their condolences. That makes me angry. At least let them say a few nice words. No one came to us."

The morning after, occupants of the building came back to see the devastation. People tried to salvage a blanket or a shirt, to poke through the rubble to find a document or a certificate, maybe a photograph, amid the piles of stones and mounds of dirt and dust. They found only shreds of blankets and tatters of clothing. Nothing was left of the furniture or the utensils. The destruction was total. The best air force in the world.

The IDF Spokesperson's Unit this week issued the following statement to *Haaretz*: "The building in question is one that had been under the control of Hamas since it was erected in 2010, and was used for the digging of an important network of tunnels beneath it. Hamas used the building for military purposes in clear exploitation of the local population living within and around it as a means for hiding and protecting the terror infrastructure under its authority.

"It must be stressed that before the attack, precautionary evacuation measures were taken in the area in order to prevent harm to uninvolved individuals as much as possible. (This was done several hours before the attack and not five minutes beforehand, as is claimed in the article.)

"The IDF plans its attacks in a way that will ensure operational achievements while minimizing harm to citizens and their property."

According to UN data, about 100 buildings, containing a total of 33 residential units, were completely destroyed by Israeli bombing in the recent round in Gaza. Fifty-two families, 327 individuals, including 65 infants and toddlers under the age of 5, were left homeless. Hundreds of other apartments and buildings sustained damage.

The junk dealers started to show up at the site with their mule-drawn carts to try and pull out metals and other construction materials from the wreckage. This week, the rubble was still there, where the apartment building stood until a month ago.

What does he miss most? "The photos," says Ziada. "The photos of my father, of my mother, of my wife and of the children. Everything that reminds me of the days that are gone. My heart is burned. Life for us is burned. They burned everything that was beautiful in our life. Like paper they burned it.

"How can the Israeli people be silent about what happened? We are the closest peoples to one another. We worked together, ate together, slept together, lived together. You used to come to our weddings. How can the Israeli people be silent when it sees what is happening to us? You used all the missiles in the world against us, including some that are banned. Where is the Israeli people when it sees its government doing this? In Gaza there are people with no arms, no legs; there isn't a home without someone dead. How can you, a democracy, behave like that?

"I only hope this gets to the government, that this article will reach Netanyahu and the Israeli people. We've been left with nothing. People are wandering around here with diseases and can't leave; in some cases their children have died. Are you pleased about that? Are you pleased at what you are doing to us? We are not animals. We are human beings, just like you are human beings.

"Don't you want us to live? Do you want us to die? You're toppling buildings on our heads? Leave us alone to live. The same way you live—we want to live.

"We are all cripples in Gaza. You close the sky to us, close the sea to us, close the land. What do you want from us? You are making us hate all Israelis," Ziada says. "We don't want that. Open Gaza and let us live, and maybe we'll forget what you did to us."

"My Future Turned Black"

July 12

According to the United Nations, 327 residents of the Gaza Strip lost their homes in the wake of bombing by the Israeli Air Force during the latest round of fighting, in May. In new testimony, compiled by Olfat al-Kurd, a field researcher for the Israeli human rights organization B'Tselem in Gaza, the occupants of two large apartment buildings that were bombed and left in ruins recall the moments of horror when they were forced to leave and the devastation wreaked on their lives.

Al-Khazandar building, Gaza City, May 4, 2019
Mahmoud a-Nakhaleh, 29, proprietor of a woman's clothing store: "On May 4, 2019, a bit before 9 p.m., I closed my shop and went into the shoe store next to me. We heard a commotion on the street. Neighbors from the building next door were

shouting, telling us the [Israeli] military had called them and said it was about to bomb the Al-Khazandar building, which is our building, and that we had five minutes to get out. We quickly left the premises and stood about a hundred meters away.

"We saw a drone fire two small missiles [as a warning] to make people vacate the building. A few minutes later, another missile was fired on the road by the building. I tried to go back into my store to get the merchandise out, but security forces and other people who were there wouldn't let me. At 9:30 p.m., they bombed the building with two missiles. It was reduced to a pile of rubble. I felt like I was about to have a stroke. I couldn't believe my eyes. I lost my business and the merchandise in the store. There was merchandise from Turkey on the second floor that I had received about a week ago. I was planning to sell it during Ramadan and over the holiday.

"I don't know why the Israeli military hurt us in such a barbaric way. I don't belong to any organization or faction in Gaza. I'm a self-employed young man who's working for my own and my wife's future, and for my father's, who invested in the business and is helping us make a living. I lost everything I had. All the work I put in was lost right in front of my eyes. What did I do? My future had turned black.

"Everything is under the rubble. I haven't managed to salvage anything so far. I have nightmares every night because of the business and the money I lost. It was right before Eid al-Fitr, which is supposed to be the busiest time for clothing suppliers and retailers in Gaza.

"My wife and I want to leave the Gaza Strip and move somewhere where we can build a good life, make a living, and enjoy basic rights. A place with a future. I don't feel like a human being. I lost hope after my business was destroyed. The Israeli military destroyed our lives and left us with nothing."

Diaa al-Khazandar, 66, retired physician, married, father of three: "On May 4, 2019, at 9:30 p.m., I was at home in the Rimal neighborhood when I learned from neighbors of the building we own that it had been hit by two warning missiles and that, about

20 minutes later, Israeli warplanes had bombed the building and turned it to a pile of rubble. We didn't get any warning phone call from the military. I don't know why they bombed it. It's not a military installation.

"My brothers and I built that building and put all our savings into it, so that it would provide us with income and our children with apartments once they got married. Within minutes, everything we invested was buried. My life was turned upside down. My hopes were dashed. My future became dark. The building was a source of hope and income for us and for our sons.

"This wasn't the first time Israel hurt our family. In 2008, Israeli bulldozers demolished my home in Beit Lahia. It was a two-story house. We've been living in rentals ever since. They also bulldozed the tile factory my brothers and I had in the Nahal Oz area, east of Gaza City. Now they've demolished our building, too. I'm an ordinary person, a doctor. I don't belong to any party."

Amjad Jabr, 28, single, owned a shoe store: "Disaster struck me while I was in the store. The occupants of the next building were informed that they had to vacate their homes, because our building was going to be bombed. The neighbors told us. I left the business without taking a thing. We went out to the road quickly, abandoning the store and the merchandise. The building was bombed five minutes later. We were standing about 100 meters from it. We went on waiting, totally stunned, and without knowing why the building was being bombed.

"Within minutes it was a heap of rubble. Seven stories collapsed and lay level with the ground as though they had never existed. I was distressed and went into shock. Within minutes, I had lost everything I had. An hour later, after I'd lost hope of finding some of the merchandise, I went home, devastated because of the future that was wiped out. Everything went down the tubes.

"Why do they bomb us with missiles, especially when I am an ordinary resident and don't belong to any party or organization? I am a young man who wants to earn a living and is working to secure his future. My whole investment was wiped out in a minute. They ruined my business, which cost me a fortune.

"I did not lose hope. Twenty days after the business was bombed, I rented another store and laid out the expenses again. I bought new merchandise. I raised the money by selling a plot of land I owned. I had planned to build myself a house on that land and get married, but unfortunately all my dreams and plans have been wiped out. I lost the store and the merchandise. Still, my situation is better than that of others."

Al-Qamar building, Gaza City, May 5, 2019
At about 5 p.m., the Israel Defense Forces informed residents of the Al-Qamar building, in the neighborhood of Tal al-Hawa, that the structure would soon be attacked and that they must vacate it. A few minutes later, before all the occupants had managed to leave, some aircraft fired a warning missile at the building. About 30 minutes later, at approximately 5:30 p.m., the building was struck by several assault missiles and completely destroyed. According to the IDF, Hamas had dug tunnels under the building.

Ghadah al-Wakil, 30, is a homemaker, married and a mother of three. Her family had been living in a rental apartment on the building's fifth floor for some three years. Her parents and four of her siblings lived in the apartment across the hall. "I was home with the children. My sister, Shatha, came into our house yelling: 'Bombing! Bombing!' I didn't understand what she meant. I thought maybe someone in the family had been hurt in a bombing. It took a while until I realized they were going to bomb our building. I picked up my son Muhammad, who is 18 months old, and tried to call my husband, Tamer, but he didn't answer.

"In the meantime, without my noticing, my sisters had taken my other two children, Alaa, 7 months, and Yamen, who is 6 years old, and left. I started shouting and looking for the kids. In the meantime, my husband called back. I told him, while screaming in a panic, that the building was going to be bombed and I didn't know where our children were. I was terrified. I went into the neighbors' and asked them where the kids were. I was so scared, I didn't realize I was actually holding Muhammad. When my husband came, I took a last sad look at our apartment, and then we went down. All the residents were in the stairway. Everyone was shouting very loudly.

"A warning missile hit the building while we were still inside it. I went into the street. All the neighbors were there. I didn't see anyone from my family—not my parents, not my children. I was scared they'd stayed in the building and that it would be bombed with them still inside. I kept looking for my children until I found them. They were all with my parents. They were frightened, screaming and crying, barefoot and in their underwear.

"My husband's family came and took us to their house. I was crying hysterically. I had hoped the bombing would hit only one floor, or one apartment, but when I heard it, I realized the whole tower had been destroyed. I went into shock. I just sat and said nothing. Everyone tried to talk to me, but I just kept silent. I didn't understand what had happened. I still don't understand why they bombed my home, the building I'd lived in.

"We stayed in my husband's parents' home for 10 days. It was tough. The room was small and crowded. Then we moved to a house my parents had rented. Their apartment was destroyed, too. I thought we'd rent our own apartment, but our financial situation is really hard. My husband is unemployed, and rent is high—at least twice what we paid in the building that was bombed.

"Our children are in a terrible emotional state. Yamen hasn't gone to school since the bombing. They have nightmares and keep waking up at night. Yamen keeps talking about his room and his toys. They went through weeks of panic. There wasn't a lot of food. They kept getting a fever. Muhammad has become very aggressive. He keeps hitting his brothers, breaking toys and screaming. We've lost so much. There's no compensation for the memories we had in that house. The scary evacuation, the anxiety and the shouting, were all a terrible experience."

I'atimad Abu Eishah, 58, a married mother of seven, lived in a rented apartment on the second floor: "We were all at home.

Suddenly, we heard shouting in the building. I asked my son Kathem, who is 41: 'What's going on? It looks like a bombing.' Suddenly, the neighbors shouted to us: 'Get out of the house. Go downstairs. The Israeli army is going to bomb the building.' I panicked. I didn't know what to do. We all got very frightened, and the children started screaming.

"We left right away, wearing house clothes that aren't acceptable to wear outside. We put on our shoes as we were going down the stairs. My son Nael went down with his young girls, and they cried and screamed the whole way down. I needed help going down the stairs.

"When we were going down, we thought they were probably going to bomb just a particular apartment in the building. I didn't think they'd bomb the whole tower. I saw all the residents on the street, crying and shouting. About 20 minutes later, the building was bombed. I cried so hard for the house. My heart was broken, even though I didn't own it. It was my home, the roof over my and my family's head. Now I, my children, and my grandchildren have become homeless.

"We stayed with my son's friend for about 10 days, and then we found another rental apartment and moved in. It's unfurnished. There are no beds or appliances, and we don't even have kitchenware. The apartment we had before was spacious. It comfortably fit a family of 11. Now everything is in ruins.

"We all sleep on the floor, on mattresses we received from the Red Cross. I have no washing machine, no fridge. My daughters-in-law have lost their gold jewelry, and my son lost merchandise for his store that he was storing at home. We even left our IDs at home.

"My granddaughters had a room full of toys, school bags and books. Everything is gone. It's all under the rubble. They have a hard time falling asleep because of the fear. They've also started wetting their beds again. I sleep next to them. When they hear a loud noise, they wake up screaming, 'Grandma! Grandma!'— thinking it's a bombing."

The Trial of "Inmate X"

October 18

Next week, after the Jewish holidays end, the trial of Mohammed El Halabi will resume in Be'er Sheva District Court. It's either/or: Either El Halabi is one of Israel's greatest and most dangerous enemies ever, as the indictment against him indicates—or he's the victim of a cynical, cruel propaganda system that is exploiting him to stop the influx of international humanitarian aid into the Gaza Strip. Either he diverted tens of millions of dollars and hundreds of tons of iron to Hamas for tunnel-digging projects, as Israel's Shin Bet security service maintains, or he's a "humanitarian hero," as the United Nations designated him in 2014. Either he's a longtime Hamas "plant" in World Vision, the huge global aid organization whose Gaza and other branches he headed, or he's a person who has devoted his life to providing humanitarian aid to farmers, disabled children and cancer patients in the Strip.

After 52 days of interrogation by the Shin Bet—which included severe torture, according to his father, Khalil El Halabi—and more than three years in an Israeli prison, El Halabi, who used to crisscross the world, address parliaments and enter Israel itself frequently, will next Thursday be brought again from Ramon Prison in Mitzpeh Ramon to face a judicial tribunal headed by Be'er Sheva District Court deputy president Natan Zlotchover. El Halabi has been brought into the courtroom 127 times since his initial arrest in June 2016; his testimony went on for nearly a year and he denied all the charges against him. According to his lawyer, Maher Hanna, from Nazareth, when his trial began, El Halabi was offered a plea bargain that included a confession of guilt and three years in prison, but he refused. He insisted he was completely innocent. Meanwhile, in Gaza, Khalil is devoting all his time to his son's struggle. "My heart is broken," he told me this week.

El Halabi's story has been reported relatively widely in international media outlets, but in Israel he is a sort of "Inmate X," with very little published about the case.

Khalil El Halabi, 65, worked for UNRWA, the United Nations refugee agency, for 40 years as an education supervisor. This week he sent me his photograph together with former US president Jimmy Carter at a 2010 conference in the Al-Mathaf Hotel in Gaza City. Mohammed, his second son, was born in 1978 in the Jabalya refugee camp, is married to Ulla and has five children; the youngest, 4-year-old Faris, knows his father only from behind bars.

In 2003, Mohammed obtained a master's degree in civil engineering from the Islamic University of Gaza; he worked in the private sector and later in the UN's development agency. In 2006 he joined the US-based Christian organization World Vision, one of the world's largest international aid groups, and in short order became its regional director, covering the West Bank, Gaza and East Jerusalem.

In an interview published on the organization's website in August 2014, El Halabi related what had drawn him to the field of humanitarian aid: "I was born in Jabalya UNRWA refugee camp in Gaza. It is the densest area in the Middle East and there I experienced the most critical times for Gaza people." He added, "I met the children whose houses were totally demolished and lost at least one of their beloved people, yet they are singing for peace."

El Halabi left the engineering profession: "Seeing injured and killed children, and knowing my own children have been traumatized by the violence, [I] decided to fully dedicate my life to helping people and children to restore their lives."

At that time, World Vision was helping 1,500 children as part of the Child Friendly Spaces program he established in the Strip to protect youngsters in emergencies, along with 350 wounded children in hospitals. El Halabi and his staff also "helped 8,000 parents in psychological first-aid training, which significantly reduces the stress on their children during the war," he said in the same interview. This was the period of Israel's Operation Protective Edge.

Photographs from the past show a stocky, smiling young man visiting youngsters in wheelchairs, disabled athletes and farmers in their Gaza greenhouses; Khalil says his son's work also often took him abroad. Indeed, one of Mohammed's last missions was to address the parliament in Canberra; Australia is an important donor to projects he managed. He also traveled extensively in the West Bank and East Jerusalem—with Israeli authorization, of course. On June 15, 2016, when returning from a meeting with his staff in Jerusalem, he was taken into custody at the Erez border crossing into Gaza. His family only learned about the arrest three days later.

Thus began the ordeal of Citizen H. This week marked his 40th month in detention, during which he has been transferred among a number of prisons. His family is permitted to visit him only once every two months, and only three relatives are allowed to come each time, including the children.

They try to take little Faris as often as possible, so he will get to know his father. It's a grueling 12-hour trip from Gaza for a mere half-hour visit conducted through an armor-plated window. As result of the torture El Halabi endured—including sleep deprivation, being hung from the ceiling and beatings, his father says—his hearing is 40 percent impaired, which makes the phone conversations through the window during visits even more difficult.

Attorney Hanna, who visits him occasionally in prison, says his client is strong and determined, and that his spirit has not flagged. Mohammed himself always tells his father in visits that he is certain that justice will prevail.

El Halabi's trial is being held partly on camera. On November 22, 2017, he was brought before the Supreme Court for a hearing on the repeated extension of his remands, because there had been so many of them. The revised indictment against him that had been filed early that year includes the following charges, some of which are very serious: contact with a foreign agent, membership in a terror organization, aiding the enemy in wartime, using property for the purposes of terrorism, passing information to the enemy, possession of arms and ammunition, and prohibited military training.

The accused exploited his position and status in World Vision, a humanitarian aid organization, to "advance the goals of Hamas," the indictment states.

El Halabi has also been accused of diverting between hundreds and thousands of tons of iron, originally intended for agricultural purposes, to Hamas for construction of tunnels. He also allegedly "marked coordinates in Israel for operations by the Iz al-Din al-Qassam Brigades"—the Islamist organization's military wing. Moreover, he is accused of transferring funds for the purchase of equipment for Hamas's naval commandos, and even of giving the organization information about the security arrangements at the Erez crossing.

In a briefing for reporters after the indictment was filed, a Shin Bet official claimed El Halabi had transferred tens of millions of dollars to Hamas. A greenhouse project he had managed was allegedly intended to conceal excavation sites for tunnels; a rehabilitation program for fishermen was actually a cover for purchasing diving suits and motorboats for Hamas's naval force; farmers he hired were lookouts for Hamas. He even allegedly transferred thousands of food parcels to Hamas activists and their families. According to the charge sheet, El Halabi was recruited by Hamas as early as 2004 to "infiltrate" World Vision.

For his part, Hanna denies all the charges against his client. He is convinced that the purpose of the indictment is solely to intimidate aid groups and effectively halt humanitarian assistance to Gaza, so that its residents will eventually rise up against Hamas, as Israel perhaps hopes for. Indeed, since El Halabi's arrest, World Vision has suspended its operations in the Strip, until the trial is over. But a comprehensive investigation by the organization itself, at a cost of $3 million, according to Hanna, exonerated El Halabi completely: No wrongdoing was found on his part.

World Vision's current director in Israel and the territories, Alex Snary, wrote: "My dear friend and colleague Mohammed El Halabi exposed the total travesty of Israeli 'justice' for Palestinians. Three years of torture and detention, over 120 court appearances and Israel still has no actual evidence to support their outrageous allegations." Snary describes El Halabi as "a man with a big heart," especially when it comes to children, adding, "It's long overdue for Israel to admit they made a mistake, stop embarrassing its judicial system and release him to return to his family and the work he loves—improving the lives of suffering children."

In August 2016, two months after El Halabi's arrest, senior diplomats from Western countries in Israel protested to then *Haaretz* correspondent Barak Ravid that they had not been given any information or evidence about the possible diversion of aid funds to Hamas. Australia's Department of Foreign Affairs and Trade announced in March 2017 that following an investigation, it had concluded there was nothing to suggest improper use of funding or of aid to the Hamas-ruled Gaza government.

Last June 14, independent Australian journalist Antony Loewenstein published the results of his investigation on the website +972: He, too, concluded that, despite the lengthy period that had elapsed, the charges against El Halabi remained unsubstantiated.

Hanna, the lawyer, notes that a considerable portion of World Vision's budget has always been earmarked to facilitate close supervision of the group's financial activities and contractual bidding processes. He adds that the total amount donated to its activities in Gaza over the years is far smaller than the sums El Halabi is accused of funneling to Hamas.

Hanna is also highly critical of the legal restrictions he himself has been subject to: Israel has barred him from entering the Strip to meet with defense witnesses, a situation that led him to petition the Supreme Court. The court's response is expected in December—after the conclusion of El Halabi's trial. Hanna has also demanded to have several witnesses be brought to Israel to testify, but the authorities are blocking that avenue as well. His request to have them testify via video conference is expected to be addressed in next week's court session in Be'er Sheva. In the meantime, the defense continues to present its case.

Hanna: "Everything you touch in this trial is a 'creative work.'

I am not against the state. I want our judicial system to be the best and most just, but I don't even get transcripts of hearings that I conducted." El Halabi understands only about half of what is said in court, Hanna says, because of faulty translation. The Shin Bet approved only one interpreter for the proceedings, for security reasons, but she is not proficient, the lawyer says.

World Vision representatives have attended some of the hearings. None of El Halabi's family is present, of course, because they live in the Gaza Strip. There is a gag order on the principal piece of evidence in the trial, for security reasons. According to Hanna, no firm, objective proof of the charges has been presented in court so far—which may attest to the protracted nature of the proceedings.

Said Khalil El Halabi this week, "We miss Mohammed. Gaza misses Mohammed. Every day I try to stir interest and awareness of my son's case. When I was an education supervisor for UNRWA, I introduced a special chapter on the Holocaust into the curriculum. I told everyone that injustice like this is above and beyond any political dispute. I never expected that my son would encounter such gross lack of justice.

"Please write my message to Benjamin Netanyahu: Your prime minister is worried that he won't get a fair trial—Mohammed also wants a fair trial. His fate is eating me from within. I want to hold him close to my chest and tell him how proud I am of all he has done for Gaza and for the Palestinian people, without doing harm to Israel. Please, treat Mohammed as though he were your son."

2020

Happy New Year, Gaza

January 2

That's how it goes when you're having fun. Time flies. Eight years ago, in 2012, the United Nations issued a report titled *Gaza in 2020: A Livable Place?* The answer was contained in the body of the report: No. Not unless steps are taken to save it.

No real steps have been taken but the projections in this severe report were also not borne out: The situation is much worse than it predicted.

On January 1, 2020, the year of the end for Gaza began. As of January 1, 2 million human beings are living in a place that is not livable.

There's a Chernobyl in Gaza, an hour from Tel Aviv. And Tel Aviv is not bothered by that. Nor is the rest of the world. News reviews of the past decade included everything else, just not the humanitarian disaster in Israel's backyard for which Israel, first and foremost, is to blame, is responsible.

Instead of taking responsibility for expelling and driving them to Gaza in 1948 and attempting to compensate and atone for what was done, through rehabilitation and assistance, Israel is continuing to pursue the policies of 1948 in a different way: a cage instead of expulsion, jail instead of ethnic cleansing, siege instead of dispossession.

It's doubtful there are many other regions of the world where disasters have lasted continuously for over 70 years, and all of it the product of malicious human acts. The memory of Gaza should have hounded us day and night. Instead, Gaza is forgotten. Only the firing of a Qassam rocket is capable of providing a reminder that it exists.

When the UN report was written, the unemployment rate in Gaza was 29 percent. Eight years have elapsed, and now, according to the World Bank, the jobless rate there has reached an unimaginable 53 percent—67 percent among young people.

Does anybody get that? Sixty-seven percent unemployment. Does anyone understand what such a life is like, when a big majority of young people have no present and no future?

Hamas is the guilty party. Hamas is guilty of everything. And Israel? Not at all. What repression, denial and brainwashing does this require? What lies and inhumanity and cruelty? A country that has dispatched rescue missions to the ends of the earth is revoltingly apathetic to the disaster it has created on its border, and is even compounding the situation. About half of the residents of the Gaza Strip live on less than $5.50 a day. In the occupied West Bank, by comparison, only 9 percent of the population subsists on such a sum.

Hamas is guilty. As if it has imposed the siege. It is obstructing exports, imports, places of employment. It is firing at Gaza's fisherman. It is preventing cancer patients from getting medical treatment. It has bombed Gaza, killing thousands of civilians and destroying countless homes. Obviously.

The 2012 UN report predicted that in 2020, Gaza would need at least 1,000 more doctors. But in the Gaza of 2020, 160 doctors have left within the past three years. Anyone who can leaves.

A young surgeon at Gaza's Shifa Hospital, Dr. Sara al-Saqqa, told the *Guardian* last week that she earns $300 for 40 days' work. Were it not for her elderly mother, she, too, would have left.

There's worse to come. Ninety-seven percent of Gaza's water supply is unfit for consumption, as the UN report forecast. Fully 100,000 cubic meters of sewage a day flows into the Mediterranean, which is also our sea. Ashkelon is bathing in Gaza's sewage, but that isn't bothering anyone, either.

Three years after the UN report was issued, the United Nations published its 2015 report. Israel's war in the Strip, Operation Protective Edge, had uprooted half a million people from their homes in 2014 and left Gaza crushed. But that, too, prompted nothing more than a big yawn. And then came the report, this time from the World Bank: The Gazan economy was in critical condition. Let them suffocate. Israel stands with Naama Issachar, the Israeli woman in jail in Russia, who has been transferred to another prison.

Nobody Opposes the War

May 16

There's no issue that all (Jewish) Israelis agree on more than the launching of a war. Almost a week has passed and no one is opposing this horrific war, not even Yair Lapid, Merav Michaeli and Nitzan Horowitz.

They attack Benjamin Netanyahu—you don't have to be brave to do that—they express sorrow over our suffering, but not a word about this criminal war of choice whose death toll and minuscule advantage it awards Israel is yet to be determined. Yet again, this is proof that there's no peace camp in Israel, not even a tiny hut.

The TV studio commentators are à la *Apocalypse Now*, hordes of retired generals and Shin Bet agents trumpeting a uniform and repulsive chorus. The saliva flows and the eyes flash, lifted upward toward the glorious pilots who have managed to elude and destroy the enemy's sophisticated air defense: two torn kites on a good day. The bombing of the helpless favela of Gaza is "proof that our air force is the best in the world," one senior newscaster said in a voice trembling with emotion.

And the results aren't being displayed. Israelis don't have a clue about what's happening in Gaza, not a notion of what the military is doing in their name. That's why they're clamoring for more, why they're so certain of the justice of their cause.

We can assume that if more Israelis saw the pictures from Gaza, at least some of them would cry out and call for a halt to this horror. I've received photos of the mangled bodies of 40 children, Friday night's harvest in Gaza. You can't remain silent after viewing these pictures. Let's leave aside humaneness for now, it's irrelevant in wartime. The question is, what is it all for? What would have happened if Israel hadn't provoked the Palestinians in Jerusalem? And what would have happened if even after these provocations it had swallowed its pride and removed its aggressive police officers from the Al-Aqsa compound, or not bombed high-rise apartment buildings in Gaza, to avoid a war? What would have happened if it showed restraint? Is it more powerful now? Is Hamas any weaker, or has it been weakened militarily but bolstered politically to an all-time high?

Hamas is the hero of the hour, not Israel. And regarding deterrence, the mother of all excuses for every war in Gaza, look how it worked out the last time they told us about deterrence, during the 2014 war. The supposedly deterred Hamas doubled its military might, as well as its boldness.

Hamas is also responsible for war crimes, obviously, but mainly, please note, against its own people. Building an aggressive war machine without any protection for the population against the Israeli military is a crime against humanity.

But we're Israelis, so we must first discuss our own war crimes. These are piling up in the current operation, which for a moment looked like it was being conducted with more caution than its predecessors. Now the blood of dozens of children in Gaza is flowing in the streets, a result of our pilots' and soldiers' crimes.

If the pilots could see the photos of the children they killed, if the commanders of air bases who appeared Friday night in all the TV studios, with their revolting mellifluous eloquence, saw these pictures, what would they say? That there was no choice? Now we can wait for the Black Friday that always happens at the end of a Gaza war. It will improve the balance of blood that has already assumed monstrous proportions.

Of all the terrible photos, one video from northern Gaza, taken Thursday night, has been etched in my memory. The camera was stationary, recording masses of people fleeing south, fearing an airstrike. It was late at night, and people were carrying plastic bags and babies, a sea of people fleeing for their lives, not for the first time, not for the last, with most of them not having a place to return to. One of them suddenly jumped onto the road to save a kitten—a rare moment of humanity.

We should look squarely at these pictures. What gives us the right to do all this? Where does it come from?

2021

One Image, 2 Million People

October 10

This image should haunt every Israeli, wherever they may go. Haunt them, disturb their sleep, torture their conscience, destroy their peace of mind. A mass of people crowding in front of the chamber of commerce in the Jabalya refugee camp, in a desperate attempt to get a permit to work in Israel. You need to look at the expressions, the bleary eyes, the stubble, the beseeching, the despair showing on the face of every person on line, fighting for his life and livelihood. The papers they wave, as though these will help them achieve their dream. The hands outstretched, as though someone's long arm will help him to reach his dream. But it is Israel's long arm, serving these people all these ills. For decades Israel has abused them, their parents and their children. There is no place like Gaza to tell this story of evil, from the expulsion and flight in 1948, through the reprisal actions and the conquests to this 15-year siege. This is Israel's true long arm, which shapes its moral profile.

Each man is looking in a different direction, left, right or skyward—from whence his help may come, perhaps. The crush is terrible. The photograph recalls the live shipments of livestock to Israel. The sadness in the eyes of these helpless people and the shock they arouse are so similar, calves and people. Here they are people without dignity. Israel has shorn them of the last vestiges of their dignity. Khoury reported that some are willing to work

12-hour construction shifts for 20 shekels [$6.20], and for that privilege they crowd tightly like beasts. The war is over 3,000 permits that Israel has oh-so-graciously offered. At least 300,000 job seekers competing for 3,000 permits. One in a hundred might win. In a territory where unemployment has reached 48 percent overall and 66 percent among young adults, self-respect has been lost. How easy it would be to restore to these wretched men their dignity and livelihood. Open up the Gaza Strip, reconnect it to the West Bank and allow these people to work in Israel, which imports laborers all the way from China.

About half a million workers entered Israel from Gaza every month until 2000. Some grew up here, between Tel Aviv's Carmel and Hatikva markets, befriended Israelis and built their lives in what was once their parents' country. The most beautiful pictures of their lives were sadly similar. They, too, packed in tightly at the Erez checkpoint in the dead of night on the way to work in Israel, and on their way back they stood like wraiths on the side of the road, carrying their junk. Those were their finest hours. There was hope in it. We were appalled by their living conditions, sleeping in warehouses, and crowding at checkpoints. To them it was the best of times, which have not returned for 20 years.

According to figures from Gisha, an Israeli nonprofit dedicated to the freedom of movement of Palestinians, in 2019 some 15,000 were still allowed into Israel. Only 6 percent of this number are permitted today, under the guise of COVID-19 restrictions. In other words: jail. Furloughs from Israeli prisons are more frequent. Seventy percent of Gazans rely on humanitarian aid, in a place that a United Nations study from two years ago declared unfit for human habitation.

How do we sleep at night with all this? This misery is on our hands. And please don't start with Hamas and the rockets. Gaza is occupied territory. Israel is responsible for its fate. Gaza is Israel's trash can, and Egypt's to a lesser degree. Gaza is the land of refugees who fled or were expelled from the land because of Israel. Israel bears a heavy responsibility for their fate.

A different photograph was published in the *Marker*: It, too, shows a mass of people, but they are waving and smiling at the camera. An hour's drive from Jabalya, the Israeli employees of Moon Active, the company whose *Coin Master*, a "light and addictive" mobile game, became a sensation earning billions of dollars. And how did Moon Active become such a sensation? "By creating a feeling of near-victory that produces a tremendous thrill, eventually leading to addiction."

Congratulations: The Gaza Ghetto Now Has a Fence Around It

December 9

They are celebrating inside the bunker: A new fence around the Gaza Strip was inaugurated. Fence? A terrifying barrier. All the honored guests of the Defense Ministry were invited to the event declaring the completion of the project—"not including the leprous Benjamin Netanyahu," who holds founding shares in the project and was, of course, not invited. They hugged each other, the way only the old boys know how, slapped the back of "Mr. Fence," Brig. Gen. Eran Ofir, who has the poetic title of "head of the border and seamline administration"—in a country that has no border, and barely has a seamline. Naturally, sliced-up vegetables with dips and petits fours were served as refreshments, Defense Minister Benny Gantz said the barrier was "creative," as if it was a work of art, and everyone was delighted and bursting with pride.

After all, how is it possible not to delight in the face of the 3.5 billion shekels cast away? In other words, buried deep down in the ground, and in return for which Israel received 2 million cubic meters of concrete, 140 tons of iron and steel that will never rust, including sensors that are sensitive to any hoe used by a Hamas member, and security forever for the children living in Israel near the Gaza border—which is, of course, "priceless."

They even came from Donald Trump's America at the time to look at the wonder—the pride of Israel. Every Qassam rocket volley passed by there and saw the three concrete plants built there, the tons of cement and iron poured into the ground in a country that pays its disabled 3,200 shekels a month and demands that they make do with this to live on, because it has no money.

While the iron and concrete monster was being buried in the earth, not even a single public discussion was held on this insane enterprise. Because what was there to discuss? Security. It's unlikely there are even 1,000 Israelis, not including the contractors and their families, who even heard about any of it. It's ridiculous to demand a public debate on the matter, which only brigadier generals understand, and characters like Trump are so thrilled about.

It's exciting to see the fence now in all its glory. It can serve as a new national monument to memorialize the temporary sanity that the country has lost. A convoy of limousines will bring the official guests from abroad—directly from Yad Vashem—to view the wonder. Here is buried the sanity of Israel. Here it has buried its head as deep as possible in the sand, and here it was finally declared an insane nation. A sophisticated military state, which surrounds itself with fences that have no rival anywhere in the world, facing barefoot militias, who will never stop harassing it for as long as they are imprisoned inside the Gaza Strip. A country that invests tens of billions of shekels more in preparations for a no less crazy attack on Iran, knowing that it will never carry it out, needs a monument to sanity—and its place is on the border with the Gaza Strip.

Behind the crowded facades of the iron grilles, it is no longer possible to see what is on the other side. But no one wants to see, either. There is a huge concentration camp for people there.

When the fence was built around Qalqilyah in the West Bank it reminded one of a concentration camp. Whoever dared to make the comparison was immediately condemned, of course. Facing the Gaza fence, it is no longer possible to deceive anyone: This is what the fence of a ghetto looks like, of a prison, of a concentration camp. Only in Israel do they celebrate the building of a concentration camp. Only the skies of the ghetto are somehow still open, and that is in a limited fashion, too. Coming soon, the next devilish invention of the defense establishment: A dome of iron, a huge ceiling over the skies of Gaza. The head of the "border and seamline" administration is already working on it. First, he will just finish with the intimidating wall being built on the Lebanese border, and then he will be free to do that, too.

Two million people have been imprisoned continuously for 15 years—there has never been another concentration camp like it. The fence that was inaugurated on Tuesday is obdurate: It will remain forever. You will never be released, Gazans. After all, you don't throw a billion dollars into the garbage.

The Bar-Lev Line in the Sinai proved to be a death trap, the separation barrier on the West Bank has been wide open and ripped up for a long time, and no lessons have been learned. But the Israelis are celebrating. There is an abundance of security in the south, too—so much security that there is nothing left for anything else.

2022

The Only Way

March 31

The way of terror is the only way open to the Palestinians to fight for their future. The way of terror is the only way for them to remind Israel, the Arab states and the world of their existence. They have no other way. Israel has taught them this. If they don't use violence, everyone will forget about them.

This is not hypothetical speculation; this has been proven in reality, again and again. When they are quiet, interest in their cause evaporates and fades from the agenda of Israel and the rest of the world.

Look what happens to Gaza between the rocket barrages. Who pays any attention to it? Who cares about it? Everyone already wants to forget about the Palestinians' existence. People are tired of hearing about Palestinian suffering, and the quiet makes this possible.

Only when the bullets fly, the knives strike and the rockets boom do people remember that there is another people here with a terrible problem that must be resolved. The conclusion is harsh and terrifying: Only through terrorism will they be remembered, only through terrorism will they possibly obtain something.

One thing is certain: If they put down their weapons, they are doomed.

One can argue about the legitimacy of Palestinian terror and its definition: Who kills more and who is more brutal, Israel or them?

In recent weeks, we've reported here about a Palestinian student who went out for a hike and was shot to death in the head, about a boy who held up a Molotov cocktail in front of a 20-meter-high wall and was shot to death in the back, about a Palestinian man who was returning from a workout when soldiers fired 31 bullets at his car, and about a teen who was fleeing for his life from Border Police officers who fired 12 bullets at him and killed him. Isn't this terror, too? How is it different from Bnei Brak?

Violence is always brutal and immoral: the violence of the terrorists who fire indiscriminately at innocent passersby and the state-sanctioned uniformed violence against Palestinians, including innocent ones, as a matter of routine.

The Palestinians were relative quiet for months, as they suffered violence and buried their dead and lost their lands, homes and last shreds of dignity. And what did they get in return? An Israeli government that declares that the issue of their fate will not be discussed anytime in the near future because it is not comfortable for the government in its current composition.

Then they got the Sde Boker summit. Six foreign ministers all telling them: Your fate doesn't interest us. There are more urgent matters and more important interests.

What were they thinking there, at the Kedma hotel? That they'd have their pictures taken, smile and embrace and visit the grave of Israel's founder, the commander who oversaw the Nakba—"This is where it all began," as Yair Lapid said—and the Palestinians would cheer? That the Palestinians would see how they were being left bleeding at the side of the road and stay quiet? That maybe they'd be satisfied with the colorful candies the government tossed at them in honor of the event—20,000 work permits for laborers from Gaza? And what about the other 1,980,000 residents there living under the blockade?

The terror attacks are the punishment, the sin is the arrogance and the feeling that nothing is that urgent. Israel is in an uncomfortable situation now. The coalition is sensitive. Things have never been comfortable for it. Now there is Iran and a new

Middle East, free of Palestinians. It's not working. And it apparently will never work.

The Palestinians have no way to prove this aside from shooting in the streets. An unknown young guy from Yabed, who killed civilians and a police officer, made Israel see this. Otherwise it would not have.

Terrorism must be fought, of course. No country can allow its people to live in fear and danger.

Summits like the one in Sde Boker are also an encouraging development, and the Emirati foreign minister Sheikh Abdullah bin Zayed is a very impressive, smart and warm person.

But when Lapid said, "This is where it all began," he might as well have meant that this is where another wave of terror attacks began, one meant to remind him and his colleagues that even though they dined on fish kebab on an olive leaf, "Ben-Gurion" rice and late-winter pomelo—just two hours away, a people continues to suffocate under the brutal, totalitarian Israeli occupation.

The War of Change and Healing

August 7

Thus wrote Labor Party chair Merav Michaeli, a few minutes after Israel once again launched a criminal assault on the Gaza Strip, a moment before the killing of the first Palestinian toddler, who won't be the last: "The residents of Israel deserve to live in safety. No sovereign state would agree to a terror organization besieging its residents. . . . I support the security forces."

Benjamin Netanyahu hadn't yet reacted, Itamar Ben-Gvir hadn't woken up, Yoav Gallant didn't yet threaten the head of the snake, and already the leader of the Zionist left falls in line with the right, salutes the military and supports a war that hadn't even begun. This time she got there even before Shimon Peres.

Michaeli cannot be forgiven for her unbelievable lack of awareness: After four days of a voluntary partial lockdown in the south, the leader of the left says that no state would agree to a "siege." Without blinking, no state. A member of the government that is responsible for a horrific 16-year siege dares to be shocked by a two-minute, voluntary, partial lockdown. Instead of supporting the government's momentary restraint, which lasted the eternity of the life of a butterfly (time's a-wasting, the election is nigh), the Labor Party once again supports a foolish war of choice, as did all its predecessors. The Zionist left once again gives the concept of a double standard a bad name. Perhaps at least now the penny will drop for more supporters of the center-left: There's no real difference between it and the right. Israel can no longer even pretend that it didn't start this war—whose infantile name, Operation Breaking Dawn, was given to it at birth—or that it had no choice.

This time they even forwent the advance saber-rattling and got straight to the point: the arrest of an Islamic Jihad leader in the West Bank, which they knew ahead of time would provoke a severe response, and the assassination of a senior commander in the Gaza Strip, after which they knew there was no way back, and Israel is already waging a "defensive war," a just war of a state to which everything is permitted. The peace-loving country that only wants security for its inhabitants—such an innocent. The state that has everything except deterrence: There is nothing or no one to deter Israel from attacking Gaza.

But this time, the government is one of "change and healing." Fifteen months after the last delight, Operation Guardian of the Walls, dawn has broken. Five weeks after the fastest gun in the West took office, Prime Minister Yair Lapid is already sending the army to war. Never in Israel's history was a prime minister in such a hurry to kill. All the Netanyahu cases pale in the face of the crime of launching a needless war that will contribute nothing but more bloodshed, most of it Palestinian. And all of Netanyahu's failings pale in the face of his relative restraint in using military force while in office. Keep on getting riled up about the cigars—at least Netanyahu doesn't have to prove his macho credentials, as Lapid does.

It's true that the analysts, the old boys' club and the mayors in the south pressed for this war, as they always do, but never was there such a rapid capitulation to the caprices to launch a war; Israel was hardly given a minute for passionate excoriations on the air. Now, when only a few months separate one attack in Gaza from another, there's no point in even asking what the goals are.

There are no goals, except the desire to prove that ours is bigger. If there were goals, and if quiet were one of them, and if this were a government of change, then Lapid would have taught Israel a lesson in restraint; and if Lapid were also a courageous statesman he would have led to change by recognizing Hamas, lifting the siege and making an effort to meet with the Gaza leadership. Anything less than this is a direct continuation of the policies of all of Israel's governments, in whose DNA baseless wars run deep. That's why there is no need for a government of change. Just be sure to remember who started this war, and who supported it.

When Roger Waters Cried

August 11

Roger Waters cried Wednesday. It was on his Twitter page, as he read, on camera, an essay he had read on the Mondoweiss news website the night before. It was about a boy from the Gaza Strip.

"I really wish I could rest, or have some psychologist help me like other people in the world who 'suffer wars,'" said Mohammed. "No one during or after the war asks me or my family 'How are you doing?'"

He's the family breadwinner, a boy of 13. And only his crying, wrote Tareq Hajjaj, "melts the manly shield" he is forced to wear. "I do not want my mother to suffer like the mothers of the kids who were killed," the boy sobbed.

Mohammed wished he could have grown up somewhere else, where he would only die "when his body is fully grown," Hajjaj wrote. And this is where Waters could no longer restrain his tears and burst out crying. No decent person could remain indifferent to the sight of the musician's tears.

Waters, the great man of conscience.

But for Israelis, this was a performance from a different planet. They have a thousand defense mechanisms against Waters's tears. Let's even assume that Waters really is an "antisemite" and someone "who hates Israel"—which he isn't. But crying over a boy from Gaza? What about the children of Sderot?

Has any Israeli shed tears for a boy from Gaza? Are many Israelis even aware of what happened to children in Gaza during those three days of colossal success that deluged Israel in waves of pride and self-satisfaction such as we haven't seen here in a long time? There hasn't been a success like this since Israel's victory in the 1967 Six-Day War. Another few days of fighting and there would even be albums.

Only the death of Zili, a Border Police dog, in Nablus—which garnered a front-page headline in the *Yedioth Ahronoth* daily, along with his funeral, the tears, the grave, the eulogies and the official statement of mourning by the prime minister—weighed a bit on the intoxicating mood of victory. It wasn't disturbed for a second by the scenes from Gaza, because scenes from Gaza were never shown here. Never before has there been such a sterile killing operation here. The Israeli media showed nothing this time, absolutely nothing. This was one of the most corrupting operations in Israel's history.

Instead of being priced at a steep discount, like its predecessors in Gaza, it was completely free. Not a drop of Israeli blood, not a single destroyed home and no condemnations from the world, not even lame ones. With a zero cost like this, the appetite for further operations will obviously grow. In Nablus on Tuesday, it would at least have been possible to argue about the results.

The usual arrogance was accompanied this time by the addictive feeling of a sweet, easy victory.

Just bring us more wars at rock-bottom prices. After all, no one was killed and almost no homes were damaged in last weekend's

Operation Breaking Dawn. But it's impossible to ignore another factor that fed these feelings of victory. This time, the operation was launched by the good Israelis. They're the ones in power now. Look at how they embarked on this war, with flying colors.

Consequently, this was the most political war Israel has ever fought. The right was united; it can never utter a word of criticism about killing Arabs. The center-left was bursting with pride —what a success, what management, what daring. The flattery for the operation's commanders—Prime Minister Yair Lapid and Defense Minister Benny Gantz, who are two of our own—ran overtime.

Yossi Verter described how Lapid's wardrobe changed due to this success. His "empty suit has been filled," he wrote understatedly. And the next day he added, "Without a doubt, this is a feather in the cap" for Lapid. The suit that was filled (with blood) and the feather in the cap are the real spoils of this war, which ended in "a dream for Israel." A dream of war.

Verter was soon followed by Uri Misgav, who shed all the disguises. The real victory picture from this war, he wrote, was that of Lapid briefing opposition leader Benjamin Netanyahu (*Haaretz* in Hebrew, August 7). It was worth going to war for this victory picture. For Misgav and his ilk, nothing could be sweeter.

Roger Waters cried. "What is wrong with the fucking Israelis? What is wrong with them?" he asked, in anger and despair. I just wish I knew how to answer him.

An Election for Whites Only

October 30

"Laugh, laugh at all my dreams," wrote the poet Shaul Tchernichovsky. The election to be held here on Tuesday is not a general election, and hence not a democratic one. Apartheid South Africa had exactly the same deception: The regime was defined as a parliamentary democracy and later as a presidential democracy. Elections were held in adherence with the law, with the National and Afrikaner parties forming a coalition. Only one thing separated South Africa from democracy—elections were meant for whites only.

"Laugh, laugh at all my dreams." In Israel, too, only whites will take part in the election. Israel currently rules over 15 million people, but 5 million of them are prevented from participating in the democratic process that chooses the government that runs their lives. The masquerade in which Israel plays at democracy should finally be ended with an unmasking. It's not a democracy.

A regime in which elections are held only for whites, namely Jews, or for people with citizenship that is not bestowed on all subjects, including the native ones living under the permanent rule applying to their land, is not a democracy.

When an occupation stops being a temporary one, it defines the regime of the entire country. There is no such thing as a partial democracy. Even if there is democracy from Dan to Eilat, the fact that between Jenin and Rafah there is a military tyranny sullies the regime in the entire country. It's amazing how for decades Israelis have knowingly lied to themselves, just like the whites in the parties of the Afrikaners.

Qaddum and Kedumim, two adjacent villages, exist side by side. Qaddum has been around since the second century CE, and it currently has a population of 3,000. Kedumim has been around for less than 50 years, and now has a population of 4,500. Only several hundred meters separate the two communities. The Jewish village was built on the lands of the Palestinian one, choking the village when the exit road from Qaddum was blocked by Kedumim.

On Tuesday, only the inhabitants of Kedumim will be voting. The residents of Qaddum will stay home. If that weren't enough, they'll be under a closure order, in order to ensure the safety of democracy. The fate of Qaddum's residents will be impacted by the results of the election much more than that of their neighbors from Kedumim. No government will dare harm Kedumim or torment its residents. But Qaddum has no voice, no voting rights, no freedom to choose or a right to wield influence.

An election in which only one community can vote, while its older and indigenous neighbor is prohibited from participating, is undemocratic. How can Israelis deceive themselves so brazenly? How can one say that this is not what apartheid looks like? In the name of what value do the residents of Kedumim have the right to vote, while that right is denied the residents of Qaddum? Are the Jews in Kedumim superior to the Palestinians from Qaddum? After all, they share the same land and live under the same government. But Zionist propaganda always has an appropriate answer to any evil perpetrated in its name.

Participating in an election in an apartheid regime is problematic, almost impossible. Nevertheless, we'll all dress up as democrats on Tuesday and go vote. No person of conscience can vote for anyone supporting the continuation of the current regime, in which parts of the people of this country are living under a military tyranny. No true democrat can vote for a party which has etched on its banner the continuation of Jewish superiority, which is what Zionism entails. All the Jewish parties, from Otzma Yehudit to Meretz, support the continuation of a Jewish state, which dares call itself a democracy, within a binational reality. This is why they cannot be considered by anyone making a conscientious decision.

It's not easy to say this, it's hard to write it, but any vote for a Zionist party is a vote for a continued tyranny posing as a democracy.

2023

The People of Israel Will Remember Its Children

April 23

May the people of Israel remember its sons and daughters, the faithful and the brave, who sacrificed their lives in the war for the rebirth of Israel, and may the people of Israel remember the sons and daughters, the faithful and the brave, of the Palestinian people, who sacrificed their lives in the war for the rebirth of their people and their land.

May Israel remember and mourn the beauty of youth, the heroic passion, the sacred will and the self-sacrifice of those who perished in the weighty battle—Jewish and Palestinian. Their dead, too, had the beauty of youth and heroic passion and sacred will and self-sacrifice. May the people of Israel also remember the Palestinian victims, its own victims.

When the siren sounds Tuesday, I will be thinking, as I do every year, of Pvt. Gideon "Pauli" Bachrach, who was killed at Tantura in 1948 while trying to rescue wounded comrades, and whose namesake I am, and also about the tens of thousands of Palestinians who died in all of Israel's wars and in between them. It's impossible not to think about them as well, especially on Memorial Day.

How can you not admire their determination and courage, the righteousness of their struggle and the unbelievable personal sacrifice that went with it?

On Holocaust Remembrance Day, the image of fire burning my grandmother and grandfather always appears before my eyes. On Memorial Day, what comes to mind are the images and the people I have written about during more than 35 years of covering the occupation and the struggle against it.

After all those long, damned years, it's impossible to stand still on Memorial Day and think only of the young people of your own nation who fell, ignoring those of the other nation.

On Tuesday, I will think about Ayid Salim from Azzun, the most recent fatality I have written about. Soldiers fired five bullets into his torso as he fled, because they thought he threw firecrackers at them. I will think of 16-year-old Hamza al-Ashkar, the fifth fatality in a year from the Askar refugee camp in Nablus, who had thrown a stone at an armored military jeep. In any other occupied land—Ukraine, for example—we would consider a boy like him a hero; here he is considered a terrorist and his killing an act of heroism.

I will also be thinking of Yousef Muhaisen, who was shot dead two days before his 23rd birthday. His friends called him "Chik Chak"—Israeli slang, meaning "very quickly"—because that's how everything went with him, including his death at the hands of soldiers.

And about Omar Khmour, 14, from the Deheisheh refugee camp, who in January was shot in the head by a soldier and killed, and whose classmates bring food to his grave every day, because one of them dreamed that Omar was hungry.

It's impossible not to think about them, and even more so on Memorial Day. And also about the fallen from further back in the tunnel of time: about the son of Faiza Abu Dahuk, who was born and died in the late 1980s at an IDF checkpoint whose soldiers refused to let her get to the hospital; about Kamala Sawalha, a 21-year-old student with two babies, who died after soldiers fired at the taxi she was riding in; about all the dead Gazans whose stories I tried to make public over the years including thousands in the 17 years since Israel stopped allowing Israeli journalists into the Strip—to do their jobs.

Who knows what has happened since to Hassan Abu Hajer, who was injured as a child? Both of his legs and one arm were amputated, and he lost his sight in one eye.

For five years, while using a wheelchair and with his remaining arm, he took care of his son Mahmoud, who was shot in the head by IDF soldiers in Gaza and became comatose. I met him for the first time in June 1994, in Room 602 at Gaza City's Shifa Hospital. The boy died five years later.

Is it possible for me not to think of him on Memorial Day? For me not to remember him, just because he's not Jewish? Not to mourn his fate and that of his father, who is unlikely to still be alive after all his tribulations?

These thoughts and memories are considered heresy in Israel, a desecration of a holy day; a mental defect at best, and treason at worst. They are neither. On Memorial Day, one can and should commune with the memory of the fallen—all of the fallen.

I Was Wrong About Netanyahu

May 11

I was wrong, I erred, I misled, I sinned. I thought Benjamin Netanyahu would adhere to the line that has guided him over the years—with one terrible exception, the 2014 Operation Protective Edge war with Gaza—and demonstrate restraint. The prime minister's momentary restraint has now been shown to be a ploy. On Tuesday he ordered a criminal targeted killing [of three Islamic Jihad leaders], and on Wednesday Israel incited a "fully full" war of choice.

The person who is responsible for this terrible chain of events is the prime minister. If we do indeed descend into another war in Gaza, as he presumably intends, it will be impossible to forgive him for this. All his years of relative restraint in the use of force would pale in the face of the current warmongering, which is more pointless and illegitimate than all its predecessors. In the winter of his career and its nadir, Netanyahu decided to join his predecessors in office and to say it solely with airstrikes in Gaza.

Tuesday's assassination operation bears a painful resemblance to the one that targeted Salah Shehadeh in July 2002. In addition to the Hamas military leader in Gaza at the time, 14 people were killed, 11 of them children. On Tuesday 10 noncombatants died, including women and children who were killed in their sleep.

The only difference is that in 2002 Israel and the world still erupted at the killing of innocents, while Israel cheered as one Tuesday, from National Security Minister Itamar Ben-Gvir to Labor Party MK Efrat Rayten, the self-righteous auntie from United for Israel's Soldiers. In 2002 there was a niggling doubt as to whether the pilots and their commanders knew they were about to kill innocent civilians—the military tried to lie at the time, claiming it thought the apartment buildings that were bombed were "uninhabited huts." On Tuesday there was no longer any doubt: From the prime minister on down, the pilots, drone operators and their commanders all knew full well they were about to kill human beings indiscriminately—and still they bombed. Netanyahu also knew, of course, and still gave the order.

The pictures of the children who died that were published Wednesday, the children of the physician and those of the Palestinian Islamic Jihad commanders, prove like a thousand words that an appalling war crime was committed. The child does not exist whose killing in his sleep is worth these assassinations, which lead nowhere and serve no purpose apart from satisfying the thirst for revenge and braggadocio in Israel.

Netanyahu decided Tuesday to be Benny Gantz and Yair Lapid, Ehud Olmert and Ehud Barak. He would bomb battered, besieged, impoverished Gaza, because that's what Israel wants. Sometimes it's hard to understand how a state can persist in conducting the same idiotic, failed policy, time after time, government after government, learning nothing and also forgetting nothing. Was there a single war in Gaza that did anyone any good, except the lords of war? Was there one bombing, one targeted killing that solved anything?

Now Netanyahu is to blame; this time there's no one else. He could have prevented it, as he did before, yet he gleefully started a war.

When I tried at the beginning of the week to put in a good word for Netanyahu, due to the restraint he had shown for a moment, the best of *Haaretz*'s readers were enraged, of course. Toxic responses and despicable comments were abundant, but there was also one response that touched my heart, by Yishai Sarid, the author whose opinion I value and hold in the highest esteem. He permitted me to publish it: "[W]riting to you after hesitation, and with affection and immense appreciation of your life's work. Also as Yossi's son . . . The time has come to renounce Netanyahu for good. The compliments don't align with the piles of bodies from this morning."

Correct, Yishai. You are right and I made an egregious, critical error that is perhaps unforgivable. As I write these lines the skies are beginning to thunder and the sirens to wail even in Tel Aviv. Gaza has been trembling for three days and three nights, and it appeared—despite last night's reports of an impending cease-fire—that soon the dead children Hajar, Miar and Ali would be joined by many other children. Their blood, the blood of young children, for which Satan has not devised proper retribution, will be on the hands of Benjamin Netanyahu. He and no other.

Do You Really Want to Go On Living Like This?

May 14

Do you really want to go on living like this? Living by the sword, war after war, one more unnecessary than the one before, all of them wars of choice, Israel's choice, with no future and no purpose? This is the 17th operation in Gaza in 19 years. A war almost every year. Sometimes, like in 2004, even two wars. The last one was set to end Saturday night, the eve of its sixth day. A six-day war.

This was perhaps the most pointless and banal of them all. An aimless war, in which few took an interest. While it was going on, Tel Aviv enjoyed an Aviv Geffen concert in the park, and later they watched Eurovision. The war broke out because a detainee was intentionally allowed to die.

Even the official reasons given for it have become insignificant. What happened next repeated itself with bloodcurdling precision, the beginning, the middle and the end, as in the previous round and the one before that. Only the amounts of blood and destruction have changed from war to war—the overwhelming majority of which is always Palestinian.

The appalling banality of this latest war makes it so dangerous. The Israelis got used to the idea that this is how it is—that there's nothing to do about it. Rain in the winter and war in the summer.

A war each year, with no cause, with nothing to gain, with no results, no winners and no losers, just periodic bloodletting, like a 10,000-kilometer checkup for your car. Do you really want to go on living like this? This question is more crucial than any other, including the judicial upheaval, and it doesn't even come up for discussion.

Continuing to live like this means accepting the situation as a decree from heaven, or from hawkish and cynical politicians, with the enthusiastic encouragement of warmongering commentators and reporters, the cheerleaders of every Israeli war. There's no opposition to the war in Israel, certainly not at its preliminary stages, and therefore no alternative is presented.

Do you really want to live like this? The answer is always "What choice do we have?" There's an alternative, one that has never been tried, but it cannot even be offered. The spectrum of options presented to the Israelis ranges only between massacre and killing, between an airstrike and a ground operation. We're at war. There's nothing else.

Continuing to live like this means killing people in horrific numbers, including children and women; to satisfy the warlords, and occasionally also to get killed, and then, of course, playing the victim. It means to live in terror in the south and occasionally in the center of Israel and to ignore with appalling opacity the terrible terror in Gaza. It means to be enslaved by the media, which on most occasions doesn't report the suffering in Gaza, and, when it does, it would've been better if it hadn't done so.

Again, there was no way to understand the extent of the horror of this little war without Al Jazeera. While the Israeli media were busy reporting about weddings being postponed and concerts being canceled, Al Jazeera showed the horror in Gaza. The world wasn't interested this time. It's tired. Let them bleed. A condemnation, yawn, pee and to bed.

When Israelis start asking themselves if they really want to continue living like this, alternatives will pop up. There are no miracle solutions and no guarantees of success. There's only one thing for sure: The alternatives have never been tried. We never thought about acting with self-control and restraint. It's for the weak. We never asked what's the outcome of all the killings and the assassinations. We never probed whether these wars contributed anything to our security, or whether they only fractured it. Now the jihad is already coming at Tel Aviv, and from under siege.

One day people will learn to appreciate the determination and courage of those who managed to establish such a resistance force while inside a cage, even if we continue to scream and scream "murderous organizations."

Do we want to continue living like this? Yes. Without a doubt. If we wanted to live differently, we would have changed direction a long time ago, lifted the siege on Gaza and talked to its leaders about its future. If we haven't tried yet, it's a sign that we want to continue living like this.

PART II

PART II

October

Israel Can't Imprison 2 Million Gazans Without Paying a Cruel Price

October 9

Behind all this lies Israeli arrogance; the idea that we can do whatever we like, that we'll never pay the price and be punished for it. We'll carry on undisturbed.

We'll arrest, kill, harass, dispossess, and we'll protect the settlers busy with their pogroms. We'll visit Joseph's Tomb, Othniel's Tomb and Joshua's Altar in the Palestinian territories, and, of course, the Temple Mount—over 5,000 Jews on Sukkot alone.

We'll fire at innocent people, take out people's eyes and smash their faces, expel, confiscate, rob, grab people from their beds, carry out ethnic cleansing and, of course, continue with the unbelievable siege of the Gaza Strip, and everything will be all right.

We'll build a terrifying obstacle around Gaza—the underground wall alone cost 3 billion shekels ($765 million)—and we'll be safe. We'll rely on the geniuses of the army's 8200 cyber-intelligence unit and on the Shin Bet security service agents who know everything. They'll warn us in time.

We'll transfer half an army from the Gaza border to the Hawara border in the West Bank, only to protect far-right lawmaker Zvi Sukkot and the settlers. And everything will be all right, both in Hawara and at the Erez crossing into Gaza.

It turns out that even the world's most sophisticated and expensive obstacle can be breached with a smoky old bulldozer when the motivation is great. This arrogant barrier can be crossed by bicycle and moped despite the billions poured into it and all the famous experts and fat-cat contractors.

We thought we'd continue to go down to Gaza, scatter a few crumbs in the form of tens of thousands of Israeli work permits—always contingent on good behavior—and still keep them in prison. We'll make peace with Saudi Arabia and the United Arab Emirates, and the Palestinians will be forgotten until they're erased, as quite a few Israelis would like.

We'll keep holding thousands of Palestinian prisoners, sometimes without trial, most of them political prisoners. And we won't agree to discuss their release even after they've been in prison for decades.

We'll tell them that only by force will their prisoners see freedom. We thought we would arrogantly keep rejecting any attempt at a diplomatic solution, only because we don't want to deal with all that, and everything would continue that way forever.

Once again it was proved that this isn't how it is. A few hundred armed Palestinians breached the barrier and invaded Israel in a way no Israeli imagined was possible. A few hundred people proved that it's impossible to imprison 2 million people forever without paying a cruel price.

Just as the smoky old Palestinian bulldozer tore through the world's smartest barrier Saturday, it tore away at Israel's arrogance and complacency. And that's also how it tore away at the idea that it's enough to occasionally attack Gaza with suicide drones—and sell them to half the world—to maintain security.

On Saturday, Israel saw pictures it has never seen before. Palestinian vehicles patrolling its cities, bike riders entering through the Gaza gates. These pictures tear away at that arrogance. The Gaza Palestinians have decided they're willing to pay any price for a moment of freedom. Is there any hope in that? No. Will Israel learn its lesson? No.

On Saturday they were already talking about wiping out entire neighborhoods in Gaza, about occupying the Strip and punishing

Gaza "as it has never been punished before." But Israel hasn't stopped punishing Gaza since 1948, not for a moment.

After 75 years of abuse, the worst possible scenario awaits it once again. The threats of "flattening Gaza" prove only one thing: We haven't learned a thing. The arrogance is here to stay, even though Israel is paying a high price once again.

Prime Minister Benjamin Netanyahu bears very great responsibility for what happened, and he must pay the price, but it didn't start with him and it won't end after he goes. We now have to cry bitterly for the Israeli victims, but we should also cry for Gaza.

Gaza, most of whose residents are refugees created by Israel. Gaza, which has never known a single day of freedom.

The Reckoning Must Be with Hamas, Not with All Gazans

October 12

Human beings live in Gaza. Right now, it's hard to even mention this fact. When the talk of "animals" is even heard coming from the—very experienced—defense minister, and is the predominant theme on the street and in the television studios, it's hard to talk about Gaza residents as human beings.

The truth is, "animals" isn't even an appropriate term for the crimes committed by the Hamas invaders on Saturday: No animal commits such acts of savagery as they did. Still, Gaza is home to more than 2 million people, about half of whom are descendants of refugees, which is something that should also be kept in mind now, despite the difficulty.

Gaza is plagued with Hamas, and Hamas is a despicable organization. But most residents of the Gaza Strip are not like that. Before we start flattening and destroying and uprooting and killing, we should take this into account. The reckoning must be with Hamas, not with all Gazans. One's heart must go out to them, regardless of one's profound solidarity with Israel's victims.

It should be possible to stand with the residents of the south, while still remembering that living on the other side are human beings just like them. We should be able to fear for the fate of Gazans and distinguish between them and their Hamas leadership. It should be possible, even in the current atmosphere, to speak about Gaza in human terms.

I visited the south this week, from Sderot to Re'im, and was completely horrified. It was impossible not to be. I met people who went through an unforgettable nightmare, and my heart goes out to them. But I also couldn't help thinking that just a few kilometers away from them, a much bigger disaster is befalling the inhabitants of Gaza. The images from Gaza are already shocking. Rumor has it that there is already white phosphorus in the streets. But most of all, it's the helplessness of the people who have nowhere to run to, no way to protect their children, nowhere to hide. In Gaza there is no refuge and no way out.

This week in the south there was a Red Alert and we ran to a safe room every few minutes. The sirens wailed in Tel Aviv, too. In Gaza, there is no Red Alert, no siren and no safe room. Hamas is the one criminally responsible for this, but the population is completely abandoned to its fate—women, children and the elderly with nothing at all to shelter them from the bombardments. Try to imagine it: relentless bombardments with no prior warning. Indiscriminate bombings, as the IDF spokesperson says, "The emphasis is on damage, not on precision."

It's hard to imagine the terror in Sderot. It's even harder to imagine the terror in Gaza's Rimal district. There needn't be a competition over which people are suffering more in order to recognize that the suffering in Gaza is staggering, too. For years, I visited homes there. I met honest, brave, determined people with a special sense of humor. I've documented terrible suffering in many places in the world, but the people's spirits there never fell.

Seventeen years of the blockade closed Gaza off to me. I presume it has changed since then. A new generation was born into even greater despair. But is it possible to remain indifferent, even to joke in some cases, at the sight of the images from Gaza? How is this possible? How is it possible to forget that these are human beings whose ancestors were expelled from their land and placed in refugee camps where they would remain?

These were human beings whom Israel dispossessed and expelled, whom it conquered again in their land of refuge and then turned into animals in a cage. They've experienced indiscriminate bombardments before, but now the worst of all is ahead of them. Israel has already announced that all the restraints it supposedly used in previous attacks will be lifted this time. Yes, hundreds of Gazans committed atrocious crimes, an outgrowth of 17 years of blockade and 75 years of suffering, with a bloody past and no present or future. But not all of Gaza is to blame.

As I sit in my neighbor's safe room in Tel Aviv, I can't help thinking about my friend Munir, who has nowhere to run to in his home in Lakiya, or even the ability to run after the stroke that he suffered. I am thinking about the Gazans now when it seems like no one else in the world cares what happens to them anymore.

A Bloodcurdling Visit to Israel's South After the Hamas Attack Evokes ISIS and Ukraine

October 14

On the side of the road, at the entrance to Kibbutz Re'im, there were two abandoned Toyota pickup trucks—a Hilux and a Land Cruiser—that looked as if they could have been stuck to each other. Both trucks had green-and-white Palestinian license plates. In the back of one were packs of bottled water, made in Gaza, and plastic bags full of dates. Someone had been planning to stay here a long time, judging by the quantity of dates. Next to the driver's seat was a rolled-up prayer rug. Camouflage army pants, bulletproof vests and other gear were strewn on the road. A machine gun had been affixed to the second truck, though it had been removed in the meantime. Affixed to the gas-tank cover was a VIP sticker.

On Monday afternoon, an Israeli army jeep approached the spot, and the soldiers it was carrying emerged to examine the abandoned vehicles, whose passengers were almost certainly the same age. The latter had plotted to infiltrate the kibbutz, slaughter and kidnap, as it happened in many other kibbutzim in the vicinity. The pickup trucks resembled those we associate with Islamic State vehicles. The south is now littered with images reminiscent of Islamic State, or more recent scenes from Ukraine, like that of the burned and destroyed police station in Sderot, where the only reminder that we are in Israel, not Ukraine, is a tattered blue-and-white flag hanging out front.

The trip around the south is bloodcurdling, shocking, upsetting and frightening. Nothing like this has ever happened in Israel. Early on Shabbat, as the two ISIS-like trucks drew close to the gates of Re'im, hundreds of young people situated a few hundred meters to the west were celebrating in what was intended to be the climax of a "nature party." The rave was scheduled to end at noon, with the partygoers' last spurts of energy. It ended earlier than expected, with human horror. Re'im was the Ground Zero of our October 7. Two days later, it was still not possible to approach the dozens of burned cars parked along the side of the road, and the stench of blood of remained in the air, because not far from here, another gun battle was being fought, whose echoes could be heard well.

Nothing here is over yet. Everyone knows that we're only at the beginning.

All the cities of the south are now ghost towns. We barely saw anyone in Ofakim, the same for Sderot. But something about the latter's proximity to Gaza made it the scariest place we visited. There is not a second of quiet here. If it's not a Red Alert, then it's the echoes of Israel's nonstop bombing over Gaza. And if it is a Red Alert, it's over in the blink of an eye, as locals have but 15 seconds after the siren sounds to run to a protected space. For a resident of Tel Aviv who is not used to such conditions, it's a difficult experience. But it is also unbearable for longtime residents of Sderot, such as Shula and Elisha Dahan, in whose apartment we were stuck for one of the alarms, taking refuge for a moment in their safe room.

The Dahan couple lives in a home opposite the city's police station. In normal times, and there are not many of those in Sderot, it was a relatively safe place to live, across the street from the police duty officer, a position that is manned both day and night. But on the first day of the war, the police station was the center of a nightmare, where the bitterest battle in the city took place.

The Dahans have lived in the city since 1956, five years after its founding. Both are 68 years old, both natives of Morocco. Elisha is retired from his job at Spectronix, a company in Sderot that manufactures firefighting systems for the military's tanks, submarines and missile boats. She is now a cancer patient, a horror that grips her, just like the nonstop shaking in her hands. Pale and terrified, she sits on the sofa next to the safe room, the one they didn't leave for two days, while there was fire and shooting at the police station. She listens to her husband's descriptions. He recalls how on Saturday morning, he saw below their window an ISIS-like truck with a MAG machine gun sticking up from its body, and carrying some 20 armed men with white ribbons tied around their heads. He couldn't believe his eyes.

"I thought I was in a movie," he recalled. They rushed into their safe room and didn't emerge until Monday—other than when Elisha would go to get Shula some water. Now they go in and out depending on the Red Alert, and there were many of them in Sderot city on Monday.

The heavy shooting taking place across the street at the police station brought Elisha back to his military service in Sinai during the Yom Kippur War. On Shabbat, the electricity stopped, and at a certain point so did the water supply. They didn't have contact with the world, and gradually also lost contact with their children across Israel. Another Red Alert cuts off our conversation.

Keren, a neighbor from one floor up, burst into the stairwell in a fit of panic. Her entire body shakes and she screams in terror. Even after all her years living in Sderot, she says she still suffers a panic attack with every alarm. The sight of the woman, lying on the floor of the narrow stairwell and crying bitterly, was difficult.

The Dahans offered her water. Elisha said that when trauma enters life, it doesn't leave.

"I was once angry at you on television," Elisha told me. "You said that the residents of Sderot are pampered [relative to the suffering of Gaza residents]. At the time, I wished that you could be here and see the reality we live in."

How many alarms were there in the last day? "Pick a number." Both the glass and the frame of the Dahans' windows were shattered from the shock waves. They are waiting for the assessor from the tax authorities, and they don't intend to leave, not even this time. They have never left.

Moshe Sabag, a neighbor from the third floor, is also still here. He, too, is 68 and Morocco-born, and has worked as a carpenter for 50 years at nearby Kibbutz Sa'ad. He said that on Saturday morning, he saw one of the armed Palestinians approach a car that was stopped in the street, kill the female driver, whom he knew, and then turn to the back seat, where her two daughters sat, one 8 and the other 4. The man paused for a moment, and then he left, without shooting the girls. "God probably told him no. Maybe he has children, too." Another armed man entered their stairwell, but then appeared to change his mind, and retreated. There is a God, is the inevitable answer here.

Now, across the street, a bulldozer is clearing away the wreckage of the police station. Two days earlier, bodies of dead from both sides were piled on the lawn in front of the station. Those of the Jews were removed as soon as it was possible, the Palestinian bodies were there for a day before being cleared away. Now a police officer emerges from the rubble he has been inspecting, with a blue ID card in his hand. Perhaps it belonged to a police officer, perhaps to a citizen who had filed a complaint or was being questioned, before everything began. An ambulance from the private Yossi firm parks on the side and waits for the bodies that may yet be pulled from the rubble.

There's a familiar face here in the street next to the station: Bernard-Henri Lévy. The French philosopher caught the first flight he could. In his trademark white shirt and with his thick,

graying hair, which is always tidily arranged, he receives explanations from the army's public diplomacy officers. He listens, quiet
and forlorn, and says to a soldier standing in front of him: "You
are a soldier of Israel and a soldier of civilization." He says to
me: "No matter how much we have been critical of Israel, you
even more than me, now is the time to be unified."

The last time we met had been in the exploding streets of a
besieged Sarajevo, precisely 30 years ago—and the scenes are
similar.

Meanwhile, Sderot mayor Alon Davidi runs around bleary-
eyed in the yard outside the improvised municipal command post,
wearing a protective vest, showing everyone a pleasant face. This
charismatic mayor tries to get the city's supermarkets to reopen,
even if just for a few hours, after two days during which residents
have not had any access to provisions. They say that Eyal Ravid,
CEO of the Victory chain, is on his way. Some hours later, we saw
that the Rami Levy branch had opened. Armed soldiers stood at
the entrance with their weapons drawn, also something we had
never seen before. It was only an hour later that a rocket would
hit the supermarket, shattering the Rami Levy sign.

Sderot. In the battle for this city, like in the other battles fought
on Shabbat, it was apparently the police officers who fought
fiercely in the first hours until the army arrived. The police sapper,
who lost many comrades, tells us heroic stories.

At the gas station at Orim Junction, there are bloodstains all
over. Some of the injured from the musical event at Rei'm, as well
as some of the fatalities, were brought here. A pair of Blundstone
boots, bloodstained white socks thrust inside of them, are strewn
in the parking lot.

On Sunday, armed militants hid in the thicket across the street
from here. A day before that, in Ofakim, armed militants with
hostages entrenched themselves in a house at the corner of Tamar
Street and Hahita Street, and there was a bitter fight to rescue
those being held. Remnants of the battle are visible on the walls
of the brown, two-story house, which is riddled with dozens
of bullet holes. Students from a religious mehina (pre-army

academy) are covering the door of the now-liberated house with an Israeli flag, though there's no longer anyone living inside.

On Kibbutz Be'eri, Time Stood Still: Traces of the Life Before the Massacre

October 19

A copy of *Haaretz* from Friday, October 6, 2023, still lies on the dining room table in one of the houses, open on Yossi Verter's column, as if waiting for its reader to return to it. It is highly doubtful this reader is still alive. On Saturday morning, maybe he rose from the table only for an instant, leaving behind the column with the coffee cup, but apparently he will never return. The column's headline is blood-chilling: "The borders of surrender." Verter had written about the borders of the surrender to the ultra-Orthodox, eons ago.

Handwriting in an open notebook on a nearby table reads: "We killed the terrorists, hope you're okay. Love, Regiment 890." A path of blood leads from the safe room to the house's door. Here a dead or wounded person had been pulled out, leaving a coagulated trail along the entire house. We saw trails like this in many of the houses we saw this week.

In the yard lies the corpse of a large, light-colored dog, shot in the head. The dog is covered with a towel and the flies swarm on the carcass. In the nearby house lies another dog's corpse, also big and light, also shot in the head. Perhaps these two beautiful dogs were friends in their lives.

The smell of death is everywhere, in the turned-over, burned-out houses and outside them, on paths, some stained with blood, and in the ruined gardens. Maybe it's the smell of death and maybe it's the smell of the blood that was everywhere here, the smell of hundreds of killed and wounded people in the killing fields of Be'eri.

Such gruesome sights I've never encountered. In besieged Sarajevo there was less blood in the streets; the destruction in Japan after the Fukushima nuclear disaster wasn't man-made;

the war in Georgia wasn't as brutal—and in all of Israel's wars, nobody had seen such sights. What I saw this week in Kibbutz Be'eri are Bucha sights, no less.

In the Yom Kippur War, when Kibbutz Beit Hashita lost 11 of its sons, the whole country was outraged and the kibbutz became a legend; in Be'eri, 108 bodies were found, and many other members are still missing and abducted. The numbers are as inconceivable as the spectacles of Be'eri.

Now the thriving kibbutz named after Berl Katznelson is a ruined place that has turned into a crowded military camp. Tanks are parked in the local bike park, well known to cyclists in the area. Armored vehicles stand in sharp contrast to the kibbutz members' abandoned mobility scooters. The areas that remain unharmed tell what the kibbutz looked like before that Saturday, and the ruins are its current face. Green grass, blooming gardens, houses filled with precious objects face off against dozens of crushed cars, chopped trees and bushes, burned houses and, above all, the terrible smell.

There's no better simile for a pastoral than a flourishing kibbutz, and nothing like today's Be'eri as a simile for a human and environmental horror. Nothing like the houses, gardens and paths that hadn't been touched demonstrates how beautiful and calm it had been here, and how it will probably never be again.

The word "cleared" is painted on most houses, those that remain intact, too, indicating they are clear of explosives or bodies. But something in the inscription is disconnected, as though the houses had committed some sin. Some of them have red writing in Arabic by Hamas smeared on them.

Yaniv Kubovich, *Haaretz*'s military reporter who has been visiting here daily since that Saturday, says we are stepping on a path of death and blood. He saw the dozens of bodies piled on the lawns and the knives dripping with blood in the living rooms. "Almost everyone who entered here was killed," he says in one of the neighborhoods where the most bitter battles took place.

The roofs in that neighborhood were burned, red tiles blackened and disappeared over the houses. A pitchfork is thrown in one of the yards; maybe, in desperation, it was used for self-defense, and now remains as a chilling association to the Grim Reaper.

The expression "time stood still" was never as accurate and as moving as when we step into some of the houses. Wine glasses after Friday night's dinner still stand next to the sink in one of the houses, waiting for someone to wash them. A flag of the Brothers and Sisters in Arms protest group stands ready in the electrical closet, waiting for the next demonstration. The residents of this house will not be participating in this demonstration. The antacid medicine on the counter will no longer help anyone.

All the houses are a chaotic mess, even those that weren't set on fire. Entire lives thrown on the floor. The refrigerators are full of food but have been cut off from power for 12 days and the smell rising from them is intolerable. Most ghostly are the houses where the power hasn't been cut off, or where it was reconnected. The ceiling fans turn quietly over the death, the lamps light up the horror.

Protected rooms that were supposed to be the safest places are now ruins. One of them, where young adults probably lived, has a list of kibbutz members' birthdays hanging on the closet. We read two names in October—one of them is two days before the massacre, another less than a week after it.

A terrible silence prevails everywhere. Only soldiers wander on the paths, alert to the slightest sound. Inside one house, soldiers of the anti-terrorism unit are investigating the events. Every now and then, the noises of explosions from nearby Gaza disrupt the deathly silence. A grenade lies in a house's yard, beside munitions and an Israeli soldier's bulletproof vest with blood marks and a hole in it.

The structure where the great battle of Be'eri took place is completely burned out. The adjacent dining room has become the resting room for hundreds of soldiers gathered here for the great entrance—if there is one. "Remember how after we shot at al-Arroub, we did a barbecue?" one soldier tells another, referring to a Palestinian refugee camp in the West Bank. "That's what we'll do here also."

It's hard to feel pre-battle joy or bloodthirst here. What is going through the heads of those hundreds of reservists? It's hard to tell. How many of them won't return? Better not to think about it. Meanwhile, they're upgrading their equipment and tying it to their person, so they don't lose it in battle.

It Is Forbidden to Even Empathize with Innocent Gazans

October 26

And darkness was upon the face of the deep. Upon the face of the abyss of the massacre in the south, darkness is taking hold of Israel. Now it is still a gathering of clouds, but it may turn to darkness: Israel is going mad. The left is "wising up," the right is growing more extreme, and McCarthyism and fascism reign.

Wartime is always a time of silencing, uniformity of opinion, racism, incitement and hatred; absolute enlistment in service of propaganda, the end of tolerance and the persecution of anyone who dares step out of line. The atrocities perpetrated by Hamas in the south brought all of these manifestations to extreme levels, as if the atrocities justify the loss of all restraint.

The emotional turmoil is, of course, understandable, but not the totalitarianism that has followed in its wake. If it is not stopped, the danger posed to democracy will be a thousand times that posed by the government coup, which made the whole system here go haywire.

The first to lose their minds were, as usual, the leftists. They "wised up." Those who before the war set out with determination to fight for democracy are now sabotaging it with their own hands. Those who before the war considered themselves liberals, people of peace and human rights, are now adopting an updated worldview: They are indifferent to the atrocities taking place in the Gaza Strip; a majority even want to see them intensified.

Why? Because they perpetrated atrocities against us. For how long? Until the end. At what cost? At any cost. This left now

THE KILLING OF GAZA

thinks about Gaza exactly as the right does: Strike and strike, it's the only option.

Those who before the war underestimated the importance of addressing apartheid and the fate of the Palestinian people now think, To hell with everyone. They can go hang. Let them suffocate. Let them die. Let them be expelled. Those who before the war considered themselves enlightened now support consensus.

Hamas also turned the Israeli left upside down. From now on, Israel is permitted to do anything to Gaza; the left will even give its blessing. From now on, it is forbidden to even empathize with the residents of Gaza.

Human rights activist and former Peace Now director Yariv Oppenheimer watched Amira Hass shedding inspiring tears over the fate of Gaza's inhabitants and hastened to write: "I admit that I have grown numb."

Even in the face of the bodies of 2,360 children, according to the Palestinian Health Ministry as of Tuesday, the left's heart is sealed. As at the start of every war, this left is for it. The left "wises up," and afterward somehow returns to itself. That seems unlikely this time.

The situation is even worse outside of the left. Fascism has become the only proper position. The local TV stations aligned themselves with Channel 14; when it comes to Gaza there's no difference. Reporters and anchors call Hamas Nazis in a repulsive display of Holocaust trivialization and denial, and the crowd cheers. Hamas did abominable things, but they're not Nazis.

Any other opinion is now condemned to persecution. United Nations secretary-general António Guterres spoke truthfully and courageously about the context of the October 7 atrocities, and hastened to stress that nothing can justify the horrific attacks by Hamas; Israel responded with a frenzied attack on Guterres, whipped up by the media. Every diplomatic correspondent who never expressed an opinion on anything knows that the secretary-general's remarks were "outrageous."

I, for one, was not outraged. They were true. The actor Maisa Abd Elhadi was detained by police and held overnight over a social media post that broke no law, and Israeli TV channels are removing her films from their streaming archives. McCarthyism would be proud.

The ransomed captive Yocheved Lifshitz gave a moving performance, and the mainstream journalists complain because she told the truth. PR consultant and internet personality Rani Rahav sees a video of the destruction in Gaza and writes: "That's how I like it!!!" (All of the drooling exclamation marks are in the original text.)

Journalist Zvi Yehezkeli urges Gaza's destruction nightly. The entire Gaza Strip. And his Channel 13 News colleague Netali Shem Tov sees "too many buildings standing in Gaza." Such is the distilled evil in the face of the Gaza catastrophe, the horrors of which are almost never shown to Israelis.

This is the dark time. The time of the barbaric attack by Hamas and the time of the lost conscience and sense of reason in Israel.

Northern Inexposure: Former "Peace" on Lebanon Border Replaced by Deathly Silence

October 29

We're in a narrow and cramped apartment on the third floor of a former railway building in Kiryat Shmona, a city of 22,000 in Israel's far north. A woman is lying in her bed, unable to move or utter a word.

She has been lying like this for five years since suffering a stroke, and she's lying there now, even though most of her neighbors have fled. When the sirens wail, her husband carries her to the dim stairwell whose floor is black with dirt; there they shelter from the rockets and hope for the best.

In Kiryat Shmona there is no time to run to the shelter behind the house, and it's certainly impossible to carry a disabled woman down three flights of stairs. In Kiryat Shmona the sirens sound and the boom follows immediately. There is no time for anything. I experienced this last Monday; the city was evacuated, but nobody has evacuated Esther Tubiana.

The nation of Israel may be alive, but Kiryat Shmona is dead. It's the epitome of a ghost town; you only see the soldiers and police at the city's entrance. Twelve kilometers (7.5 miles) south of the city they've installed a yellow iron gate to block traffic, like the ones that surround villages and cities in the West Bank.

Although a few thousand people remain in Kiryat Shmona, no one knows exactly how many. The people are hiding in their apartments in a terror and silence that casts a deathly pall over the city.

The same deathly silence envelops the entire Upper Galilee. As you head north, the traffic gets thinner and thinner. Not a soul is on the road up to Metula, the town at the very top of the Galilee Panhandle on the Lebanon border. Two elderly members of the town's security squad stand by the barrier at the entrance to Metula and pleasantly prevent the entry of strangers.

To the southeast, near the locked gate of Kibbutz Dafna, reservists from the Golani Brigade stand and pray; it's the evening service. On neighboring Kibbutz Dan, the biologist of the kibbutz's trout and sturgeon farm, Avshalom Hurvitz, sits at home; he's almost alone in the sleek, green neighborhood of the kibbutz's old-timers. It's quiet everywhere, maybe the calm before the storm. Either way, it's certainly a deceptive silence.

The sign at the entrance to the city announces "Kiryat Shmona, a realm of opportunities," and this, too, is deceptive. So are the campaign posters that adorn the sides of the roads in preparation for Israel's local elections that have been postponed. The slogans promise everything good, under candidates' pictures comically photoshopped.

No less misleading are the advertisements for the north's many attractions, from guesthouses to kayaking to hiking. Now the deception has ceased, and, with it, the delusion of the beautiful and secure life here. Almost everyone has fled south. This region has never seen such flight or, to be politically correct, maybe we should we say evacuation.

"Red zone: You are entering a zone under threat" is written on the concrete blocks at the barriers. On the wall of the mall there's a different message: "OMG, we've opened a branch of Urbanica."

The iron door of Shelter No. 512 on Lebanon Street is open. Steep stairs lead down to a spacious room with folding iron beds, on which blankets and sheets are strewn as if the place was hastily abandoned. An unpleasant odor hangs in the air, and water bottles bide their time on the side, as does a children's board game, the Israeli version of "Operation."

The desolation outside, in front of the houses on Lebanon Street, stirs the emotions. Old sofas thrown out into the yards give the last remaining people a chance to breathe some fresh air. Trash is accumulating and only the cats are enjoying the quiet hours of grace.

Almog Shema, 30, works at a company that provides rehab for people with disabilities. He's now sitting on one of the sofas, alone in the yard. He and his mother, Luna, were born here, and neither wants to leave. During the 2006 Second Lebanon War they fled south, but not this time.

"My conscience won't let me leave," says the 64-year-old Luna. "I was born with all these wars and Katyushas and sirens. But I never thought about an infiltration. Now I'm more afraid of infiltrations than missiles." But until she sees a "really difficult situation," she won't leave. Her daughter-in-law is a police officer who can evacuate her south to Tiberias on the Sea of Galilee, but she's staying here, almost alone in the building.

The mother and son's main concern now is to evacuate the disabled neighbor on the third floor. They've phoned everyone, including the Home Front Command and the municipality. Everyone promised to get back to them, but no one has come.

We go up to the third floor. The husband, Yaakov Tubiana, opens the door, unshaven, his face showing signs of despair. He's 66, an employee of the Jewish National Fund. His wife is 67 and both were born in Kiryat Shmona. The poverty and need cry out here, even before you see Esther lying motionless on her side, casting a blank stare that's in its fifth year now.

"It's hard for us. Take care of yourselves," Yaakov whispers at the door as we leave.

A bit to the northeast, one of the two entrances to Kibbutz

Dafna is blocked by an iron gate and decorative rocks that now serve a different purpose. Near the kibbutz's second entrance, which is manned, a company of Golani reservists has gathered. Amid the nearby signs that promise leisure activities, entertainment and healing, the religious soldiers in the company pray their evening prayer.

The signs advertise things like tours, camping trips, shiatsu, acupuncture and yoga, and in front of them the soldiers are chanting, "Blessed art Thou, O Lord, who destroys enemies and subdues the wicked." From a soldier whose eyes are closed, his body rocking back and forth, we hear "Holy, holy, holy, Redeemer of Israel."

It's very doubtful that such a prayer session had ever been held at Dafna's gates. The soldiers pose for a group photo. It has been two and a half weeks since they were called up, and you can't help but wonder how many of them won't return home safely. "We'll do what we have to," they say, the soldiers' cliché.

The yellow gate at Kibbutz Dan is also locked, and the security squad prevents outsiders from entering. To prepare for a possible attack, they placed in front of the gate large plastic fruit crates filled with black gravel.

I haven't seen Hurvitz for nearly 50 years. He's the son of a founder of the kibbutz Elimelech Hurvitz, who also founded the Beit Ussishkin natural history museum.

Avshalom Hurvitz is one of the few members who didn't leave, because of his job at the trout and sturgeon farm. Those fish—the latter for caviar—can't be neglected, nor can Kibbutz Dan's large bee yard. Oh yes, then there's Hurvitz's dedication and courage.

We walk along the kibbutz's paths; they were always quiet, but now their silence is deafening. One kibbutz member asked Hurvitz to turn off the boiler at his home, another asked him to water his lawn. This meticulously kept green neighborhood of the kibbutz's veterans is a small piece of heaven.

I couldn't tread Dan's paths without recalling a similar walk at Kibbutz Be'eri near Gaza the previous week. Those were paths of blood. Even though Be'eri is three times larger than Dan, it's natural to compare Be'eri's paths before the killing and destruction to these quiet paths on Dan. This is exactly how Be'eri looked, and my memories of the sights there are unrelenting.

A neighbor's clementine tree is covered in netting because of noxious flies. The water in the small fountain at another house in the row is bubbling softly. Hurvitz's house is spacious, renovated and beautifully designed. It's impossible not to compare it to the poverty on Lebanon Street in Kiryat Shmona 11 kilometers away, but now the fate of those remaining is a single fate.

Hurvitz met his wife, Lea, at a soldiers' party in Gaza while serving in the reserves in 1973, the year of the Yom Kippur War. But the current war brought him back to the days of waiting in 1967 before the Six-Day War. He was a high school kid who, while waiting for the war, was drafted into the kibbutz's security squad.

He says that on June 7, 1967, the third day of the war, "when an attack by two Syrian infantry companies that came to occupy the kibbutz began, the IDF wasn't present here. Kibbutz members with machine guns and 91mm mortars stopped the Syrians here. The attacks reached the kibbutz's outskirts. They placed charges on fences.

"Since then, my feeling has been that this would never happen again, that the army would always be here around us. But after the events in the south, that sense of security has been shaken. And now they're fortifying the kibbutz instead of giving us the security that stops the enemy at the border.

"This is constantly with me. For the veteran members of the kibbutz, this is the context. It's part of the feeling in our DNA and it's impossible not to make the comparison. The paradigm that the army protects us has collapsed, and no one will agree to live like that, like sitting ducks—even if we're stronger ducks. There's no fence that the Radwan Force can't breach," Hurvitz says, referring to Hezbollah's elite unit.

In the past there was an armory on Dan, many of whose members had guns. About a decade ago, the guns were taken away following break-ins and thefts at the armory.

Now Hurvitz sleeps alone in his house, almost alone on his kibbutz, without a gun. He promises his wife—who left with one of her daughters, her daughter's family and the other kibbutz members for Haifa's Dan Carmel hotel—that he's sleeping in the safe room.

I doubt he's always sleeping there. Hurvitz says he's not afraid. He's only concerned that the recent events might halt the kibbutz's expansion.

As in the south, here, too, there is a desire for the army to enter Lebanon, even expressed by kibbutznik Hurvitz, a veteran of the left-wing Hashomer Hatzair youth movement who looks younger than his 75 years.

"There will be no choice but drastic action in Lebanon. Solve it once and for all," says Hurvitz, who adds that he always voted for Mapam in the past and now Meretz, parties to the left of the Labor Party.

"I believed in peace and the Oslo Accords. But in today's situation, the illusion of peace is no longer with us. Now you have to do what's necessary for security. The threat must be removed both here and down there. I'm a simple farmer, not a politician or a general, and that's what I think."

Only 2,680 meters (1.7 miles) separate Dan from the border. This kibbutz has never been evacuated, not even during the two Lebanon wars or the heavy shelling in the '60s. But when Kibbutz Dafna, which is 1,980 meters from the border, was evacuated on October 20, some Dan members requested the same.

"I ask myself: Did they evacuate us due to knowledge that Hezbollah is going to enter and they're worried about our safety, or was it an exaggerated panic because of what happened in the south? They've never evacuated Dan; only during the War of Independence they evacuated the women and children."

From Dan to Kiryat Shmona. Suddenly, a siren and, right after it, a terrifying explosion. The soldiers at the barrier quickly jump into the concrete cubicle there. We lie down on the road. And Esther Tubiana no doubt remains motionless.

November

These Are the Children Extracted After the Bombardment of Gaza's Jabalya Refugee Camp

November 2

A Hamas terrorist was taken out of the debris, carried in his father's arms. His face is covered with dust, his body jerking like a sack, his stare blank. It's not clear if he's alive or dead. He is a toddler of 3 or 4, and his desperate father rushed him to the Gaza Strip's Indonesian Hospital, which was already bursting with wounded and dead people.

Another terrorist was extracted from the wreckage. This time she's clearly alive, her fair, curly hair is white with dust; she's 5 or 6, being carried by her father. She looks right and left, as though asking where help will come from.

A man in a tattered vest scribbles here and there, a white sheet folded like a shroud in his hands, covering an infant's body, and he's waving it in despair. It's the body of his son, a newborn baby. This infant hadn't yet had a chance to join Hamas's military headquarters in the Jabalya refugee camp. He had only lived a few days—a butterfly's eternity—and was killed.

Dozens of youngsters continued digging in the rubble with their bare hands in a desperate effort to extract still-living people or the bodies of neighbors, raising destroyed walls from the hand of a child sticking out of the ruins. Perhaps this child was a terrorist in Hamas's Nukhba force.

All around stood hundreds of men, dressed in rags, clasping their hands together hopelessly. Some of them burst into tears. An Israeli solar heater with a Hebrew sticker lies in the rubble, a reminder of days gone by. "We have no time for feelings now," says camp resident Mansour Shimal to Al Jazeera.

On Tuesday afternoon, Israeli Air Force jets bombed Block 6 in the Jabalya refugee camp. In Israel, it was barely reported. Al Jazeera reported that six bombs had been dropped on Block 6, leaving a huge crater, into which a row of gray apartment buildings fell like a house of cards. The pilots must have reported successful hits. The sights were horrific.

When I went to Gaza's Daraj Quarter in July 2002, the day after Salah Shehadeh's assassination, I saw harsh sights. But they were pastoral compared to what was seen in Jabalya on Tuesday. In Daraj, 14 civilians were killed, 11 of them children—about a tenth of the number of people killed in the bombing on Tuesday in Jabalya, according to Palestinian reports.

In Israel, they didn't show the Jabalya scenes. And yet, hard to believe, they did take place. A few foreign networks broadcast them in a loop. In Israel, they said the commander of Hamas's central battalion in Jabalya, Ibrahim Biari, was killed in an air force strike in the most crowded refugee camp in Gaza and that dozens of terrorists had been killed. Shehadeh's killing was followed by a penetrating public debate in Israel.

What took place on Tuesday in Jabalya was barely even heard about here. It happened before the bad news about the Israeli soldiers who were killed was released, while the wartime campfire was crackling away.

According to the reports, about 100 people were killed in the Jabalya bombing and some 400 were wounded. The pictures from the Indonesian Hospital were horrifying, no less. Burnt children thrown one beside another, three and four on one filthy bed; most of them were treated on the floor for lack of enough beds. "Treatment" is the wrong word. Due to the lack of medicines, life-saving surgery was carried out not only on the floor, but without anesthesia. The Indonesian Hospital in Beit Lahia is now a hell.

Israel is at war, after Hamas murdered and kidnapped with barbarism and brutality that cannot be forgiven. But the children who were extracted from the debris of Block 6 and some of their parents have nothing to do with the attacks on Be'eri and Sderot.

While the terrorists ran rampant in Israel, Jabalya's people were huddled in their huts in Gaza's most crowded camp, thinking how to pass another day in these conditions, which were worsened by the siege of the last 16 years. Now they will bury their children in mass graves because in Jabalya, there's no room left for individual ones.

If We Can't See the Eyes of Gaza's Dead Children, Can We See Children at All?

November 5

Is there a difference between children and children? Are the photos of children killed in Jabalya supposed to shock us less than those of children killed in Be'eri? Are photos of dead children in Jabalya even supposed to shock us, and is it legitimate to be shocked by them?

Our own children are dearer to our heart than anything in the world, and the heart of every Israeli is more shocked by Israeli children who have been killed than by any other dead child. That's human and understandable. But we cannot refrain from leaving room for shock at the mass slaughter of children in Gaza, only because our children were also killed.

The killing in Gaza should weigh particularly heavily if we recall who these children are and who brought their disaster upon them. (Answer: Israel and Hamas.) What did their lives and deaths look like? (Answer: Children who lived in poverty, misery, under siege, seeking refuge with no present and no future, overwhelmingly due to Israel.)

A good friend, a famous lefty, wrote over the weekend: "At war I can't pity both sides equally. Maybe in Ukraine, but not here. Gideon Levy describes a burned baby, and I see the baby from Nir Oz."

The baby in Nir Oz was murdered by Hamas scum with indescribable cruelty. The Israel Defense Forces kills the babies in Jabalya coolly, without any particular malice, but in gruesome numbers. Seeing only the baby in Nir Oz and not the one in Jabalya? That veers into twisted morality, especially as the number of dead children in Gaza reaches an unprecedented toll —3,900 children as of Saturday, according to the Hamas health ministry.

The weekend in Gaza was blood-soaked, and the videos emerging from there were among the most shocking we've seen in this horrible war. The torn bodies of eight infants embracing one another put into two white plastic bags, four infants per bag, zippers close the bags forever, en route to a mass grave. They were Gazan babies. Someone killed them. This is war, but even in war, limits need to be set.

In another video, screams were heard next to ruins strewn with dozens of bodies, mostly of children. The areas around Gaza's hospitals are bombed incessantly. On Saturday it was the al-Nasser children's hospital, where children with cancer are treated and five people were killed. It's not hard to imagine the terror of the hospitalized children. This hospital was also required to evacuate, as though there was where to, or how.

An ambulance with wounded people en route to the Rafah crossing was bombed by the air force. Israel claims there were terrorists in it. The coastal road on which the displaced are trying to flee south, at Israel's command, was strewn with bodies, including many children. Each bombing in Gaza kills children.

All this is not supposed to shock any Israeli, for Israel is mourning its dead. Not only should it not shock—shock has been banned and criminalized. Those expressing shock are arrested, particularly if they are Arab citizens. You must not be shocked at the carnage in Gaza, not even of children about whose innocence and lack of guilt there can be no debate; protesting their killing is full-on treason. They are Gazan children, and in Israel they are un-children, just like their parents are un-human; Our children were killed more cruelly.

"How can we not?" US secretary of state Antony Blinken asked on Friday, in response to the bodies of Gazan children pulled from the rubble. Blinken expressed how shocked he was by images of Israeli children whose father was murdered and his murderers opened the fridge and ate indifferently in front of the two crying orphans. Then he spoke of the dead children of Gaza: "When I look in their eyes, I see my own children—how can we not?" he said.

And when we look at the eyes of the dead children of Gaza, we don't see our own children. It is doubtful whether we see children at all. How can we not?

If Israel Resists Examining Its Own Failures, Another War Awaits Us

November 9

The war is still raging, the guns are roaring, but Israel is already wrapping itself up in cushioning layers to protect itself from real soul-searching.

The initial shock is now replaced by countless tales of heroism and rebirth, alongside the horrifying, intolerable stories of disaster. One month after the war started, not a moment goes by without a weeping face on television, not a newspaper page without a heroic story.

In the tearjerker called *Yedioth Ahronoth* every soldier killed is an "Israeli hero"—a soldier who carried out an amazing act of heroism. The moving, exciting displays of volunteering are also over-covered—look how beautiful we are and how good we feel about ourselves. Beside them the reports from the front stream in, all—but all—heralding a great success: Victory is on the way.

All these have, of course, a place of honor. A grief-stricken society and a state at war crave and need all those. But when they completely take over the discourse, one suspects the addiction to the tales of heroism is also intended to conceal reality and blur it. Quiet, we're wallowing in our disaster and feeling impressed and amazed by ourselves.

Notice how the incredible fiascoes of October 7 are slowly fading in our consciousness, perhaps deliberately. People are talking less and less about the surprise to Israeli Intelligence, and, when they do, they disregard the all-knowing, omnipotent Shin Bet security service's role. They hardly talk anymore about the helplessness of an equipped, budgeted, mighty army, about its inability to save a kibbutz that had been conquered for 12 whole hours.

A few more thousand Palestinian fatalities in Gaza, and the debacle will fade away even more; the IDF is winning. The army's corrective experience, if it is indeed as successful as the story they're telling us so far, could make us forget the botch-up. Who will call to account the great Israeli heroes who serve us the head of Yahya Sinwar on a silver platter, and maybe even free the hostages? We'll forgive them anything.

The preoccupation of wallowing in grief and patting ourselves on the back is intended to cover the black holes, not only about what has happened, but about what is happening and mainly about what will happen.

The first black hole is what's happening now in Gaza: The endless verbosity in the Israeli media almost ignores the horrific bloodbath. Not a word about Gaza's disaster. Not that it's justified or unjustified—it simply doesn't exist. The disregard is deliberate. There are no reports. No images. Barely even lip service. Nor is there any mention of the morning after. Reams of words, and nobody has yet to say what will happen after the great victory.

We all want to hear more and more tales of heroism—true stories, certainly true—and to share with everyone the horrifying disaster of so many Israelis who were killed, kidnapped, wounded, bereaved, orphaned and who will remain crippled and scarred.

There isn't an Israeli who doesn't want every bit of information about the hostages and their families, about those who were killed, the bereaved and the missing. But the mourning and heroism cannot totally dominate public discourse for a month and beyond, and still not make room for any other matters.

Alongside the heroism and rebirth, we must also deal with the debacle and those who are to blame for it, already now, before the severity of it is blunted due to a military victory, real or simulated. Nor can we hesitate to tell Israelis what is being done now in their name in Gaza.

The Israeli heroes are killing tens of thousands of people there wholesale. It's all right to justify it, one may say there's no choice, or even be glad, driven by bloodthirstiness and feelings of vengeance. But it cannot be concealed, not only because the whole world is dealing only with that, but because it's the moral imperative to look reality straight in the eye.

A month after the beginning of the war, Israel is not looking reality straight in the eye. The chance for real soul-searching after the war is therefore diminishing. We'll probably have to meet again in the next war.

A Population Transfer Under the Cover of War: A Visit to the Forsaken Land of Settler Militias

November 18

As we descended with difficulty down the road, moving large rocks placed by settlers there out of our way, we spotted two intimidating figures heading toward our car. They arrived from the main road. One was wearing an Israel Defense Forces uniform, was armed with a machine gun and had long ear locks; the other was dressed in civilian clothes. The Palestinian passengers who were accompanying us grew visibly tense. Never has there been such fear of settlers here.

The settler in the T-shirt jumped on the hood of the car and blocked our way with his body. He held his cell phone close to us to take photos in a threatening way, as if he had caught us in some sinful act—and then pushed additional rocks onto the road with his foot so we couldn't go on. His armed, uniformed friend asked us in an entitled manner what we were doing there and demanded that we show our IDs. We were on our way back from visiting one of the last shepherding communities that has yet to flee the region, Khirbet al-Tiran, south of Dahiriya, in the South Hebron Hills. The night before our arrival, its residents received a threat, delivered in person, demanding that they leave their village within 24 hours, otherwise they would be killed.

We somehow got through the rocky roadblock, ignored the soldier-settler's rude demand that we tell him what we were doing there, and continued on toward the main road. The passengers in our car recognized the soldier as a settler from Yehuda Farm, describing him as one of the most violent settlers in the region. Now he is a member of the settlement's community defense squad, the latest scourge to plague the shepherding communities here. "With the [regular] military security coordinators we knew what to do and what to look out for," says Nasser Nawaj'ah, a B'Tselem field researcher who lives in nearby Susya. "The community defense squad has the authority to arrest anyone they want and do whatever they want."

On the perpetually deserted roads of the South Hebron Hills, what you mainly see now are cars with yellow flasher lights— the standby squad vehicles that have significantly multiplied in number recently. Under the cover of the war, settlers have grown wilder than ever. New shacks turn up on every hilltop, flying an Israeli flag, harbingers of a forthcoming outpost. Settlers are armed and wear IDF uniforms instead of civilian clothing over their fringed religious garments. Nawaj'ah calls them "criminals in uniform."

In recent weeks, all of the roads leading to the shepherding communities and other villages here have been blocked by settlers with large boulders. For example, Susya, a village that's home to more than 300 people from 32 families, has been obstructed by 16 such roadblocks, some of them even in its fields, so that it's no longer accessible by car.

"Not even a fly can get here," Nawaj'ah says, in Hebrew. According to B'Tselem's data, 16 communities of shepherds have fled their villages across the West Bank since the war broke out, six of them in the South Hebron Hills. Now there are 149 new families who have run for their lives, who will never be able to return to their villages. A population transfer under the auspices of war.

The system repeats itself in every Palestinian village: The settlers turn up mainly at night, sometimes in uniform, sometimes masked, threatening and menacing. Sometimes they hold a gun to a child's head, destroy cars and other property, open the taps of water tanks and empty them, tear open and empty sacks of grain, scare the cattle, smash everything in sight and inform the terrified residents that if they don't leave their village within 24 hours, they will return at night and hurt them.

Residents of these tiny communities are the weakest and most helpless link in the Palestinian food chain, and they have no choice but to give in and flee from the place where they were born and where they live under near-biblical conditions. There's no one to protect them, their children or their property. In this forsaken land, there's no army, no Israeli or Palestinian police or any other agency that defends residents. The settler bullies exploit the weakness of the residents and the chaos of war to expand the population transfer. Their goal is to cleanse the entire South Hebron Hills and other areas of their Palestinian residents. Their success can already be observed. In the territories south of the town of Samu and the city of Dahiriya, and in Masafer Yatta, abandoned tent villages were visible this week, with the flag of the occupier and expeller flying above them.

This latest round began two weeks ago, when the residents of the villages of Zanuta (27 families) and Inizan (five families) were expelled by settlers who apparently came from Meitarim Farm, the bane of the Palestinians' existence. The village of Razim, near Samu, was also emptied after settlers threatened its residents. They fled, leaving behind even the contents of their tents. At night settlers with bulldozers arrived and destroyed all of their property, meager as it was. Ten tons of barley were destroyed.

The last resident of Razim, Issa Safi, 77, ultimately had to leave after threats on his life intensified. One night he called Nawaj'ah crying, and the next day he left as well. His donkeys were stolen by settlers from Asa'el, he tells us.

The community of Maktel Amsalam also ceased to exist. Amar Awawe, a 38-year-old shepherd, escaped with his family. He was forced by the settlers to walk barefoot over thorns and was abused in other ways until he managed to flee, according to Nawaj'ah. Nawaj'ah says that many of these villages are tiny, with two or three families each, and they have no option but to flee.

Two months ago, four families lived in the village of Atiria. Now an Israeli flag is flying over its shacks, near the road.

Brothers Tawfik and Rafik Zarir, 47 and 55, respectively, live in Khirbet al-Tiran. Each has 12 children, and together they own 500 sheep. The main tent in their village was partly made of a giant tarp originally intended as an advertisement for an Israeli mortgage bank. Yehuda Farm, one of the most violent outposts in the area, overlooks from a nearby hilltop. Five families, 100 people, live in Tiran. Odeh Abu Sharah is 75; his father was born here 110 years ago. He has yet to receive threats, unlike his neighbors Tawfik and Rafik.

On November 11, a Sabbath, at 10 a.m., two armed settlers arrived in the village, driving their truck wildly into the herd of cattle, aiming to spook them. According to Rafik, one of the settlers jumped out of the truck and held a gun to the head of one of the children, screaming at him: "You have 24 hours to get lost!" They asked the youngsters where the owners of one of the dwellings were, and then repeated their threat, before leaving.

In the afternoon two other settlers arrived from Yehuda Farm, again threatening and harassing, and declared: "We'll return tonight." They in fact returned the next night. On Sunday, between 7 and 10 masked men, some wearing military uniforms, used clubs and rocks to smash the windows of two parked cars and destroyed a tractor engine. They emptied the village's water tank and its sacks of grain. They ordered everyone to gather in one tent, where they then cursed and threatened them. No one opened their mouth out of fear. "We gave you 24 hours to leave, why didn't you leave, ya sharmutot [you whores]? You have another 24 hours."

"What are you going to do?" we asked them the next day. "What are we going to do? If they continue to hurt and threaten us, we'll leave. We have no one to protect us from them," says Rafik.

We sat in the shadow of a berry tree, as air force planes, apparently on their way to a bombing raid in Gaza, flew noisily overhead. It was clear to everyone that within a few days this community, too, would be abandoned, and the greedy settlers would take the land as spoils.

Some residents have tried to leave the area at night, when attacks are more likely, and to return at daytime to herd their cattle and guard their property. That's what Mohammed Jabarin, a 47-year-old shepherd, did. But after a week, he arrived home one morning to find that all the doors and windows had been removed forcibly and smashed. His washing machine was broken, and his cauliflower patch was uprooted. He's also left now.

Susya, whose residents were expelled by settlers a few years ago from the nearby caves where they were born—forcing them to relocate across the road—also cannot be accessed by car. Nawaj'ah has to park his car a kilometer and a half from his home. When he is carrying heavy things, he needs to put them on the back of a donkey. The settlers have sent him back to the Stone Age.

Giora Eiland's Monstrous Gaza Proposal Is Evil in Plain Sight

November 23

Giora Eiland is one of the "thinking officers" to have come out of the IDF. Pleasant and eloquent, his demeanor is all moderation and sound judgment. He had an impressive military career, was head of the military's Operations and Planning Division and head of the National Security Council. He is constantly being interviewed and hailed by the Labor movement. He isn't inarticulate and ignorant like Brig. Gen. Amir Avivi and isn't bloodthirsty like Itamar Ben-Gvir. Middle of the road, moderate right.

Eiland, not a well man, who has even written a book about his suffering, has an idea: Epidemics in Gaza are good for Israel. "After all, severe epidemics in the southern Strip will bring victory closer and reduce fatalities among IDF soldiers," he wrote this week in *Yedioth Ahronoth*. One only has to wait for the daughters of Hamas's leaders to contract the plague, and we've won.

Eiland didn't detail which plagues he recommends—pestilence, boils or cholera, maybe a cocktail of smallpox and AIDS; perhaps also starvation for 2 million people. A promise of Israeli victory at rock-bottom prices. "And no, it's not cruelty for its own sake," he stressed, as though anyone thought otherwise. In fact, it's rare kindness and humaneness, which would only save human lives.

Eiland, in the role of Mother Theresa, an officer and a gentleman in the world's most moral army, made a Nazi proposal and no storm broke out. Anyone who attributes genocide to Israel is antisemitic, after all. Just imagine a European general proposing to starve a nation, or to kill it with an epidemic—the Jews, for instance. Imagine spreading a plague because it would promote the war effort. All is fair in war, and now it's okay to suggest anything and everything you've dreamed of and never dared to bring up. Political correctness has been turned upside down. Anyone can be Meir Kahane, nobody may be human. It's okay to propose genocide, but wrong to pity the children of Gaza. It's okay to propose ethnic cleansing, but it's wrong to be shocked by Gaza's punishment.

It's no longer only the right. It's the mainstream. Yesh Atid's MK Ram Ben Barak supports voluntary transfer; the moderate minister Gila Gamliel is also in favor. The foreign minister said she doesn't represent the government. Yes, she does, and not only the government.

Monstrousness has become correct, diabolism has penetrated the center and even left of center. Another war or two, and everyone will be Kahane.

We haven't yet recovered from Hamas's brutality, and already we are being inundated with all this goodness—not only from the extreme right and the settlers, but from the heart of the Israeli center. Apparently, there is horrific cruelty and correct cruelty. Hamas are animals, but the proposal to spread disease is legitimate. One of the most dangerous occurrences to be born in this war is unfolding before our eyes: the standardization, legalization and normalization of evil.

This evil grew out of the ground of the unbelievable disregard and pathological indifference in Israel to what's happening now in Gaza. Foreign journalists who come here can't believe their eyes: Gaza's suffering doesn't exist. Israel hasn't killed thousands of children and didn't evict a million people from their homes. Gaza's sacrifice is totally out of the picture, gone not only from public discourse but even from the daily news. On Israeli television, alone in the world, we didn't kill children. According to the Israeli media, the IDF hasn't committed in this war even one tiny little war crime.

A society that so disregards reality and is so indifferent to the suffering of the nation it declared war on raises moral mutations like Eiland. You can be sure he thinks his suggestion isn't in any way tainted, all he did was make a reasonable suggestion that serves Israel's interest. What other consideration is there, anyway, except Israel's interest? International law is for the weak, morality for the philosophizers, humanism for the bleeding hearts. And really, what's wrong with a plague in Gaza? Only one thing: It could infect Israel, too. In fact, it already has.

Forty-Two Palestinians Killed in Seven Weeks: A Visit to a West Bank City That Has Become a Firing Zone

November 25

On the main road leading from the town of Anabta to the city of Tulkarm, near the entrance to the Nur Shams refugee camp

THE KILLING OF GAZA

east of the city, one needs to drive slowly and maneuver between potholes, puddles and piles of mud.

Israel Defense Forces bulldozers have destroyed this part of the road, to facilitate the army's frequent incursions into the camp (every other night, according to residents). Due to the risk of improvised explosive devices being embedded in the asphalt, roads are ripped up and then left unpaved. As a result, cars move only haltingly, stuck in a perpetual traffic jam.

The two main roads within the camp have been torn up as well, repaved by the Palestinians, and then again torn up by the army. The infrastructures in the camp—water, electricity and sewerage—have been seriously damaged by army bulldozers. Blocks of concrete and piles of dirt have been placed at the Einav checkpoint since the start of the war, to make it difficult for cars to pass there, too. The West Bank is still relatively quiet, but the IDF is more active there than ever, sowing destruction under the cover of defensive measures.

The already difficult financial situation in the West Bank has been compounded by the wartime lockdown, which prevents tens of thousands of laborers from going to work in Israel. Even those who in the past would risk sneaking into Israel illegally for work are now scared of passing through the breaches in the security fence due to the dangerous atmosphere. A few laborers have already been beaten up on streets in Israel. Israeli Arabs have stopped coming to Tulkarm to shop, afraid of the checkpoints, soldiers and settlers. The West Bank is heating up, albeit quietly. The feeling is that the IDF is not only working to keep Israelis safe, but also taking advantage of the war to oppress the Palestinian residents even more than usual—to torture them. Support for Hamas, it can be assumed, has skyrocketed here since the war broke out.

The residents are glued to the images being broadcast from Gaza. The shock over what happened on October 7 in the Negev, and its scale, is evident here as well. Conspiracy theories are rampant, considering how the army was taken by surprise and overcome by the attackers, suffering a grave, initial failure on that fateful Shabbat. No one imagined such a thing happening. Everyone understands that things will never be the same, that that Saturday was a watershed moment.

But just how will things change? No one knows.

B'Tselem field researcher Abdulkarim Sadi, who lives in the nearby village of Attil, says that on October 7 he woke up when his son called him, agitated, from Ramallah, telling him to turn on the news. Sadi couldn't believe what he saw: Hamas in Sderot.

No few roads have been closed to Palestinian traffic; only Jews are allowed on them, here in the land of "no apartheid." This includes the roads between Barta'a and Jenin and between Jit and Hawara, which itself was under siege even before the war.

Cow heads are strung up on hooks in butcher shop windows in Tulkarm. A drawing of Umm Kulthum hangs from a hot dog stand called Inta Omry—"You Are My Life." Traffic in the city is bustling, despite everything. In the Nur Shams refugee camp, 14 people were killed in one night, which we will get to later. In Tulkarm, "only" 42 people have been killed since the war began. More than 200 Palestinians have been killed across the West Bank.

People were gathered this week, as always, at the entrance to the Thabet Thabet hospital in central Tulkarm. Behind the hospital lives the Awad family. Innocent paintings of snowy mountain peaks, forests and lakes adorn the walls of their house; a blue sky is painted on the ceiling. Birds are chirping from a tiny cage. A meager house in the back of a hospital. Here lived "the engineer-shahid Majdi Awad," as he's described in the death notice. Awad is certainly a shahid (Muslim martyr), but he was never an engineer. He studied engineering in Jordan when he was young, but after suffering a psychotic breakdown he dropped out. He was diagnosed with schizophrenia, and never worked after that. His only daughter, Atidel, 36, and her husband, Mohammed Barake, 50, sit in the tiny, kitschy living room, recalling her father's life and death.

After his diagnosis, four decades ago, the father stayed isolated, living on the ground floor, enveloped in his silence. He wasn't violent, but communication with him was minimal. Nevertheless, he married Samira, now 55, and fathered Atidel. Samira made a living cleaning houses in Taibeh, Kalansua and Tira, Arab towns within Israel. Madji would sit at home or head to the market. People would give him food and drinks. He was 65, and in the photo on his death notice his face looks anguished.

On November 1, he got up as usual before dawn, before the muezzin's call. Just after 4 a.m., he took his regular route along Mukataa Street: He got an order of hummus and ful (fava beans) at the hummus place, a pita at the bakery, and sat down at the entrance to the mosque to eat his breakfast. When he finished, he got up and walked toward the road. Footage from a security camera shows him taking his final steps: Awad is walking slowly, heavily, and then in the blink of an eye he falls on the road, his face hitting the asphalt, as a blue light illuminates the street in the background.

At the corner is an army jeep, some 100 meters from Awad. His slow walk left no room for doubt that he was an older man, and that he wasn't holding any sort of weapon. Nonetheless, one bullet hit his head. The soldiers entered the city that night to arrest a Palestinian operative, Kasab Zakot. He was indeed arrested. Awad died on the spot.

The way to the Nur Shams camp is short. In a house at the edge of the camp resides the Mahamid family, above an abandoned shop. Nahida, 54, and Ibrahim, 58, have nine children. Ibrahim is a former journalist and publisher of a local weekly. A couple from the Israeli-Arab village of Jatt, old friends, are visiting them, which they've been doing frequently since tragedy struck the family. The woman from Jatt explains that she comes even though she has been scared of traveling here since the war broke out.

Taha was 15 years old. A 10th-grader. On the night of October 19, the family was awakened with the rest of their neighbors when fighters from the camp triggered an alert indicating that IDF forces were heading that way. This time, it was undercover troops in cars with Palestinian license plates.

Taha was playing a computer game with his sister Shimaa, 32. He told her he was going to see what was happening on the main road nearby. Two minutes later she heard gunshots. His other sister, Sara, 18, was on the porch and saw everything. Taha merely peeked into the road—and was shot immediately. Two bullets hit his head, one under his eye and another above it, in his forehead. Another bullet hit his leg. It was 3:35 a.m. Sara screamed for her father. "Dad, Dad, Taha fell."

Ibrahim ran from the house toward his dying son, a distance of 20 meters or so. Ibrahim didn't see the soldiers who shot his son, but he yelled in the direction the shots came from, in Hebrew and in Arabic, that he was the father, and also waved his hands, to no avail. The moment he tried to turn his son over to see his face, the soldiers shot Ibrahim as well. He was seriously wounded in his abdomen and was hospitalized at Thabet Thabet for two weeks. Now he can only walk with difficulty, leaning on a cane, thin and pale.

Father and son both lay on the road without medical treatment for an hour before an ambulance was permitted to evacuate them. The ambulance first took Taha, whose death was pronounced at the hospital, and then his father, who was rushed to the operating room.

Asked about both incidents, the IDF issued the following statement: "Security forces were active on the specified dates in foiling terror and in arresting wanted figures in Tulkarm and in the Nur Shams refugee camp. During the fighting, terrorists fired at the forces massively, and threw numerous [explosive] devices at them. Security forces fired at armed terrorists, at the sources of the fire and even at the devices, to preemptively detonate them.

"We are aware of the claims about the wounding of both Majdi Awad and of Taha Mahamid and his father. The details of the incidents are being checked."

On the night Taha was killed and his father wounded, a total of 14 residents of the refugee camp were killed, 10 by an Israeli missile. On Wednesday this week, another six people were killed at the Tulkarm camp, also by a missile fired from the air. Dozens of fatalities in a month and a half. This is the new normal.

Is It Permissible to Rejoice in the Joy of Palestinians Released from Israeli Prisons?

November 26

This was a roller coaster of a weekend which left no one unmoved. The images of the released hostages, old women and little children, were the stuff of a thousand telenovelas with happy endings.

To see 6-year-old Emilia and cry; to see 9-year-old Ohad and shiver; to see the release of Hannah Katzir, who was declared dead by Palestinian Islamic Jihad, and Yaffa Adar, who survived captivity at 85 years old, and feel a lump in the throat.

The fact that all are in good medical condition is cause for relief and happiness. This is what national joy looks like, mixed with the grief, anxiety and discomfiture that have prevailed in Israel since October 7. Just let them all come back already.

Israel in its mixed joy, and the Palestinians in their mixed joy. Is it permissible to rejoice in their joy? Who is even allowed to rejoice in this country? The emotional police has set boundaries: Palestinians may not rejoice.

Israeli police representatives visited the homes of those released in East Jerusalem, warning the occupants to refrain from any display of joy. We are allowed to rejoice in the return of our children; they are not allowed to rejoice in the return of theirs. But the prohibition does not end here. We are not allowed to watch them rejoice, either.

The day after the hostages returned, the sun rose on Gaza. It was the first morning in 50 straight days that Gaza's skies weren't covered in plumes of smoke and dust from the bombings. People weren't fleeing back and forth for their lives, helplessly trying to escape bombs that could fall at any moment without warning. Children, anxious at nighttime, still wet their beds (those who have beds), but less than before. Is it permissible to rejoice over that in Israel?

About an hour's drive from the hospitals where families were reunited, sparking national joy, similar sights could be seen in East Jerusalem and the West Bank. A father who hadn't seen his daughter in eight years reunited with her in a teary embrace. A woman ran hysterically toward her daughter, who had been incarcerated for seven years.

I saw the mother of Malek Salman of Beit Safafa hugging her daughter, weeping and shouting. "Mama, mama," Malek yelled, and I felt joy. Is that a transgression? A psychological defect? A moral defect?

Thirty-nine Palestinian women and minors also made their way from prison to their families and to freedom. Some were convicted of stabbing attacks, possession of a knife, or attempted murder, others of throwing rocks or minor peccadilloes. None are innocent of the crime of violent resistance against the occupation, and the state was within its rights to try and punish them. But they are also human beings.

The children are certainly children, even when we talk about young rock throwers, sentenced in Israel to disproportionate prison terms and to far worse conditions than Jewish defendants of their age. I was also happy to see them walk free. I know that's not permitted.

In one of the exceptional moments of the painfully one-sided TV coverage in Israel, Channel 13 News showed a very brief moment of Palestinian joy at the return of a daughter. Channel 13's Almog Boker, a field reporter in his soul, who from war to war is becoming even more nationalistic, and can't utter the word Hamas without tacking on the word "Nazis," cried out in indignant fury, "We mustn't show that."

Journalist Raviv Drucker tried to convince him that it's important to show that the Palestinians are happy in order to reveal their true face—this, after failing to persuade him that everything should be reported, simply because that is what journalism is about.

Boker thinks that during war the only things that should be shown are those that serve Israel's interests. And, indeed, in the Israeli media not only is Gaza's suffering banned from the screen, so is the joy of parents upon their daughter's return from prison, lest we be tempted to think that they, too, are human beings, with feelings and all.

These are the days of intense emotional swings. The roller coaster goes up and down, and it's okay to leave a small place in it for the small joy of Palestinians. The war, the government keeps telling us, is against only Hamas.

December

While War Rages in Gaza, Israeli Troops and Settlers Grow Trigger-Happy in Ramallah

December 2

The traffic jams in the center of Ramallah are on a Tel Aviv scale. Likewise, the crowds in the stores, restaurants and gyms. But not far away is another traffic jam—of a kind you won't see in Tel Aviv: the ever-present, kilometers-long logjam of cars snaking toward the Qalandiyah checkpoint, en route to Jerusalem. It's always congested, but since October 7, the situation has become much worse.

Israel blocked most of the entrances and exits from the unofficial Palestinian capital when the war began, including the northern entrance to the city (the District Coordination Office checkpoint). So everyone who is authorized and who seeks to enter or leave Ramallah these days—generally, East Jerusalemites wanting to go home—must do so via the Qalandiyah checkpoint, one of the most miserable places in the West Bank, with its depressing developing world feeling, abutting a modern cityscape.

The war isn't felt in the center of Ramallah—try and find a parking space—but in its periphery it is very much present. The list of blocked thoroughfares and of villages whose access roads are now locked with imposing yellow iron gates is very long, and thus the trips local folk must make to work, school and shops and to visit families have also become arduous.

But the most serious problem is not that the roads surrounding Ramallah have been closed off to Palestinians, or the fact that Palestinian workers have been banned from entering Israel—it's that in this part of the West Bank many people have been killed since the war broke out on October 7—far more than usual. According to data collected by Iyad Hadad, the regional field researcher for the B'Tselem Israeli human rights organization, 31 people have been killed here in less than two months. And in contrast to the Tulkarm area, which we wrote about here last week, where most of those killed were armed, here, in and around Ramallah, none of the victims was armed and none were active in resistance organizations.

Hadad's estimate is that six of the dead were probably killed by settlers, or by settlers and soldiers together. The most recent case was last Saturday evening, when the body of a Palestinian was found next to the settlement of Psagot in circumstances that have yet to be fully clarified. In his office in El Bireh, adjacent to Ramallah, Hadad has a thick folder documenting the investigations he is conducting of every case of killing since the war erupted in the Gaza Strip. The folder just keeps getting thicker.

The Ramallah region, like the entire West Bank, is bleeding profusely under the cover of war in Gaza and far from outsiders' eyes. The fact that there are a great many settlements and settler outposts in the area only heightens the violence further. And here, too, like everywhere in the West Bank, the soldiers' fingers on the trigger seem far twitchier since October 7. In war as in war.

On the evening of October 12, five days after the Hamas attack in the south, Randa Ajaji, 40, a mother of seven children, was traveling with her husband and two of her children, the younger one just 18 months old, in the family car. Outside the village of Silwad they saw an improvised checkpoint, where soldiers were stopping cars headed in the opposite direction. Many such surprise checkpoints are springing up in the West Bank today.

After they drove a few more meters, the family saw figures signaling them to stop with a flashlight. Certain that these were also soldiers, they slowed down almost to a standstill. They then saw that the figures were civilians and figured that they were set-tlers. At once they started driving again, but their car came under fire. First the older boy was wounded, in the leg. The father sped toward the clinic in Silwad, where he discovered, to his horror, that Randa, who had been sitting in the back with the toddler, had been shot and killed, reportedly by soldiers. She was pro-nounced dead in the clinic.

For his part, Hadad says there was no apparent reason for the majority of the killings he has investigated recently. Another incident occurred on October 8, the day after the massacre in the south. Yasser Kasba, an 18-year-old resident of the Qalandiyah refugee camp, threw a makeshift Molotov cocktail at the fortified concrete tower manned by Israel Defense Forces soldiers at the nearby checkpoint. The bottle shattered, smoke curling upward, but no damage was caused. As Kasba fled he was shot in the back by soldiers in the tower. He collapsed, bleeding.

The shooting was broadcast live by the American Arabic-language satellite TV channel Alhurra, which also filmed Kasba as he was carried to a car by friends. He died very soon after-ward. Later that same day, an incredible scene unfolded. It was 9:15 p.m. and cars were passing by across the road from Border Police personnel stationed at the Qalandiyah checkpoint, who were standing on the sidewalk. For no apparent reason, the troops sprayed one of the passing vehicles with dozens of bullets—and then reprised that act with the next car. Both cars continued traveling until they slammed into the separa-tion barrier. In the first car was Mohammed Hamaid, 25, from Beit Anan; in the other, Amjad Hdeir, 36. Both were killed, and Hdeir's brother, who was sitting next to him, was wounded.

The Israel Police sent this statement: "Following a report that an Israeli vehicle had mistakenly entered Qalandiyah and a lynching was being perpetrated on its passengers, Border Police arrived to rescue them. During the fighters' activity a violent dis-turbance erupted, during which explosive devices and Molotov cocktails were thrown and shots were fired. In addition two vehicles began speeding toward the fighters in an attempt to run

THE KILLING OF GAZA

them over, at which point Border Police officers opened fire at the suspects and neutralized them."

Another incident: on October 29 at 2:30 a.m., in the town of Beit Rima. Social media had been warning about an Israeli invasion, and an army force indeed arrived in three vehicles, from the direction of Nabi Saleh. A group of 15 to 20 young people took to the streets to meet the troops with stones. One jeep started to move forward, and the Palestinians thought the force was leaving. What they didn't know was that another group of soldiers was lurking nearby, in an ambush, under the cover of darkness, near the skeleton of an unfinished building.

The young people came under heavy fire from the group of soldiers and 12 were hit. One—Nasser Barghouti, 29—was killed, three were seriously wounded and four more lightly wounded.

On the morning of November 9, the army arrived to make arrests in the Al-Amari refugee camp, outside Ramallah. Snipers were scattered on rooftops and shot at virtually anyone who was outside, according to B'Tselem's Hadad; a number of residents were hurt as they left their homes for work or to shop. A woman who went out to buy bread was shot in the leg. Mohand Jad al-Haq, who was standing with a group of workers in the street, wanted to look at what was going on and was shot and killed. Another seven wounded residents were left behind by the troops as they departed town.

This week we also visited the town of Beitunia, on Ramallah's western outskirts. An apartment building with an elevator, a bourgeois home on the third floor. This is the residence of 15-year-old Suhaib Sus, a 10th-grader and the son of Iyad Sus, a senior official in the Palestinian water company, 48, and of his wife, Saida, a 45-year-old homemaker. The couple has three other children. Early on Friday, October 20, a large army force, traveling in some 15 vehicles, made its way from the nearby Ofer facility toward Ramallah. They initially passed through Beitunia at 4 a.m., made arrests in Ramallah and returned to Ofer. At 9 a.m. they returned for round No. 2.

Posts on social media in Beitunia said that the troops had returned and Suhaib left home to see what was happening. He and a few friends waited for the soldiers' arrival some 40 minutes later and threw stones at the first vehicle in the convoy. A video clip shot by a bystander shows a soldier opening the door of a jeep and shooting the teenager, who then ran about 100 meters with two other young people, clutched the right side of his chest and collapsed on his back, bleeding profusely.

Some minutes beforehand, his father, Iyad, read on social media that Suhaib had asked where the soldiers were. With a sense of foreboding he phoned his son a few times but got no answer. Shortly thereafter Iyad heard shots and then, horrifically, he saw an image on Telegram of his son lying in the street, oozing blood.

The IDF Spokesperson's Unit stated this week, in response to a query from *Haaretz*: "On October 20, forces of the IDF operated to arrest a wanted individual in the village of Ein Mesbah. As the troops were leaving, via the village of Beitunia, a violent disturbance erupted. The force responded with crowd-dispersal measures and by firing, in order to end the disturbance. A hit was observed. We are aware of the allegation of the death of a Palestinian during the event. The circumstances of the case are currently being clarified."

Iyad hurried down to the street; a neighbor had called to say that Suhaib had been wounded lightly. The son had been evacuated to the local clinic and from there to a hospital in Ramallah, where he was undergoing the first of two operations when his father arrived. Toward evening he died from his wounds.

He was a quiet, introverted boy who liked to help others, his father tells us. After he was killed, his friends refused to return to school, and only when social workers were called in to talk to them did they agree to go back—two weeks after the incident.

Israel Has Turned Its Back on the Hostages in Favor of Destroying Gaza

December 2

Israel's resumption of the war is its biggest mistake since October 7. A war "heavy in days, heavy in blood," in the wondrous words of Moshe Dayan regarding another war, has become a war that is even heavier in days and blood, with its goals receding and its crimes accumulating.

Returning once again to the awful scenes in Gaza—the first two days of the renewed phase looked horrible—is tantamount to a return to a loss of humanity. On Saturday, children were again dying on the filthy floors of Gaza's hospitals, with their parents bent over them crying out in anguish. People with head injuries, covered in dust from collapsed buildings, were brought to clinics where no help could be provided.

Gaza can't take it anymore, and after the pause, human suffering is even more unbearable. Go tell a family that has already fled for its life, finding a puny shelter for itself, a scrap of a tent, to move south again. Go tell that family to move south while the south is being bombarded indiscriminately, almost like the northern part of the Gaza Strip.

The interactive escape route map, the glory of the IDF's technology and ethics which was disseminated in Gaza over the weekend, cannot save even one soul. It's dubious that it was even meant to.

Israel is not interested in punishing Gaza, only in attaining its goals. In resuming the war in Gaza, Israel has admitted that it prefers one goal over all others. Gone is the talk about liberating the hostages at any price, before anything else.

The die has been cast and there is no way of obscuring this. Israel clearly prefers to "pulverize" Hamas, whatever that term means, over saving the hostages. No word games will help here, this is the naked truth. In resuming the war, Israel is not only endangering the lives of the hostages, it is also thwarting any attempts to free them. And all of this while the process of exchanging hostages for prisoners was going better than expected.

After long days of celebrating the return of hostages, with TV panels and newspapers squeezing out every possible drop of emotion, with news broadcasts becoming reality shows, in which every distant cousin of a released hostage repeats the story over and over; when a horrifying reality is turned into a telenovela, with a happy ending that becomes kitsch—after all that, the negotiations blew up, and with them went the myth of freeing the hostages at any cost.

According to some reports, Hamas was interested in moving to the release of male hostages, whose price was higher, and Israel wanted to complete the release of women first. To scuttle negotiations over this issue while returning to full-blown war is a clear statement of Israel's priorities, which even before that showed signs of preferring war over releasing hostages.

Israel's moment of truth arrived, and the choice was made. It is an infuriating one. Israel should have no goal more important than securing the release of hostages. There is nothing more grave than severing the unwritten pact between a civilian (or soldier) and his state, abandoning the hostage to his or her fate.

From now on, we can no longer talk about releasing them at any price. Israel is for releasing hostages, obviously, but not at any price. In its perception, there are more important issues. It will not agree to a deal of exchanging all hostages for all prisoners, including a permanent cease-fire, in order to save 136 Israelis.

In the TV panels of death and kitsch they tried to blur this choice. Only some family members of the hostages, not all, dared oppose the renewal of the war, while armies of commentators and correspondents continued to recite hollow slogans supporting this choice.

There are very grave questions that no one is raising regarding its horrific methods. Israel embarked on a just war using patently unjust methods. Even in just wars, not everything is permissible, certainly not the killing of 15,000 people and then continuing without end, only in order to achieve goals that may not be attainable. Even if they are achieved, nothing will be solved.

Let's set aside the justice of this war and its methods for a moment. It's imperative to return the hostages, before anything else. It's still possible, on condition that the war stops.

The Israeli Army's Incursions Are More Frequent and Violent; the Jenin Refugee Camp Is Now Little Gaza

December 8

Hamudi is dead.

A shoe found amid the rubble of the house, which was destroyed by a missile, bears witness that he was indeed liquidated, as the Israel Defense Forces announced. It's a black Nike Air, with a black hole and stained with blood, exactly like what Hamudi wore. Mohammed (Hamudi) Zubeidi, 27 at the time of his death last week, was the No. 1 wanted individual in the Jenin refugee camp since being released from an Israeli prison two years ago.

The last time we were in the camp, a few months ago, it was Hamudi himself who drove us through the alleyways in his car, his rifle slung over his shoulder. Together we drove to the new cemetery of the camp's fallen, on its outskirts. That cemetery, the second one built since the beginning of the second intifada, has also already filled up with graves. And after the war broke out in the Gaza Strip two months ago, a third cemetery was inaugurated, alongside the other two. Scores of fresh graves have already been dug there, and this week relatives and friends gathered in hushed tones to commune with their loved ones. But Hamudi, whom I've known since he was 5, and who spent five years of his life in Israeli prisons, isn't buried here. The IDF snatched his body and departed.

The way into the camp is worse than ever. To get to Jenin from Tulkarm these days, you have to pass through many villages on narrow, twisting roads, like in the worst days of the intifada.

Palestinians are banned from using the main highway in the area. In the camp an appalling experience awaits. First, there is the pervasive stench. In its latest incursions the IDF tore up the camp's roads and seriously damaged its sewage system. The rancid water now flows in the muddied alleys, and a nauseating smell wafts from the streets. The streets themselves are almost impassable with their mud and rocks strewn all over; vehicles bounce from side to side as they pass the rubble of homes. The word in the camp is that in recent days the army trashed some 80 apartments, leaving them unfit for habitation. The camp's Ansar mosque also lies in ruins.

In early May 2002 I arrived here to witness the total destruction the IDF sowed during Operation Defensive Shield. The sights I saw this week reminded me of what I saw then. After that operation, the United Arab Emirates helped to rehabilitate the camp—but now that it's been destroyed again, who is going to rehabilitate it? Residents say the army issued orders not to start rebuilding, because it intends to return soon. Thus it was on Tuesday, the day after our visit: Army bulldozers rumbled back in and wrought even more destruction. The Jenin camp is now Little Gaza. No one in Israel takes any interest in the fate of either place.

In the Faluja neighborhood, named for the lost village of the parents of Jenin's current residents, Jamal Zubeidi, the man with the aristocratic demeanor, awaits us as usual. Hamudi is the second son Jamal has lost, in addition to a son-in-law, sister-in-law and nephew. All told, nine members of this fighting family have been killed over the years by the army. Most of its remaining male members are in Israeli prisons, among them Jamal's famous nephew Zakaria, whom he raised from childhood.

Hamudi, Jamal's youngest son, joined Islamic Jihad less than a decade ago; his father did not oppose his sons' decisions to become fighters. Islamic Jihad has become the leading organization in Jenin in recent years, more because of its militancy, less for its religious piety. All the fighting forces in the camp have been united under the umbrella of one command center, the Katiba (Battalion).

Along with Mohammed Zubeidi, his friend Hussam Hanun was also killed last week. Aged 28, with a law degree from the American University in Jenin, Hussam was a member of the Popular Front for the Liberation of Palestine, a secular organization. His only brother was killed by the army 29 days earlier. Mohammed and Hussam fought together despite their affiliation with two very different organizations—and together they lost. Two children were also shot to death during the liquidation action, but we'll get to them later.

About one-third of the camp's inhabitants haven't slept at home since the war in Gaza started. The army's incursions have become more frequent since then, and above all more violent, so people spend the night with relatives in the nearby city of Jenin. Jamal and his wife, Sanaa, have adopted this habit as well: The IDF often arrests the parents of wanted individuals, and the health of 67-year-old Jamal—who worked in Israel as a young man and was a fan of the Maccabi Haifa soccer team—won't allow him to undergo yet another arrest after all the ordeals he's been through.

About a month ago he got a phone call from "Captain Iyad" from Israel's Shin Bet security service, who asked him how Mohammed was feeling. "We've stopped playing around," the agent said. "Tell Mohammed to come to the Salem checkpoint tomorrow morning." Jamal indeed delivered the message to his son, but Mohammed ignored it, of course.

In the guest room in the parents' home—which long ago became a shrine for all the relatives who have been killed or are in jail—Hamudi's memorial poster has been added to the portrait gallery. In four days of mourning Jamal received thousands of people from all across the West Bank who came to pay their respects. But this past Monday, he was alone and worried about our safety. The camp has banned the entry of Israeli journalists, apart from two; its residents are sorely disappointed by the reporting of what they see as the "mobilized" media in Israel.

On Tuesday, November 28, Sanaa and Jamal spent the night in their daughter's home in the city. It was then that the special-ops force carried out a massive invasion of the camp—with 1,500 soldiers, according to the locals—accompanied by heavy bull-dozers and other machinery of destruction, and with drones and helicopters hovering in the sky. As far as is known, this massive force arrived in order to liquidate Mohammed Zubeidi. Although most of the alleys in the camp are covered with tarpaulins to prevent the aircraft from spying, that didn't help, of course. The soldiers were able to track down Mohammed and Hussam and two other armed men, even though they tried to evade them by moving from house to house.

According to testimonies collected by Jamal and by Abdulkarim Sadi, a field researcher for the Israeli human rights organization B'Tselem, the four men ran to take cover in a house in the Damaj neighborhood in which an army unit was concealed. Mohammed and Hussam fired at the soldiers and ran on to the next house. Three missiles launched from the sky struck it; it was also tar-geted by ground fire, and an IDF bulldozer completed the work. The two men were killed; the army unearthed their bodies from among the rubble and took them away. When local residents found part of an M16 rifle in the ruins, they took it as a definitive sign that Hamudi was dead.

Jamal, who didn't yet know that his son had been killed, tried to enter the camp later that night, but all the entrances were blocked. The District Coordination and Liaison Office then informed the residents that two bodies had been taken and that two others—of the other wanted individuals who had been with Mohammed and Hussam—might also be lying beneath the ruins. Later, however, the two men turned up in the camp, alive and unharmed, after somehow escaping the inferno.

Mohammed's father saw him around midday on the day he was killed. As usual, he came home then to shower, change his clothes and eat. There was no water in the house, but he con-nected a hose to the neighbors' home.

"That was the last thing he did," says Jamal.

The wife of Mohammed's older brother, 37-year-old Anton, prepared a meal for him that would be his last. The brown wooden chairs in the living room came from the café that Mohammed had once opened in the camp. Before that he ran a juice stand, between one period of incarceration and the next. He was released for the last time in 2021, from Damon Prison in northern Israel, but was subsequently declared a wanted individual by the Israeli security forces.

Five months after his release, Mohammed's cousin Daoud, who was also his brother-in-law, was killed by the army. Half a year later, in early 2022, Na'im, Mohammed's brother, was killed. He was 34, the father of two daughters; the first was born while Na'im was in prison, the second after he was killed.

On October 26, a month before Mohammed's death, he was badly wounded in an Israeli missile attack. He suffered a ruptured spleen and for a time walked about with a stoma bag for collection of bodily fluids. Sometimes, Jamal recalls, his son held the bag with one hand and his rifle with the other. Aysar Amar, who rescued Mohammed after that missile strike, was killed two days later, while Mohammed was in intensive care, unconscious. Aysar's brother, Ayham, was killed less than two weeks later, at the age of 23, two months after he was married.

Mohammed and Hussam never married. It's no simple matter for a woman to marry a wanted person whose fate is sealed—a dead man walking.

Jamal's eldest son, Anton, was also wounded this year, by a drone-launched missile, and lost part of his lung. Jamal's daughter Safad was widowed when her husband was killed by the army. Mohammed Zaidan, 32, the husband of Jamal's second daughter, Rafah, is now the No. 1 wanted individual in the Jenin camp. The Zaidans have six children, including a set of triplets. Mohammed Zaidan's brother, Ahmed, was killed in 2004. Jamal's third daughter is married to Zakaria's brother, Jibril Zubeidi, who spent 14 years in prison and who for the past year has been in administrative detention—incarceration without trial.

On one of the walls in Jamal's home there are three photographs of wanted persons, around whose faces Israeli soldiers drew a circle and marked with an X: Daoud, Ahmed Zaidan and Na'im. None of them is alive. And while we're on the subject of people in the family who have been killed, Zakaria Zubeidi's mother Samira was killed on the balcony of her home during the second intifada.

"Everyone who became close to this family has ended up in the cemetery or in prison," says Jamal, a refined person who doesn't like to show emotions. He has already seen everything and endured everything; words fail now in the face of the spiral of death in his family. Hamudi was his youngest child, and everyone pampered him.

Jamal: "Maybe outside he was a big-deal commander, like the Shin Bet says, but at home he was Hamudi, the baby. He was 27, but for us he was a child. I used to send him to buy cigarettes for me, and his mother sent him to get things in the grocery store."

After Mohammed's release from prison, his father wanted to start building a house for him. "Wait," his son told him. He apparently knew he would not have a long life. "We thought he would die before Na'im and Daoud, the army always looked for him first, but he surprised us," his father says.

Hanging on a wall in the camp, which has lost more than 200 of its sons since the early days of the intifada, are photographs of the latest victims. The wall is perforated with bullet holes. Soldiers have smashed all the memorials in Jenin, including the sculpture of a horse created by a German artist from parts of wrecked Palestinian ambulances, which stood at the entrance to the hospital at the outskirts of the camp. Last week the IDF also shattered the camp's gate with its famous bronze "keys of return." A woman in black passes through the alley. Her son was killed three months ago, we are told.

A forward emergency room is due to be built in an open field opposite Jamal's house, as the army prevents those wounded in its incursions from getting to the hospital outside the camp.

We ride through alleys where Zakaria once drove me, careening wildly, on an all-terrain vehicle. Never had I been so frightened. In the Ansar mosque, where Jamal prayed, a wanted individual was liquidated with a missile that destroyed the building completely in late October. Prayer rugs are still lying outside. As we pass the decimated structure in which Hamudi and Hussam were killed, Jamal falls silent. The whole alley is in ruins here, its homes ripped open.

As the long convoy of armored IDF vehicles pulled out of the camp on the afternoon of Wednesday, November 29, after the efficient liquidation operation the night before, children threw stones at them, as usual. One jeep stopped; from inside a soldier fired off a few rounds. Two children were killed on the spot: Basel Abu Alufa, 15, and Adam al-Rol, an 8-year-old boy in the third grade. Afterward the driver got out of the vehicle and photographed Basel's body, sprawled on its back in the street, perhaps as a memento.

The IDF Spokesperson's Unit this week provided the following response to *Haaretz*: "During activity by the IDF in the Jenin refugee camp, in the [sector of] the Menashe Brigade, a number of suspects threw explosive devices at the forces. The fighters responded with fire at the suspects; hits were observed. Claims of the death of Palestinians are known to us. The circumstances of the case are under clarification."

In the home of the dead 8-year-old, Adam, his father, Samar, is grieving. The 49-year-old owner of a store in Jenin that sells pet birds has two other sons and a daughter.

"Those children will never forgive the soldiers," he says bitterly. "The children in Gaza and here, too, will not forget. Now these children want Israeli children to be killed."

By Trying to Humiliate Gaza to Its Core, Israel Is the One Being Humiliated

December 10

As if all this were not enough—the thousands of dead children, the death toll nearing 20,000, the hundreds of thousands uprooted from their homes, the tens of thousands of wounded and the starvation, disease and destruction in Gaza—on top of this, they must also be humiliated. Humiliated to the core, so that they learn.

We must show them (and ourselves) who they are (and who we are). To show how strong we are and how weak they are. It's good for morale. It's good for the soldiers. It's good for the home front. A Hanukkah gift of humiliated Palestinians: What could bring more joy?

There is no greater proof that we have lost our way than the despicable attempts to humiliate the Palestinians for all to see. There is no greater proof of moral weakness than the need to humiliate them in their defeat.

Images and videos from last week: dozens of men on their knees, wearing only underpants, their hands tied behind their backs, their eyes blindfolded, their gazes lowered. One group is on a razed street, another in a sand pit, soldiers standing over them.

Bingo, a victory image. A few of the soldiers are masked; perhaps they are ashamed of their behavior—we can only hope. Their victims are young men and also older ones; some are fat, with potbellies, others gaunt, some have pale skin and others are scorched by the hardships of the war. Perhaps their children watched them, perhaps their wives; that would heighten the achievement.

According to reports, they were removed from a UN Relief and Works Agency shelter in Beit Lahia and detained for questioning. No one knows for sure if any of them were even Hamas members. After the victory photo, they were taken to an unknown location, their fate unclear. Who even cares, besides their loved ones?

What good does it do? This isn't the first time the Israeli army has stripped Palestinians this way in order to humiliate them. Such "walks of shame" were held in the past in the Gaza Strip, the West Bank and Lebanon. Wanted and unwanted men in underpants, for all to see.

That's what Israel does, and it's important to record the event and to spread the images. But the truth is that the images

humiliate the Israel Defense Forces much more than they humiliate its naked victims.

But even this public undressing was not sufficient humiliation
of them in this accursed war. Two weeks after the war broke out,
IDF and Shin Bet security service forces took over the home of
senior Hamas official Saleh al-Arouri, in the West Bank of village
of Aroura—Arouri is now based in Lebanon—and attached to its
facade an enormous Arabic-language banner that reads: "Here
was Arouri's home, which became the headquarters of Abu al-
Nimr of the Shin Bet." Poor agent Abu al-Nimr: His HQ was
destroyed a few days later, and with it the spectacular display,
but the taste of the infantile humiliation remains.

In Gaza, our forces destroyed the parliament building and the
courthouse. Why? Why not? In the Jenin refugee camp, in the
West Bank, they smashed all the monuments, including the "key
of return" at its entrance.

The army also destroyed and plundered the great tin horse at
the hospital entrance, constructed by a German sculptor from the
wreckage of destroyed Palestinian ambulances, a monument to
the dead. In Tulkarm it demolished the Yasser Arafat memorial.
Soon we'll scorch their consciousness, too.

And the height of the grotesquerie: The commander of the
Nahal Infantry Brigade's 932nd Battalion, in an IDF Spokesperson's Unit video, flaunts Ismail Haniyeh's credit card, which
expired in 2019. Kudos to the IDF. "You fled like cowards and
we even got to your credit card," the officer babbles.

Commentators explained that perhaps it was the credit card of
someone with the same name: Our Haniyeh hasn't lived here for
a long time. But Haniyeh's son lives here, and the IDF spokesperson neither rests nor sleeps: Here are the receipts that prove he
bought jewelry. The great victory is closer than ever.

If Settler Violence Wasn't Enough, Israel Is Now Depriving Jordan Valley Palestinians of Water

December 16

Twelve forty-five, this past Monday, in the northern Jordan Valley. The northern section of the Allon Road (Highway 578) is deserted, as usual, but by the roadside, between the settlements of Ro'i and Beka'ot, a small convoy of water tanks, pulled by tractors and trucks, is standing and waiting. And waiting. Waiting till the sheep come home. Soldiers of the Israel Defense Forces were supposed to come a few hours ago to open the iron gate, but the IDF isn't showing up and isn't calling, either, as the song goes. When the number listed by the army on the yellow gate is called, the phone on the other side of the line is answered and then immediately disconnected. An activist with Machsom Watch: Women for Human Rights, Tamar Berger, has tried three times this morning, and each time, as soon as she identified herself, the other side slammed the phone down demonstratively. The Palestinian drivers are afraid to call.

This is the time of the yellow wind, the time of the water carriers in the northern Jordan Valley, who are compelled to wait for hours upon hours until the army force that holds the key arrives and opens the gate for those hauling the water to enter. In this parched region, Israel doesn't allow the Palestinian residents to hook up to any water supply network: They and their sheep must depend on the expensive water that's transported in the tanks, and the drivers of the trucks and the tractors are totally dependent on a soldier with a key.

The soldier with the key was supposed to be here in the morning. Drivers have been waiting here since 8 a.m.; in a few minutes it will be 1 p.m. After the gate is opened, they will wind their way to Atuf and fill the tanks with water, then return via the dirt road on their way to the villages on the eastern side of the road, where they must again wait for a soldier with a key who will deign to open the gate for them, so that they can deliver the water to humans and animals that have no other source for the commodity.

Since the start of the war, this barrier has been locked by default, after having stood open for years. Since the car-ramming attack that occurred here two weeks ago, in which two soldiers were lightly wounded, the troops with the key have been late in coming or haven't come at all. During this latest period, entire days have gone by with the gate remaining locked and the inhabitants left without water. The truck drivers and the shepherds need to be punished for a (non-fatal) terror attack perpetrated by a resident of the town of Tamun, west of here, who was himself shot to death. So now the Palestinians are being hung out to dry, so to speak.

The eastern side of the road is officially water-denied. It's forbidden to drink and forbidden to irrigate, by order. That's what Israel decided, with the unspoken aim of embittering the life of the shepherds until it becomes untenable for them, and then of removing them from this area. The settlers, too, are terrorizing the Palestinians with the aim of expelling them, even more intensely under the cover of war's darkness. As at the other, far end of the occupation, in the South Hebron Hills, here, too, at its northernmost point, in the area called Umm Zuka, the overriding goal is to be rid of the shepherds—the weakest and most helpless population group—and to seize their lands.

New fences have already been erected along the side of the road, apparently by settlers, around the entire area, with the aim of completing the cleansing process. To date, around 20 families, constituting almost 200 people including children, have fled, taking their sheep with them and leaving behind, in their flight, slices of life and property.

Back to the yellow gate. Dafna Banai, a veteran of Machsom Watch in the Jordan Valley, who has been assisting residents here with endless devotion for years, has been waiting with the truck drivers since morning. She and Berger were detained by soldiers at the Beka'ot checkpoint on the false grounds that they had entered Area A. "I know who you are, and what you're doing," the unit's commander snapped at them. Rafa Daragmeh, a truck driver who has been waiting since 9:30, is supposed to do four rounds of water deliveries every day, but now it's the middle of the day, his tank is full and he hasn't yet finished even one round. On one occasion he asked a soldier why they don't show up. "Ask whoever carried out the terrorist attack," the soldier replied, which makes it sound like collective punishment—but that can't be, since collective punishment is a war crime.

On the other side of the checkpoint, an empty water tanker has also been waiting since morning. The driver, Abdel Khader, from the village of Samara, has been here since 8 a.m. Another truck is packed with animal feed—it's doubtful that the soldiers will let it through. Its driver has to bring the cargo to a community that lives 200 meters to the east of the barrier. Two flytraps hang alongside the checkpoint. Time creeps along.

After 1 p.m., a civilian Nissan Jeep with a flashing yellow light pulls up. From it the force emerges, determined and confident: Four soldiers, armed and protected as if they were in Gaza. Quickly they take up positions. One soldier climbs onto a concrete cube and aims his rifle at us unflinchingly; his commander, who is masked and wearing gloves, asks us "not to interfere with the work," and threatens that if we dare to take pictures the trucks will not go through. Maybe he's ashamed of what he's doing.

A third soldier opens the Nissan's baggage compartment and from it takes out a key that dangles at the end of a long shoelace. This is the coveted key, the key to the kingdom. The soldier strides to the barrier and opens it. Now comes the stage of the security check. Maybe the water is poisoned, maybe it's heavy water, maybe it's an explosive device. With Arabs you never can tell.

To pass through here you need "coordination." An Israeli Bedouin driver from the north of the country says he has coordination. His truck is carrying construction materials. The driver of the tanker tells us that the shipment is intended for settlers; the Bedouin driver denies that and says it's for shepherds. But there isn't a single shepherd in these parts who has permission to build even a tiny wall.

A German shepherd warms itself in the sun and observes the goings-on with wonder. One tractor goes by smoothly; one truck, the one coming from the west, is delayed and its driver sits on the ground at the checkpoint while he waits. But the grotesquerie has barely begun. The peak comes when a minibus bearing Israeli license plates arrives and disgorges a frolicsome group of Haredi yeshiva students equipped with an amplifier that plays Hasidic music and with a tray of sufganiot, Hanukkah donuts. The Palestinian drivers who are still waiting can't believe their eyes—they thought they'd already seen everything at checkpoints.

The yeshiva students, who are from the town of Migdal Ha'emek in northern Israel, are doing a mitzvah by distributing donuts that were dispatched from the Chabad center in Beit She'an for the soldiers at this and other checkpoints, to the astonishment of Palestinian water carriers who want only to cross over and deliver their cargo of water.

The soldier with the rifle that's aimed at us chews his donut lazily, one hand holding it, the other on the trigger. All together now: "Maoz tzur yeshuati"—"O mighty stronghold of my salvation." The truck with the animal feed doesn't get through. No coordination. An officer wearing a kippa is summoned to the site and from a distance takes our picture with his phone.

The IDF Spokesperson's Unit, in response to an inquiry from *Haaretz* about the irregular operation of the checkpoint: "In the wake of a number of security events that have occurred here, the gate was blocked in part. Passage through the gate is with coordination only, and is permitted according to the operational situation appraisal in the sector."

A few kilometers to the north, there are remnants of life on the roadside. Here two sheep-herding families lived for years, but settlers from nearby outposts made their lives a misery until, two weeks ago, they left, abandoning their meager property. A playpen, two refrigerators, a rusting iron bed, two wrecked animal pens, a couple of children's books and a drawing of socks captioned by the word for socks in Hebrew, probably from a schoolbook.

Dafna Banai explains that the settlers have fenced off the entire area of the Umm Zuka nature reserve, some 20,000 dunams (5,000 acres), to cleanse it of its shepherd inhabitants. It's the same old system, Banai explains: First the sheep are prevented from grazing and the pasture lands are downsized, then the people in the tiny communities are attacked almost every night—sometimes the assailants urinate on their tents, sometimes they also begin to plow the soil in the middle of the night, in order to create "facts on the ground." Tareq Daragmeh, who lived here with his family, couldn't take it anymore and left, and so did his brother, who lived next to him with his family. This isn't Gaza, but here, too, people are being forced out of their homes with threats and violent assaults.

Farther north still is a well-appointed shepherd community that is bustling with life. This is El-Farsiya, in the far north of the Jordan Valley, almost the outskirts of Beit She'an. Three shepherd families live here and two others not far off. Two families left. One came back after Israeli volunteers started to sleep here nightly after the start of the war, to protect the inhabitants bodily. There are 30 to 40 of these beautiful Israelis, most of them relatively advanced in age (60 or older), who divide the shifts to protect the Palestinians in the northern part of the Jordan Valley, stretching from the settlement of Hemdat to Mehola. "But how long will we be able to safeguard them 24 hours a day?" asks Banai, who organized this volunteer force.

Three of the volunteers descend from the hill. Amos Megged from Haifa, Roni King from Mazkeret Batya and Yossi Gutterman, the veteran of the group, from Rishon Letzion. There are two or three of them in every 24-hour shift. King was until recently the veterinarian of the Nature and Parks Authority; Megged, the younger brother of writer Eyal Megged, is a historian who specializes in the annals of the Indians of Mexico; and Gutterman is a retired psychology lecturer. He is equipped with a body camera.

Today they're here, having returned from an incident of sheep rustling from the Palestinians, and there aren't any volunteers yet for the coming night. Since the start of the war it has become an urgent necessity to sleep here, Gutterman says. "Settler violence has become a daily matter, taken for granted, and includes nighttime invasions of the tent camp, the breaking of objects, smashing of solar panels. I don't think the purpose is to cause damage as such—it's the wearing down, the intimidation, the creation of despair."

One family left, the volunteers relate, after settlers from Shadmot Mehola and their Shabbat guests from a religious boarding school at Kibbutz Tirat Zvi broke the arm of the father of the family. "Two weeks ago," explains Gutterman, "when three friends of ours were here, settlers roused the whole tent camp at 2:30 a.m. with shouts and flashlights, and frightened everyone. Then they started to plow a plot of private land that had recently been declared 'abandoned land.'"

Less than two weeks ago, two volunteers were attacked here. One was beaten with a club and was pepper-sprayed in his eyes, the other took a stone to the head. "There is a campaign of ethnic cleansing going on here," Gutterman says.

A phone call sends the three scurrying to their car and north toward Shdemot Mehola. A shepherd tells them that settlers have just stolen tens of goats from him. Police and army came to the site, and with the aid of the three volunteers, 37 goats were found and returned to their owner. They weren't all the goats that were stolen.

In the meantime, the tractor and truck drivers finished filling up with water and hurried back in order to go through the same gate, which was supposed to remain open for an hour. When they arrived, at 2:30 p.m., they discovered that the gate was locked and the soldiers gone. They waited four hours, until 6:30, for their return. Undoubtedly due to the operational situation appraisal in the sector.

Would Israel Be Any Different Without Netanyahu?

December 21

What if Benjamin Netanyahu hadn't been prime minister for 16 years—would this terrible war not have broken out?

Would the war have looked different? Can we be sure the surprise and fiasco of October 7 wouldn't have happened? The hostages wouldn't have been taken? Israel wouldn't have carried out such a gruesome mass killing in Gaza?

These aren't "what if" questions, nor are they meant to reduce by one iota the hugeness of Netanyahu's responsibility and the severity of his blame for what has taken place. Netanyahu has to go, yesterday, today, tomorrow, like the entire insane government of zeroes he formed, which has brought us to the brink of the abyss.

But are there any leaders in Israel who would act in a fundamentally different way toward Gaza and the Palestinians? No way.

Placing the full blame for all Israel's woes on Netanyahu is saying that had it not been for him, everything would have been different. That's what the "anyone but Bibi" people have been doing since their first day. Had it not been for Netanyahu, Gaza wouldn't have been a prison, the settlements wouldn't have rotted Israel and the IDF would have been a moral army.

That's not true, of course. There are enough things for which, had it not been for Netanyahu, Israel would have been a better place, but lifting the curse of the occupation and the siege is not one of them.

There are decent politicians in Israel, full of good intentions, who are more modest and faithful to their positions than him—it would have been nicer to be occupiers under them.

Israel would have remained the same apartheid state, only more dolled up. Netanyahu corrupted the political system and infected it, destroyed the justice and law enforcement systems, and as for his personal conduct, it's better not to start.

But when it comes to the core of the matter, the core Israel is fleeing from as from fire, the core Netanyahu had planned to remove from the agenda—it appears that Netanyahu acted as his predecessors did and as his successors will.

Apart from the commendable efforts of former prime ministers such as Yitzhak Rabin, Shimon Peres, Ehud Barak, Ehud Olmert and Ariel Sharon to find a solution, if only partial, none of them had any intention of giving the Palestinians the minimum justice they deserve, without which there is no solution.

All the premiers sided with continuing the occupation and the siege on Gaza. None of them thought for a moment to allow a real Palestinian state, with full powers, a state like any other. It didn't occur to them to liberate the Gaza Strip from the strangling siege. Had it not been for all those, perhaps there would not be a Hamas.

The siege of Gaza wasn't laid by Netanyahu; the change government didn't think of lifting it. The money from Qatar may have flowed to Hamas in a more responsible way under Naftali Bennett, but the policy would basically have been the same. Nobody thought of opening Gaza to the world even in a controlled way—the only policy not tried, and the only one that could, perhaps, have advanced a solution.

It is also difficult to assess whether the IDF under another prime minister would have been a different army.

Would the fiasco have been avoided? It's not certain. The occupation missions that became the majority of the IDF's activity weren't invented by Netanyahu. Any other prime minister would also have directed insane forces and resources to mollify the settlers and their whims. That's how it was under all Israel's governments.

The candidates are warming up on the starting line. Each one of them will be a better prime minister than Netanyahu. Certainly more honest, modest and decent than him. But will any of them alter Israel's steep downward trajectory?

Yair Lapid announced he's in favor of bringing the Palestinian

Authority into Gaza, and immediately changed his mind, and he's already against it. Lapid has no opinion.

Benny Gantz and Gadi Eisenkot are taking part in conducting the war, with all its crimes, which will yet turn out to have been futile. Neither of them has proposed a new way, one we've never tried before. It's only force and more force.

Netanyahu has to go, there's no more doubt. But Israel will continue its course.

A Disabled Palestinian Was Carrying a Bag of Lollipops When He Was Shot by Israeli Troops

December 23

First there's the shocking video. A heavyset man with a cumbersome gait walks slowly toward two Israel Defense Forces soldiers. The iron gate at the checkpoint is behind him, shared taxis waiting for passengers are parked at the side of the road, he's holding a plastic bag. From his peculiar walk, with his body swaying from side to side, it's quite clear that he is a person with special needs. Not a moment passes before the soldiers shoot him in the leg at close range, without warning, for no apparent reason. The man collapses to the ground, goes into spasms, is writhing in pain and screaming and bellowing like a wounded animal. The two soldiers continue to train their weapons on him. He rolls around on the road, terrified and in agony. The person who shot the footage, most likely from a nearby building, is overheard saying, "It's Tariq the Azawi [the Gazan]."

Tariq the Gazan is Tariq Abu 'Abed, a 34-year-old man whose family is originally from Khan Yunis in the Gaza Strip. Tariq roamed the streets of Hebron every day trying to sell lollipops he kept in a jar for a few pennies each. The plastic bag he held that day, Tuesday, December 5, contained the lollipops he hadn't sold. It was late afternoon, he was on his way home; the checkpoint was at the entrance to Khirbet Qalqas, a neighborhood in southern Hebron, bordering the city of Yatta.

Here's another photo, taken at the checkpoint shortly afterward: A young man is lying on his stomach, both hands bound behind his back, his legs spread, a soldier standing above him and aiming his rifle at him. The man is Tariq's brother, Ziaa, 32, a construction worker employed in Israel, who tried to come to the aid of his wounded sibling. The soldiers hit him, Ziaa relates now. They ordered him to lie on the ground, shackled his hands and kicked him in the back.

In his ponderous way, Tariq tells us that before shooting him, the soldiers had struck him, too. They demanded to see his ID card, whereupon he told them that it was at home and that he passed by every day like this, on the way to work and back. The two soldiers became angry and struck Tariq, who tried to keep walking. Unable to stop him, they shot him with seemingly no hesitation.

It's safe to say that they knew he was a person with a mental condition from his behavior and manner of speaking; it's hard to mistake his disability. In the video clip the bystanders don't appear to be especially upset at the sight of this helpless person writhing in pain on the ground. Most of them go about their business unperturbed; it seems that this is routine for them. Only one tries to approach Tariq.

It turns out that you don't have to be an Israel Defense Forces soldier in the Gaza Strip in order to shoot helpless people. It's just as easy in the West Bank. Just over a month before this incident, Israeli soldiers shot to death another young man with special needs, Fouad Abu Sabha, 22, at the checkpoint at the northern entrance to Yatta, just a few kilometers from where Tariq was shot. Under the cover of the atrocities being perpetuated in Gaza, no one was unduly disturbed by that incident, either.

Since the war broke out in early October, life in and around Hebron and Yatta, two of the largest cities in the West Bank, has become particularly difficult. Yatta, with a population of over 100,000, is closed off to vehicular traffic from almost every side. Using iron gates and boulders, the army has blocked all the entrances and exits other than those on the city's eastern side.

We visited Yatta this week accompanied by Nasser Nawaj'ah, the South Hebron Hills field researcher for the Israeli human rights organization B'Tselem, whom we met at his home in Susya. Also in that village, all the entrance and exits have been blocked with boulders.

Driving to Yatta, we negotiated a narrow, difficult mountain road, which twisted and turned and stretched on and on. On the way back we looked for a different route. We drove around the city for some time until we found a barrier where one of the boulders had somehow been moved, creating a space about the width of a medium-sized car through which we were able to eke our way out.

There were fewer cars than usual in Yatta this week. The week before, the IDF had conducted an operation to impound cars without a license plate—called mashtubot, slang for "erased vehicles"—across the West Bank. That had netted about 1,500 vehicles, at least 100 of them in Yatta, where the troops also arrived at the local government hospital and seized cars belonging to patients and visitors.

There are a huge number of mashtubot in Yatta, cars sold for scrap in Israel which are then sold cheaply to residents of the West Bank. Because there is no public transportation in the city, the Palestinian Authority turns a blind eye to the illegal vehicles, in contrast to other cities, such as Hebron, where it impounds them. Now the Israeli security establishment, which is known for its sincere and devoted concern for the safety and well-being of the local inhabitants, has seized hundreds of cars in the territories that anyway were only used within the confines of villages and cities. Just one more punitive measure among the many inflicted on Palestinians since the war began.

The home of Tariq the Gazan is at the edge of Qalqas. Signs of severe distress and dire economic and social straits emanate from this building. Garbage is strewn at the entrance, flies buzz around inside.

Tariq's mother, Sumia, a 52-year-old divorcee who cleans homes in Hebron for a living, lives in one room in the cramped ground-floor apartment; his brother Samar, 21, his pregnant wife and their son live in another room; and the third room is occupied by Tariq, his wife Ayat, and their two young children— the youngest one, Maryam, was born earlier this month in the Abu Hasan Al Qassem Governmental Hospital, while Tariq was recuperating in a room on the floor below. Tariq's brother Ziaa lives with his wife and their four children in an apartment on the upper floor of the building.

The young children of the extended family scamper through the small living room, barefoot and half-naked, munching on cheap snacks and the lollipops that Tariq sells, which may on some days be their only food. Since the war broke out, Ziaa, the family's chief provider, has been unable to enter Israel—like all the inhabitants of the West Bank—and the economic crunch has become even more acute.

The family moved here 23 years ago from Gaza, in the wake of family feuds. Sumia has two sisters in Khan Yunis, and the four half-brothers and half-sisters of Tariq and Ziaa also live there with their families. With the exception of one of Sumia's sisters, Ibtisam, who accompanied her son for cancer treatments at a Hebron hospital a few years ago, they haven't met anyone from Khan Yunis since they left. Tariq and Ziaa's father, Ahmed, lives elsewhere in Hebron, and the family is apparently not in touch with him, either. It is Ahmed's children from his second marriage and their families who are now, as war rages, either alive or dead in Gaza.

Tariq is brought into the room, wearing a tattered brown galabiya. He's aided by a walker but can barely move, putting his weight only on the left foot; the right leg, shattered by bullets, has a brace on it. It's a huge effort for him to sit down. His mother brings him a filthy plastic pail to serve as a footrest, but finally he rests the leg on the walker.

Chewing gum, Tariq looks around apathetically at the scene around him. He isn't able to say how old he is, when asked, but answers other questions. He shouts when speaking, as does his mother, and the house resounds with noise. Occasionally Ziaa swats one of the little children. He also tries to keep his mother from talking, but she ignores him. Not exactly a picture of domestic tranquility, the Abu 'Abed home.

Tariq's wife, Ayat, 27, sits in a corner, rocking the cradle of their son, 1-year-old Seif, who was born with a neurological condition and has an enlarged head. His mother stares vacantly at what's going on in the room but doesn't utter a sound. Two-week-old Maryam is wrapped up, mummy-like, in a blanket and lies on the sofa like a doll.

How are you? Tariq replies that he's wounded. His mother uncovers his right hip, which is in a sling-like device. In 2019, the Palestinian Health Ministry decreed Tariq 100 percent disabled, because of his mental state. Tariq never attended school. Until the age of about 5 he was a very aggressive child. Every day he goes out to sell his lollipops, mostly just to get out of the house and have something to do. He says he doesn't make a profit. Ziaa, he adds, is calmer than he is, but still jittery. Until the war Ziaa worked in Israeli locales including Harish, Hod Hasharon, Tel Aviv and Taibeh.

Tariq would leave the house at 7 every morning, usually taking a shared taxi to the center of Hebron, but in some cases drivers refuse to let him into the car, he says, because he doesn't stop talking. In that case he walks two hours to the city center. On December 5, his mother joined him for the trip—she went to clean homes—as did 9-year-old Ahmed, Tariq's nephew, who also sold candies. In the center of Hebron they split up: Ahmed went to the market, Sumia to her cleaning jobs and Tariq proceeded to the Ein Sara neighborhood, where he sells his wares next to traffic lights.

At midday, an acquaintance of Sumia sent her a clip that was being shared widely on social media, showing soldiers beating Tariq. Sumia could not bring herself to watch. The footage was shot close to the gate at the entrance to Qalqas, which has been closed to cars since the beginning of the war. Eyewitnesses related to the family that after Tariq told the soldiers that his ID card was at home, a tall, thin soldier called him a liar and started to beat him, while a second soldier aimed his rifle at him.

When Ziaa, who was home at the time, learned that Tariq had been shot, he rushed to the checkpoint, a few kilometers away. When he got there, the soldiers ordered him to halt. He tried to explain to them that his brother was lying on the ground and that he was mentally disabled. Ziaa says he was certain that Tariq was dead.

The soldiers fired into the air to frighten Ziaa, ordered him to lie on the ground and forcefully handcuffed his hands behind his back. They kicked him a number of times, he adds. One soldier rammed his foot under Ziaa's chin. He asked them to send a soldier who could speak Arabic. They told him to shut up. He lay like that for half an hour. Finally an Arabic-speaking officer arrived. Ziaa tried to explain that his brother was mentally disabled, to which the officer replied, according to Ziaa, "If your brother is crazy, tell your mother and your father to shut him in the house and not let him go out."

The IDF Spokesperson's Unit stated, in reply to a query from *Haaretz*: "The existing preliminary information indicates that during a security check that took place adjacent to Hebron on December 5, the Palestinian was shot in the leg and was evacuated to receive medical treatment. Upon receipt of the report, an investigation was launched by the Military Police.

"As for the second case [i.e., Abu Sabha], dozens of suspects threw stones on October 30, 2023, at vehicles on Highway 317, near the Zief Junction, located in the territory of the Yehuda Brigade. A force was rushed to the site and dispersed the suspects. At a certain stage, a Palestinian threw stones at a military position, the force responded with gunfire, and a hit was observed. The Military Police have launched an investigation."

When Israel Abuses the Hostages That It Holds

December 23

Every Sunday and Tuesday, Israeli guards enter Palestinian prisoners' cells, handcuff them and beat them with batons.

That's their weekly party, according to released prisoners. Four prisoners have died since the war began on October 7, almost certainly from beatings. Nineteen guards who participated in these sick parties are under investigation, suspected of causing one prisoner's death.

Hundreds of Palestinians who were detained in the Gaza Strip have been kept bound and blindfolded 24 hours a day, and they have also been brutally beaten. Some, perhaps even most, have no connection to Hamas. Some of them—no one has even bothered reporting how many—have died in captivity at the Sde Teiman base.

Some 4,000 Gazan workers who were arrested in Israel on October 7 despite having done nothing wrong are also being held in inhumane conditions. At least two of them have died. And more than enough has already been written about the detainees being stripped and the humiliating photographs.

In this terrible competition over the magnitude of evil, there are no winners, only losers. But it's impossible to talk day and night about Hamas's atrocities—writers vie with each other over who can coin the most derogatory terms for the organization— while completely ignoring Israel's evil.

There are also no winners, only losers, in the competition over how much blood is shed and the way it is shed. But it's impossible to ignore the horrific quantity of blood that has been spilled in the Gaza Strip. This weekend, some 400 people were killed in two days, the majority of them children. On Saturday, I saw the weekend's pictures from Al-Bureij and Nuseirat, including children dying on the floor of Al-Aqsa Hospital in Deir al-Balah, and they are horrifying.

Israel's refusal to increase the amount of humanitarian aid allowed into Gaza, in defiance of a UN Security Council decision, similarly attests to a policy of evil.

And as if all this weren't enough, the voices of evil within Israel have raised the bar on satanic proposals. Journalist Zvi Yehezkeli favors killing 100,000 Gazans in a first strike. Retired Maj. Gen. Giora Eiland had second thoughts and switched from proposing that we spread disease in Gaza to proposing that we starve its residents.

Even the left's new Prince Charming, Yair Golan, who is currently winning 12 Knesset seats in the polls from people who see themselves as the beautiful Israelis, told Gazans in an interview with the daily *Yedioth Ahronoth*, "As far as we're concerned, you can starve to death. That's completely legitimate."

Yet after all this, we consider Hamas the only monster in the area, its leader the only psychotic and only the way it holds Israelis hostage as inhumane. It's impossible not to be horrified by the thought of our hostages' fate, particularly the sick and the elderly among them. But it's also impossible not to be horrified by the fate of the Palestinians whom we have kept bound and blindfolded for weeks and months.

Israel has no right to set standards for evil when its hands are also stained with wickedness. Forget about the killing, the starvation and the mass displacement. Our treatment of Palestinian prisoners should have particularly upset Israelis, if only because of the danger to the Israelis held by Hamas. What will a Hamas member who holds an Israeli hostage think when he hears that his comrades are being restrained and beaten incessantly?

We can cautiously conclude that at least some of the Israelis held by Hamas are being treated better than the Palestinians held by Israel. When freed hostages Chen and Agam Goldstein told Channel 12 News on Friday night about their treatment by Hamas and how their captors protected them with their own bodies during Israeli airstrikes, they were attacked vociferously on social media. How dare they tell the truth?

Hamas perpetrated a barbaric attack on October 7. It killed and kidnapped indiscriminately. There are no words to describe its brutality, including in holding dozens of senior citizens, sick people and children hostage for months in unbearably harsh conditions.

But does this make it legitimate for us to act similarly? Forget about morality. Will Israel's brutality in the war and in its jails do anything to advance its goals? Will Hamas free its hostages faster if Israel abuses the Palestinians it is holding hostage?

There's No Way to "Explain" the Degree of Death and Destruction in Gaza

December 28

There is no way to "explain" Israel's conduct in the Gaza Strip. Destruction, killing, starvation and siege in such monstrous dimensions can no longer be explained or justified, even by an effective propaganda machine like Israeli public diplomacy (hasbara).

The evil can no longer be hidden by any propaganda. Even the winning Israeli combo of victimhood, Yiddishkeit, chosen people and Holocaust can no longer blur the picture. The horrifying October 7 events have not been forgotten by anyone, but they cannot justify the spectacles in Gaza. The propagandist who could explain killing 162 infants in one day—a figure reported by social media this week—is yet to be born, not to mention killing some 10,000 children in two months.

Israel is already setting up its updated "Yad Vashem." Hundreds of Jewish functionaries from the United States are being flown by air shuttle to the burnt kibbutzim in the south. Natan Sharansky has also been to Kfar Azza this week, to see and show those antisemites what they did to us.

No official guest will be able to land in Israel from now on without being forced to pass through Kibbutz Be'eri. And afterward if he dares turn his gaze to the Gaza Strip, he will be labeled antisemitic. Wait for Birthright buses with a soldier watching over each one, Czech rifle drawn. They, too, are already on their way to Nir Oz.

It is very doubtful this will do any good. Hasbara is now an immoral machine. Anyone who makes do with being shocked at what has been done to us while disregarding what we've been doing since has no integrity or conscience. One cannot ignore Gaza and only be shocked by Kfar Azza. Of course, it's compulsory to tell and show the world what Hamas did to us. But the story only begins there. It doesn't end there. Not telling its sequel is a despicable act.

Alongside the awful Israeli suffering, which must not be under-estimated, the much greater suffering is now in the Gaza Strip. It's enormous in scope and causes despair. It has no explanation, nor does it need one. Suffice it for the reports coming out of Gaza and being broadcast all over the world except in one tiny state, whose eyes are shut and whose heart is sealed.

Israeli hasbara is a deception. It tells a story that isn't the whole truth. By hiding more than half the truth, hasbara should have been seen as a shameful activity. But it isn't. In Israel a preposterous figure like Noa Tishby has become the heroine of the moment. The fatuous attack on Benny Gantz, who attended a party in her honor in the home of bereaved father Eyal Waldman and was photographed smiling, a glass in one hand and Tishby in the other, missed the point.

The point is that deceivers are turned into heroes here. Browsing through Tishby's X account will make you puke. Like Nataly Dadon, but with Hollywood stardust, new age, hugs, tears and Colgate smiles, kitsch and death straight from the area near the Gazan border. The Jewish nation is the indigenous people in Israel, we're from here, says Tishby, the woman who migrated away from here. The moment she landed in Ben Gurion Airport she had to run for shelter, filming herself, of course, to make the heart of every "friend of Israel" tremble and bring them to tears.

And the jewelry, oh, the jewelry on Tishby: two Stars of David, not one, just to make sure; a Chai necklace and a from-the-river-to-the-sea map, all in gold. A quarter of a million followers. Hanukkah is a Zionist holiday. Tel Aviv is a city under attack. "You have to imagine what the Middle East will look like after Hamas is defeated," she tells Piers Morgan of TalkTV.

Want to know what the Middle East will look like? Gaza destroyed to the ground, 2 million homeless people, and opposite them, also scarred and beaten, an apartheid state, which Tishby hasn't even heard of.

The Legitimization of Evil Will Remain with Israelis Long After the War in Gaza Ends

December 31

At the end of this war, Israel will find itself in a worse situation than when the war began. Even if Israel is able to realize its goals, which appear to be receding, the country's situation will be worse than before. Since the moral aspects of this war hardly bother anyone in Israel, particularly not the media, all that remains is to honestly answer the following question: What does Israel stand to gain from this war? What exactly can it hope for?

While the chorus of army spokesmen posing as journalists cheer the army's achievements, and since almost all Israelis believe that after October 7 Israel can do anything it pleases, one can only ask about the gains. The losses are already piling up. The longer the war continues, the greater the damage to Israel.

One can hardly think of even one advantage Israel might reap from this war, even if we ignore its horrors and the indescribable suffering on the other side and focus only on "what is good for Israel," as Israelis like to frame it. It's very bad for Israel. The future of the hostages is becoming increasingly murkier, and Israel's security is growing shakier.

The facts are glaring. Hamas is growing stronger. The more it is hit in Gaza, the more its political strength grows among Palestinians, at least outside the Gaza Strip. The longer the war goes on, the worse Israel's international standing becomes. It's already reached an unprecedented nadir, not yet among governments, but certainly in world public opinion.

Israel has become a pariah state more than ever before. Reports from Gaza present a barbaric reality. The world sees it and feels loathing. How could it not? Polls of young people in the United States, including young Jews, should horrify Israel. Hamas is more popular among them than Israel is. We can thank the war for that.

Thank you, war, for making every Israeli not only a security target everywhere he or she goes, but a target of national shame. Some Israelis don't mind feeling ashamed, but not all of them.

Thank you, war, for bringing Israel to the brink of an economic abyss. The days of tourists coming here in the numbers we were used to are far off, but the greatest damage done to Israel will be felt in what is happening to it internally. More than the judicial overhaul, this war is shattering the vestiges of Israeli democracy.

During this war, civilians have been fired, interrogated or imprisoned for expressing solidarity with other human beings and horror at the killing, for simply calling for peace, for protesting about the lack of opposition to this war. Israeli Arabs are afraid to breathe. The conduct of law enforcement agencies during this war is much more dangerous to Israel's democracy than the suspension of the use of the reasonableness standard by the country's courts.

Such conduct has elicited very little protest. Not only on battlefields has Israel adopted a policy of indiscriminate killing to an extent not previously seen; it has also become sadistic in an unprecedented manner in its detention facilities.

Anything goes after October 7. It's not only the extreme right who have tainted the public discourse. The center also wants more blood, destruction, epidemics and hunger, and is unashamed to say so openly.

This legitimization of evil will remain with us long after the war is over. Gaza may be rehabilitated, but not the moral collapse in Israel. The legitimization of war crimes will not let go of us, and from now on, everything will be permitted in the West Bank as well, and subsequently in Israel itself. What begins in a detention center near Be'er Sheva will not stop there. Fewer are the number of those making an effort to stop the sadism. They have "sobered up."

Between the time you started reading this article and reached the end of it, one more child has died in Gaza, with two others wounded. That's how it is: a child fatality every eight minutes. Israel's indifference to this fact and its concealment by the press are the most irreversible damage this war has inflicted on Israel. And now, back to our military correspondent, who will tell us about the Israel Defense Forces' successes in Dir al-Balah.

2024

January

No Israeli Soldiers Have Stood Up and Refused to Participate in This Evil War

January 3

Nobody stood up. So far, as far as is known, not even one case of disobedience has been registered in the IDF since the war broke out, except for one young man before his recruitment.

The pilots bomb as they have never bombed before, the drone operators kill by remote control in wholesale quantities never known before, the artillerymen shell more than ever, the heavy-engineering-equipment operators destroy as they have never destroyed before, and even the prison guards abuse prisoners as they've never abused before—and nobody stood up.

Among the hundreds of thousands of reserve and career officers —let's leave the regular soldiers alone due to their age, status and being brainwashed—there's not even one soldier or officer, pilot or artilleryman, paratrooper or Golani trooper who has said: That's far enough; I'm not ready to continue taking part in the slaughter, not ready to be partner to causing the inhuman suffering. Nor has one prison guard stood up to tell the truth about what's happening between Sde Teiman and Megiddo security prisons and lay the handcuffs on the table.

On the face of it, the IDF should be pleased with a wholly consensual war, with no background noise. But the total lack of disobedience should raise dire thoughts; it points to automatic obedience rather than to good citizenship. Such a brutal war that hasn't yet raised doubts among the combatants reflects moral blindness. The pilots and drone operators are one thing, they see their victims as tiny dots on a screen. But the soldiers and officers in Gaza see what we have done. Most of them are reservists, parents to children.

They see more than a million people bereft of everything crowding together in Rafah. They see the bodies in the streets, the remnants of life in the ruins, the children's dolls and their beds, the tattered rags and the broken furniture. Do all the soldiers think Hamas is to blame, that all Gaza is Hamas, that they deserve all this, and that this will benefit Israel?

The absence of insubordination is even clearer in view of what happened here last year prior to October 7. Disobedience became a more legitimate and common weapon than ever before; thousands of pilots and reservists threatened to use it.

In July the Brothers in Arms movement announced that about 10,000 reserve soldiers from 40 units wouldn't volunteer for reserve duty if the regime coup passed. They joined the 180 pilots and navigators who stated already in March that they wouldn't report to training drills, along with 300 military doctors and 650 reserve soldiers from special ops and cyber. With so many people threatening disobedience, its complete absence now is especially thunderous.

The conclusion is that many of the career and reserve soldiers are convinced the regime coup was a just and proper cause for insubordination, in contrast to the bloodshed and destruction in Gaza. The army is trashing an entire region along with its residents, and that doesn't bother our forces' consciences. The reasonableness clause bothered some of them more. Where are those 10,000 soldiers who threatened disobedience because of Benjamin Netanyahu and Yariv Levin now? Where are the 180 pilots?

They're busy bombing Gaza, flattening it, destroying it and killing its residents indiscriminately, including its thousands of children. How did it happen that bombing Salah Shehadeh's house, which killed 14 residents, 11 of them children, led to the "pilots' letter," in which 27 pilots stated they would refuse to serve on attack missions—and now, not even a postcard from a single pilot? What happened to our pilots since 2003, and what happened to the soldiers?

The answer is seemingly clear. Israel says that after the October 7 horror it's allowed to do anything, and anything it does is worthy, moral and legal. Insubordination during war is also a much more drastic step than insubordination in training, and indeed it borders on treason. It could hurt the brothers in combat. But the total absence of disobedience after some 90 days of evil warfare is not something to be happy about. It is not good. Maybe in a few years, some people will regret it. Maybe some will be ashamed of it.

Someone in Israel's Army Decided to Bring This Quiet West Bank Area into the Circle of Violence

January 5

For the past few months, even prior to October 7, Nur Shams refugee camp, on the eastern outskirts of Tulkarm, in the central West Bank, has been in the crosshairs of the Israel Defense Forces. Hardly a night goes by without a brutally violent incursion; the access roads and the streets inside the camp have long since been ripped up by bulldozers.

Since the war started, the IDF has stepped up its strikes and has taken to killing from the air by means of drones. Thus began, on the night between Tuesday and Wednesday of last week, a horrific round of indiscriminate killing and abuse of the wounded that lasted until the beginning of this week. It doesn't take long for the inspiration of IDF behavior in the Gaza Strip to pass over to the West Bank: What's permitted in Khan Yunis is permitted in Nur Shams, too.

The Al Mahajar ("quarry") neighborhood lies on the northern flank of the camp, situated on both sides of the highway to Tulkarm. Al Mahajar is considered relatively quiet; until last week the IDF rarely raided it, not even during its nightly incursions into the camp's Al Manshiya neighborhood, on the other side of the main road. But someone in the army decided to bring this quiet area into the circle of violence and resistance—and what better way than to fire a missile late at night straight into a group of young people who, according to witnesses, were standing around innocently in the neighborhood. Six were killed in one blow and another seven wounded, some then subjected to physical abuse.

This past Monday, the camp's streets filled up with children; there's no school here on New Year's Day. Nur Shams is Gaza-like, with narrow alleys and garbage strewn everywhere. Next to the spot where the missile fell, across from the local grocery store, Palestinian phone company technicians toiled to repair damaged poles and lines. The crater the missile created in the road had already been filled in.

Waiting for us in the refugee home of the Shehadeh family is the son, Mohammed, 25, who walks with the aid of a crutch. A teacher in the primary school, he was wounded in the pelvis by shrapnel. He was soon joined by his cousin and best friend, Awas Shehadeh, 23, goalkeeper for the Palestine national soccer team and holder of a master's degree in physical education from Kadoorie College in Tulkarm. Awas is also the goalkeeper for the Hilal al-Quds soccer team, which is based in Al-Ram, just outside Jerusalem. On October 9, the team was supposed to have flown to Tajikistan. Today his head is bandaged and he, too, can hardly walk. Fragments from the missile struck him in the head.

The two recounted in articulate detail what happened to them on that night, and also last Saturday night. Their fathers—brothers, both of whom have worked for decades in Israel and who ask not to have their names used—listen from the side.

The invasion of the camp began around 11 p.m. on December 26, in the Al Manshiya neighborhood. The sounds of the shooting and explosions could be heard very well here and also reached the distant village of Atil, where Abdulkarim Sadi, a field researcher for the Israeli human rights organization B'Tselem,

lives. He accompanied us bravely into the center of the refugee
camp—it's no simple matter to escort Israelis to this camp during
a war.

Back to that night: About 13 young people from the neighborhood came into the street and were standing next to the grocery
store. The neighborhood is built on the slope of a hill, from which
it's convenient to observe the southern part of the camp, which
was being raided then by the army.

At about midnight, as they stood there watching events unfold,
a missile fired from a drone overhead slammed with a thunderous
roar into the group. "That was a terrible moment," Mohammed
recalls. "A scene of terror that is hard to describe." Mohammed
felt a sharp blow in the hip area and fell to the ground. Awas was
hurtled through the air and landed on the road, then discovered
that he was bleeding from the head and neck from fragments
that had struck him.

Around them were the dead and the dying. Two of the group
died immediately, one was in death throes after losing both
legs, another's face was torn apart, three others were in very
serious condition. The screams of the wounded, mingling with
the screams of people who had rushed into the street, were
unbearable, says Mohammed. Most of the dead and wounded
were younger than him and Awas.

Mohammed heard a noise in his head that was to stay with
him for a time. He felt that he was losing consciousness. Both
he and Awas say they were scared that the first missile would be
followed by a second, as occurred two weeks earlier next to the
camp, when, as the local residents were evacuating the dead and
wounded, another missile exploded in their midst. Adham Shehadeh, 33, their friend, who joined our conversation, had gone to
the toilet a minute before the missile struck and so was spared. "I
was saved by a miracle," he says in his worker's Hebrew.

Two ambulances were rushed to the site, one from the Red
Crescent, the other from Al Shifa, a private clinic. Until they
arrived, the wounded were aided by young people from the camp,
many of whom have taken first aid courses, which are now in

demand here. The first ambulance arrived after about half an hour, having been detained on the highway, and squeezed in the three most badly wounded young people before departing. The second ambulance also had no choice but to cram three of the wounded into its narrow space: Awas, Mohammed and another person, Mahmoud Rashad, 19, whose leg was bleeding. Then they faced another problem.

At the end of the road that descends from the neighborhood a large force of Border Police troops was waiting for them. Firing into the air, they ordered the paramedic to stop, turn off the engine and look only forward, according to the testimony he gave Sadi. The paramedic said that his arrival in the camp had been arranged via the Coordination and Liaison Directorate. The Border Police opened the side and back doors of the ambulance. They grabbed Mohammed, who was sitting on the seat next to the side door, and threw him onto the road. Mohammed heard one of the men say to another, "Pump a bullet into his head," and terror welled up in him. "Why? Why? I didn't do anything!" he shouted helplessly.

The troops handcuffed Mohammed behind his back, made him spread his legs to search him, blindfolded him and told him to kneel on the ground, head bent down. One of the troops asked where he had been wounded, and when he indicated the bleeding spot in his pelvis, started to kick him there. Each kick was accompanied by curses. This was the start of a round of beatings, Mohammed says, that involved being punched and kicked by many Border Police officers, who took turns striking him as he knelt on the ground. Most of the troops were masked. A few struck him in the head with their rifle butts. One kicked him in the testicles. "Do you want your leg?" another asked, aiming his rifle at Mohammed's leg.

In the meantime, they also checked and discovered that he had a clean record. The other two wounded Palestinians waited in the ambulance, dizzy and losing blood. When Mohammed told an officer who interrogated him on the spot, by phone, that he had been beaten, the troops punished him by hitting him again.

"No one is clean in Nur Shams, the whole camp is whores and sons of bitches," they told him, like their buddies in Gaza say.

An Israel Police spokesperson this week told *Haaretz*: "During operational activity of the security forces to prevent terrorism, terrorists threw [explosive] devices at them and endangered the lives of our forces. The fighters acted to preserve security, examined the suspects and allowed the wounded to be evacuated in ambulances."

When he stopped feeling woozy, he discovered that he was in the ambulance, and that his head had been bandaged. "You will stay here until you die, you won't get to a hospital," one of the troops threatened. Another took a selfie with the wounded as a souvenir. They cursed the wounded Palestinians and also laughed at them. Only after an hour or so was the ambulance permitted to leave, and it sped to Thabet Thabet Hospital, a government institution in Tulkarm.

Last Saturday night, the IDF again entered the refugee camp. There were some 200 soldiers, according to eyewitnesses. Entering the homes in the Al Mahajar neighborhood, they ordered all males above the age of 14 to gather in a single house, where they were all bound and blindfolded. This included Mohammed, who had been discharged from the hospital after two days. Around 15 men and adolescents were herded into each of the rooms, in densely crowded conditions. He heard the soldiers: "They are asshole Hamas, maybe we'll take them and throw them in the Jordan?" "No, if we throw them in the Jordan, they'll come back." "Maybe we should give each of them a bullet in the head?" "No, it's a pity to waste the money a bullet costs, 10 agurot [a few pennies] per round. We'll take them and dump them in Gaza." "There is no more Gaza. We'll take them to Sinai." "Let them go f--- themselves in Khan Yunis, and we'll level all their homes here and make the country bigger for us."

So it continued in the packed rooms from 2:30 a.m. until 10 a.m. on Sunday. Anyone who asked to relieve himself was told, "What do you think, that you're in school? Go in your pants."

The IDF Spokesperson's Unit this week gave the following

statement to *Haaretz*: "On the night of December 26, IDF, Shin Bet and Border Police forces undertook an anti-terror operation at the Nur Shams refugee camp, which is under the authority of the Menashe Territorial Brigade. During the course of the action, the soldiers identified terrorists who threw [explosive] devices at them. An aerial vehicle of the air force attacked the gang, and six of the terrorists were eliminated as a result.

"On the night of December 31, the IDF again operated in the Nur Shams refugee camp, during the course of which dozens of suspects were interrogated. Five of them were arrested and transferred for continued questioning by the security forces. Some of the suspects were held for a number of hours because of the lengthy operation and due to the nature of the interrogation. The forces allowed those who requested to attend to their bodily needs. Throughout the entire action, there were exchanges of fire, which is why the forces held some of the suspects the whole time. When the forces left, the suspects were released."

Finally the soldiers left, leaving the dozens of men still bound and blindfolded. On the way out, the troops smashed a few car windshields. We saw them this week, shattered.

Palestinians in Gaza Are Being Held Hostage by Israel and Hamas

January 11

Shai Wenkert is the father of 22-year-old Omer Wenkert, who has colitis and is being held hostage by Hamas. Colitis is an accursed chronic disease which can be aggravated under stressful conditions and in the absence of medication and appropriate nutrition. It causes much suffering to people who have it.

Omer's father has been sounding warnings from every possible platform: His son is in mortal danger. He tries not to think about his son's condition, he said in one interview, but he doesn't always manage to do that. Indeed, thinking about a person with colitis and having no medication, in Hamas captivity, is akin to thinking about hell. Omer needs to be released, or at least to quickly get the medication he needs.

One cannot maintain composure in the face of his father's calls. There is no person who would not be horrified by the thought of the young Omer's suffering. At the same time, one cannot but wonder how many people suffering from colitis there are in Gaza now, under the same conditions as Omer's, with no medication, no food and under stress.

Omer is imprisoned; people in the Gaza Strip with colitis and other chronic diseases are desperately fleeing for their lives. They have no bed on which to lay their sick, aching body, they have no home, their hygienic conditions are dreadful. They've been living for three months with a constant fear of dying, under bombardment and shelling that is unprecedented.

Omer was kidnapped and is a hostage. The residents of the Gaza Strip are also hostages, and the conditions they live in, including the sick among them, are no better than Omer's hell. They, too, need relief. They, too, must at least receive the medications they require, quickly. It's too bad that Omer's father believes that denying humanitarian aid to Gaza, including people with colitis, is the means that will lead to saving his son. However, one shouldn't rush to judge a person in crisis.

There is no difference between Omer and Mohammed, who both have colitis. They share a similar fate, an unbearably cruel one. I try to imagine young Mohammed, suffering from colitis. In the 16 years Gaza has been besieged, it is unlikely that he's received the best medications available for treating his disease. Getting him out of the Gaza ghetto for medical treatment when his disease worsened was difficult, often impossible.

Now Omer is imprisoned in a dark, scary tunnel and Mohammed is roaming the streets hungry, at risk of contracting something in an epidemic, an intestinal infection or any other ill. At any moment, the next shell could overtake him. Mohammed and Omer are suffering torments we can't even imagine.

To the 136 Israeli hostages one must add 2.3 million Gazan people, or however many of them are still alive, also as hostages.

The Israelis are hostages of Hamas, while Gazans are the hostages of both Israel and Hamas. Their fates are conjoined. When hostages released by Hamas earlier talked about the meager food they received while in captivity, one pita a day with some rice occasionally, they also related that this is exactly what their captors received. This was something to think about, which no one in Israel bothered to do. That's what there is in Gaza now, for the hostages and their captors, but no one talks about it.

Only Omer's suffering hurts, not Mohammed's. The Israelis were forcibly kidnapped to hell. The residents of the Gaza Strip were also forcibly kidnapped to the same hell. First it was Hamas's cruelty, with one of its crimes being embarking on this war without preparing its home front; Hamas knew full well how intensely Israel would respond, but they didn't bother to prepare any protection for Gazans—no hospitals, no supply of medicines or food, no shelters. That was the first kidnapping of Gaza's residents. This was joined by the renewed Israeli occupation of Gaza, crueler than any of the previous ones.

Omer's father, as mentioned, tries not to think about what his son is going through. One can empathize with him. It's beyond a father's ability to imagine the suffering of his child and feel so helpless in trying to save him. One's stomach turns on hearing the father's cries. But one cannot continue to shut one's eyes and harden one's heart in the face of the suffering of the rest of the hostages—the entire population of the Gaza Strip, including those with colitis.

If It Isn't a Genocide in Gaza, Then What Is It?

January 14

Let us assume that Israel's position at The Hague is right and just and Israel committed no genocide or anything close to it. So what is this? What do you call the mass killing, which continues even as these lines are being written, without discrimination, without restraint, on a scale that is difficult to imagine?

What to call dying children on hospital floors, some of whom have no one left in the world, and hungry elderly civilians fleeing for their lives from the unceasing threat of bombs everywhere? Will the legal definition change their fate? Israel will breathe a sigh of relief if the court dismisses the charge. As far as it is concerned, if this is not genocide our conscience will be clean again. If The Hague says "not genocide," we will once again be the most moral ones in the world.

This weekend, the Israeli media and social media erupted with admiration and praise for the legal team that represented us at The Hague. What elegant English and persuasive arguments. On the previous day, the media hardly reported South Africa's position, which was presented in even better English than the English of the Israelis and was far more anchored in facts and less on propaganda, once again proving that in this war, Israel's media has reached an all-time nadir. It sees its duty as enhancing the Israeli position and nullifying the position of "the legal arm of Hamas." Look at how much legal honor those experts have brought us.

Let's assume we're talking about a country that is on trial for the most severe violations that exist in international law. Those with the black robes and white wigs and those without them presented Israel's usual talking points, some of which are just, such as the descriptions of the October 7 atrocity.

At other parts, it was hard to know whether to laugh or cry. Like at the argument that Hamas alone is to blame for the conditions in Gaza. Israel has no hand or part in it. Saying that to a prestigious international institution is to cast doubt on and insult the intelligence of its judges.

And what to make of the remarks of the head of the Israeli defense team, Prof. Malcolm Shaw: "The actions of Israel are proportionate and only target armed forces"? But what about the truth? Proportionate with such destruction? If that is what proportionate looks like, what does disproportionate look like? Hiroshima?

"Only against armed forces," with near multitudes of dead children? What is he talking about? "Making phone calls to evacuate the uninvolved"; who still has an operating telephone in Gaza and exactly where are they supposed to evacuate in this hell where not a single piece of safe ground remains? And the ultimate: "Even if soldiers violated the laws governing war, that will be heard by the Israeli legal system."

Shaw apparently has not heard about the Israeli legal system and even less about what is called the military legal system. He has not heard that after Operation Cast Lead, the 2008–2009 conflict with Gaza, only four soldiers were indicted for criminal offenses and only one of them was sent to prison for the misdemeanor theft of a credit card (!). All the others hurling shells and bombs at the innocent will never be indicted.

And what about the remarks of Dr. Galit Rejwan, the weekend discovery who will undoubtedly be chosen to light this year's torch at the Independence Day ceremony on Mount Herzl: "The IDF is moving hospitals to a safer place." Will Shifa be moved to Sheba? Rantisi to Soroka? What safe places in Gaza is she talking about, and which hospitals will the IDF move?

None of this, of course, proves that Israel has committed genocide. The court will decide that. But to feel good about such arguments for the defense? To feel good after The Hague? To feel good after Gaza?

The Gaza I Loved Will Never Be the Same

January 24

An email in English: "My name is Yuval Caspi and I'm the daughter of Dr. Yosef Caspi. You once wrote an article about my father ... I hope you can help me locate it and the date of its publication." I had no idea what this was referring to. The *Haaretz* archive found it: On July 14, 1995, 30 years ago, I accompanied Dr. Caspi on a visit to the Nasser Children's Hospital in Khan Yunis.

Caspi, the former doctor of an elite IDF unit and the director of the pediatric surgery department at Soroka Hospital at the time, had volunteered to treat pediatric cardiac patients in Gaza.

He would transfer some of these young patients to Soroka for treatment, when he was able to obtain the necessary donations.

The search for the long-forgotten article was also like a trip back in a time machine to an equally forgotten reality. Today Nasser Hospital is at the center of the fighting in Khan Yunis. The wounded and dead are rushed there by the dozens and hundreds daily.

In this war, it's no longer a children's hospital. Hard to say whether it can really be called a hospital anymore, with people dying on the floor there without medicine and the building surrounded by the Israeli army. The hospital director, Dr. Nahed Abu Taima, told Radio A-Shams this week, "We're caught up in a catastrophe."

Nothing remains of what was found then, in the hopeful days of 1995. Dr. Caspi doesn't live here anymore, either. His daughter told me he moved to the US not long after that time, far from Soroka and from Nasser. He's 71 now.

And Hani al-Hatum should be 40 today, if he's still alive. In the summer of 1995, al-Hatum was admitted to Nasser Hospital because of a congenital heart valve defect. He had a forlorn expression and blue lips. His blood pressure threatened to burst the blood vessels in his brain. Mohammed Batash was a younger patient. He was just a baby then. He should be 29 now. Did he survive? He needed a heart transplant. The odds that he got one aren't great.

Farid Tartur, from the Bureij refugee camp, is probably no longer alive. His house is surely no longer standing. Back in 1995, he came to the hospital with his baby Yasser, who was in urgent need of a bone marrow transplant. He'd heard that there was an Israeli doctor in the hospital and thought that maybe he would save his son. He had no other way to save him. Are father and son still alive? I highly doubt it.

The children and babies of the summer of 1995 are now Hamas fighters. What other possibilities and opportunities did they have in life? They were born into occupation and grew up under the blockade, with no chance of anything. Maybe right now they are fighting against the army that invaded the remains of their land after their comrades committed the massacre in southern Israel, or maybe they're foraging through the rubble of what remains of their houses.

Since the war began, I haven't dared phone anyone in Gaza. I was afraid that none of my small circle of friends and acquaintances there was left alive. And if they were, what would I say to them? To hang on? To be strong? In the best-case scenario, they are all uprooted, with nothing left to their name.

I think about them a lot. Is there any chance that Munir and Sa'id, two dedicated taxi drivers who are dear to my heart, are still alive? Munir, from Beit Lahiya, recently recovered from a stroke. The last time we spoke, he asked me to try to arrange a work permit for him in Israel, despite his partial paralysis. He could work as a translator for laborers, he suggested. I haven't heard from Sa'id in a long time.

I loved Gaza. Every visit there was a unique experience. The Gazans are different from the West Bank Palestinians. Up until 16 years ago, this was a very warm, compassionate community, a courageous one, with a feeling of solidarity and, of course, one familiar with suffering. In all my years of visiting Gaza, I met not one "savage" or "monster."

I have no idea what the 16 years of the blockade did to it. Now the war is killing it for good. It's not hard to guess what will grow in Gaza in its memory.

Israel's Mainstream Brought Us to The Hague, Not Its Lunatic Fringes

January 28

Isaac Herzog, Yoav Gallant, Israel Katz: Israel's president, defense minister and foreign minister. The president of the International Court of Justice in The Hague, Joan Donoghue, chose to cite all three of them as evidence of suspicion of incitement to genocide in Israel.

The judge did not cite the far-right fringes, neither Itamar Ben-Gvir nor Eyal Golan; neither retired generals Giora Eiland (let epidemics spread in Gaza) nor Yair Golan, the man of peace and diagnostician of processes (let Gaza starve).

The third of the provisional measures issued by the court Friday, signed by former Israeli Supreme Court president Aharon Barak, Israel's ad hoc judge in the case, orders Israel to take all measures within in its power to prevent and punish direct and public incitement to genocide of Palestinians in the Gaza Strip.

It would appear that Israel must now investigate, and possibly punish, its president and two most important cabinet ministers, and they should have been summoned by the police as early as Sunday morning. Israel will not do this, of course, but it is impossible to ignore the suspicions raised by the court regarding the very heart of Israel.

The ICJ ruling is a masterpiece of caution and moderation. Only in Israel, which deceives itself and denies to distraction, can one "breathe a sigh of relief" and even "celebrate" in its wake. A state that is on trial for genocide in the court of the United Nations should be ashamed of itself and not celebrate anything.

A state whose president and senior ministers are suspected of inciting genocide should wear sackcloth, not marvel at its own great imaginary accomplishment. Every Israeli should have squirmed in their seat Friday from the mere fact of the trial, and felt a deep sense of shame and humiliation upon hearing the explanations for the ruling.

There may be Israelis who heard for the first time what their country has done and continues to do in Gaza in this war. This time, not even its propagandist media—which had protected them until now with infinite dedication, showing them nothing—could rush to their aid.

It is a little more difficult to accuse this court of antisemitism now, after it did not order Israel to stop the war. This did not bother the Channel 13 News political correspondent.

Moriah Asraf Wolberg, wearing a necklace with a pendant in the shape of Israel including the West Bank, did not concede to the antisemites of The Hague; she continued to recite the mantra that the court is hypocritical, and the world is hypocritical and Israel is waging the most just and moral war in the world. Anyone who wants to believe this even after the order of the court in The Hague is welcome to do so; one may believe any fiction.

Above all, however, we must pay attention to the wisdom of the court, which focused on Israel's mainstream, not its fringes. Herzog, a former Labor Party chairman and the most unifying, statesmanlike person in Israel; Gallant, whose dismissal was physically prevented by the protest of the center-left; and Katz, who despite calling Saturday for the prosecution of the head of the UNRWA refugee agency (!), is considered relatively moderate.

They are the main suspects in the incitement to genocide. The incitement to the genocide of the Palestinian people may have been invented by Meir Kahane, but it's already nearly in the public domain.

In post–October 7 Israel, the proper reaction to the punishment of Gaza is: "It is an entire nation out there that is responsible," in the words of the president who signs shells; "I have released all restraints . . . We are fighting human animals," as the defense minister said—when he was head of the IDF Southern Command he was fond of calling for cutting off "the head of the snake"; or "They will not receive a drop of water or a single battery," as Israel's No. 1 diplomat, Foreign Minister Katz, threatened on October 13, when he was serving as energy minister.

The judges in The Hague diagnosed perfectly what we here refuse to admit: Israel's problem is its mainstream, not its lunatic fringes. It is the mainstream that brought us to The Hague, it is the mainstream that incited to genocide, after Israel convinced itself with unbelievable ease that after October 7 everything is permitted. Fortunately, in The Hague they seem to think differently, very differently.

February

Israel's Dignity Will Be Damaged, Hamas Will Be Crowned Winner, but the War Will End

February 7

The terms of the emerging deal with Hamas are being presented by Israel as entailing a "painful price." It is based on the assumption that whatever is good for Hamas must be bad for Israel and whatever is bad for the Palestinians is good for us: a zero-sum game.

Israel has convinced itself that it must not sign a deal that would benefit Hamas in any way; it can only be harmful to Israel and can only exact a painful price.

We should not accept these assumptions. There are elements of the deal that are good for both Israel and Hamas. The "price" is not always really a price at all. It is not always as painful as they want us to believe.

The freeing of Palestinian security prisoners and a cessation of the fighting will be to Hamas's benefit. Perhaps they will benefit Israel, too. In any event, the alternative will be a lot worse for Israel. Hamas will not free its hostages unconditionally, just as Israel does not free its prisoners without getting something in return, and it has thousands of those right now.

Israel taught the Palestinians that they can win the early release of their prisoners held by Israel only by exchanging them for hostages. By the way, both sides have hostages: Many of the

Palestinian detainees were taken from their beds and have never stood trial.

Israeli prisons are bursting with security prisoners who, contrary to the way they are presented in the media's propaganda, are not all "terrorists with blood on their hands."

Among them are numerous political prisoners of a regime that prohibits Palestinians from any kind of organizational activity. Many others have been convicted of trivial offenses and sentenced to draconian punishments. If there is any more need to prove the existence of Israeli apartheid, it is the separate court systems for Jews and Palestinians.

In Israeli prisons, there are also despicable Palestinian murderers. But many have served their time and deserve to one day be let free, just like their fellow Jewish convicts. The release of elderly veterans of the Palestinian armed struggle will do no harm to Israel.

There are even those whose release will be to Israel's benefit, first and foremost Marwan Barghouti, but not only him. If Israel is seriously interested in finding a partner to change the reality of endless wars, he can be found behind Israeli bars. The next generation of Palestinian leaders is being held in Israeli prisons, from Megiddo to Nafha.

Liberation struggles throughout history, including that of the Jewish people, produced brave leaders who came out of the prisons of their conquerors. There will be grieving Jewish families who lost their loved ones years ago and do not want to see the killers released. That is understandable, but they certainly cannot be allowed to dictate what is in Israel's best interest.

The wisest course of action that Israel should have taken a long time ago was to voluntarily release the security prisoners as a gesture and not just as a concession in negotiations. But there is no chance of that happening—it is too smart. Freeing 1,500 prisoners, as Hamas is asking, is neither a disaster nor is it painful. It will bring the hostages home. Disaster and pain will only result if they are not rescued.

Nor would it be a disaster or painful to bring an end to this cursed war, during which Israel lost its humanity without achieving its goals from the indiscriminate killing and destruction, the likes of which have only been seen in the most brutal of wars.

Israel's dignity will indeed be damaged, Hamas will be crowned the winner of the war—a dubious winner but a winner nevertheless (except that it had already crowned itself such on October 7). Even if Benjamin Netanyahu's "total victory" were to be achieved, which will, of course, never happen, Hamas has won the war. Therefore, it is better to put an end to it.

We have to put aside the clichés and tired slogans Israelis have been fed and calmly consider important questions: Is the deal really that bad? In what way? Is there a better one?

Israeli Border Police Killed a 4-Year-Old Palestinian Girl, Then Took 10 Days to Return Her Body

February 10

Ruqayya Jahalin was going to celebrate her fifth birthday on February 9, 2024. But that will never happen because about a month ago, she was shot and killed by Israel Border Police troops. They fired no fewer than 32 rounds at the shared taxi in which the little girl was traveling with her mother, sisters and brother, on their way home, in the West Bank. Miraculously, she was the only person killed by the insane, indiscriminate gunfire.

She was sitting in the middle of the back seat of a Ford Transit when a bullet slammed into the vehicle from the back and stopped in her chest. Her body was removed from the van by the police officers and lay on the road for about six hours before her shocked parents were allowed to approach. The officers then took the body away and only returned it to the grieving family 10 days later. This is how, in both life and in death, Israel treats both the bodies and the dignity of Palestinians, even of little children who don't make it to the age of 5.

Beit Iksa is perhaps the most besieged and alienated village in the West Bank. Because of its location, northwest of Jerusalem, adjacent to the post-1967 neighborhood of Ramot, Israel closed its only entrance off with a temporary barrier in 2008, replacing it two years later with a permanent one. In the last 13 years only officially recognized residents of Beit Iksa, approximately 1,900 people—some of whom have blue (Israeli) ID cards, while others have special permits—have been allowed to enter.

The closure has become even tighter since the start of the war in Gaza. Previously, nonresidents were able to get special permission from the District Coordination Office to enter the village to attend weddings or funerals, or for other reasons, but that's no longer allowed. Cooking-gas canisters may be brought in, but only of one color; fodder for sheep is on the permitted list, but any new flocks from outside have not been allowed into Beit Iksa since October 7. The connection between bringing sheep into the village and the war in Gaza and Israel's security is obvious, right? It was into this surreal, Gaza-style reality that Ruqayya Jahalin was born.

Her family is split up. Her father, Ahmed Jahalin, a 40-year-old construction worker and shepherd, is married to two women and has nine children. Six of them live with Aisha, 38, Ruqayya's mother, in Beit Iksa. The other three live with Rabaa, 30, and Ahmed in a neighborhood called the Western Valley in Arabic, in the town of Beit Hanina in the West Bank (other parts of town are within the municipal bounds of Jerusalem). Complicated? Such is the bureaucracy of the occupation.

Aisha and her children frequently visit Ahmed in the collection of shacks where he lives with his other family. Indeed, the youngsters attend school in the Western Valley on weekdays and sleep over in their father's place, rejoining their mother in Beit Iksa on the weekends. Ahmed, who worked in the settlement of Givat Ze'ev until the war erupted, is now unemployed, as Israel has barred Palestinians from working in Israeli locales ever since. He's now forced to rely on his small flock of about 30 sheep to support his families.

Ruqayya was his second-youngest—only her brother, 3-year-old Mohammed, is younger. On Sunday, January 7, Aisha brought four of her children, who were on a winter break from school, to visit their father in Beit Hanina, which is about 15 kilometers from their home. That afternoon, they headed back to Beit Iksa. A friend of Ahmed drove Aisha and the children—daughters Marwa, 15, Rahma, 12, and the two little ones, Ruqayya and Mohammed—to the village of Bidu, where they got into a shared taxi heading to Beit Iksa, driven by a resident who is permitted to enter and leave it. The family was joined in the Ford Transit by two other Beit Iksa women; one sat next to the driver and the other was behind her. Aisha and Marwa sat in the middle row of seats, and Mohammed, Ruqayya and Rahma were in the back.

After a short drive they reached the checkpoint at the entrance to their village, where they had to undergo the usual strict procedure, waiting while other vehicles were stopped and checked before approaching cautiously and slowly. Three Border Police troops were at the checkpoint, Marwa tells us now, two men and a woman. The latter quickly checked the IDs of the passengers in the taxi, to ascertain that they were residents of Beit Iksa, then had a look inside the taxi to ensure that they weren't smuggling in sheep or other contraband. The driver was then allowed to proceed toward the iron gate at the other end of the checkpoint, which the female officer ran to open. Everything followed the usual, well-entrenched checkpoint routine.

Suddenly shots rang out. Heavy gunfire came from behind the van and the passengers had no idea what was happening, says Marwa. "We were scared, we shouted, a few bullets hit the floor of the taxi, under our feet." The driver, paralyzed by fear, stopped the vehicle immediately after passing through the gate. Aisha tried to protect her children, gathering panicky Rahma and Mohammed to her from the back seat. She then pulled Ruqayya toward her—and was appalled to see blood streaming from her back. Marwa relates that her mother screamed that she wanted to get out of the taxi and rush Ruqayya to a hospital, but the driver warned her that if she got out of the vehicle, she, too, would be shot. He summoned an ambulance from Bidu, which arrived within minutes, but Israeli security personnel prevented it from passing through the checkpoint, to reach the taxi on the other side.

Panicked and desperate, Aisha continued to scream as she saw her little daughter fading before her eyes. After about 15 minutes, Ruqayya stopped breathing and her eyes rolled back into her head, Marwa says, adding that they were forced to stay in the taxi for a total of 20 minutes, which felt like an eternity. Aisha yelled to the driver to call Ahmed. None of the Border Police personnel bothered to approach to see what had happened inside the van.

When we visited her on Monday at Ahmed's home in Beit Hania, Marwa, a shy teenager, consented to have her picture taken, but only with her father, not alone. The trauma of having her little sister shot dead next to her was still apparent when we spoke to her, along with Iyad Hadad, a field researcher for the Israeli human rights organization B'Tselem, who investigated the incident.

She recalls that the Border Police officers finally came over and asked the driver why he wasn't leaving. "We have a wounded child here," he told them. Only then did security personnel approach the dying Ruqayya. The passengers were then allowed to get out of the vehicle, says Marwa, and to carry Ruqayya to the checkpoint. Paramedics in the Israeli ambulance that had meanwhile been called to the site examined the child, but in short order told Aisha that her child was dead.

It turns out that after the Ford Transit was given the go-ahead and started to move toward the iron gate, a car suddenly appeared behind it and burst into the checkpoint area without stopping next to the Border Police. Footage from the security cameras shows the course of events: The Ford Transit advances slowly after passing the officers and then a smaller car speeds in. The Border Police open heavy fire on the car and run after it. According to Hadad's report, 32 rounds struck the taxi with the women and children in it, four slamming into the seats and 28 into the chassis. One bullet killed the little girl.

The B'Tselem researcher reports that the only passengers in the car that burst into the checkpoint area, and who were summarily shot to death, were a married couple from Bidu: Mohammed Abu Eid, 37, a gardener who was employed in Israel until the war, and his wife, Doha, 31. They had four children aged 14 and 10, in addition to 2-year-old twins, both of whom have a congenital heart defect and recently underwent open-heart surgery. What made the couple speed through the Beit Iksa checkpoint, knowing that that was basically an act of suicide? The couple had no record of security offenses or history of psychological problems. Relatives suggest that something may have gone wrong with the car, but that seems like a far-fetched possibility, judging from the way they drove.

Another possibility raised this week is that the couple wanted to die because their economic situation had become untenable, with Mohammed out of work and costly medical treatment needed for the twins. One account, which is unverified, says he took leave from some of his friends on the day of the incident. As far as is known, the Abu Eids were on the way to pay their condolences to a family in Beit Iksa—but they would have known that there was no entry into the village and that such a visit was impossible.

There is no hard evidence that this was a rare instance of Palestinians committing suicide in that fashion. What actually happened? We will probably never know. The couple were killed in the heavy volley of gunfire and Israel has not yet returned their bodies to their families.

An Israel Police spokesperson stated this week in reply to a query from *Haaretz*: "The investigation of the terrorist ramming attack at the Ras Bidu crossing is still ongoing at this time, with the aim being to arrive at the truth of the matter and to determine the precise circumstances of the incident."

It emerges that Border Police personnel kept Ruqayya's father, Ahmed, who was summoned to the scene by the taxi driver, from approaching his daughter in her final moments and trying to calm his distraught wife and children. He was compelled to wait at the checkpoint for six hours, he says, while his daughter's body lay on the road, wrapped in a black plastic body bag, next to those of the couple from Bidu. Ahmed asked to be allowed at least to stand next to Ruqayya's body, but the police refused. Finally, security personnel took the body away and told Ahmed he would receive it the next morning.

"Ten days I waited for her," the father tells us. The police wanted to perform an autopsy and the family refused, but a Jerusalem court gave the green light. An international NGO for the protection of children made a lawyer available to the family, who handled the contacts with the authorities for the return of the body.

Finally, 10 days after she died, Ruqayya was buried in the soil of her father's village.

An Israeli Incursion into Gaza's Rafah Will Be an Unprecedented Humanitarian Catastrophe

February 11

All we can do now is to request, beg, cry out: Don't enter Rafah. An Israeli incursion into Rafah will be an attack on the world's biggest displaced persons camp. It will drag the Israeli military into committing war crimes of a severity that even it has not yet committed. It is impossible to invade Rafah now without committing war crimes. If the Israel Defense Forces invades Rafah, the city will become a charnel house.

Around 1.4 million displaced people are now in Rafah, sheltering in some cases under plastic bags that have been turned into tents. The American administration, the supposed gatekeeper of Israeli law and conscience, has conditioned the invasion of Rafah on an Israeli plan to evacuate the city. There is not and cannot be any such plan, even if Israel manages to come up with something.

It is impossible to transport a million entirely destitute people, some of whom have been displaced two or three times already, from one "safe" place to another that always turns into a killing field. It is impossible to transport millions of people as if they were calves meant for shipment. Even calves cannot be transported with such cruelty.

There is also nowhere to evacuate these millions of people. In the devastated Gaza Strip, there is nowhere left to go. If the Rafah refugees are moved to Al-Mawasi, as the IDF will propose in its humanitarian plan, Al-Mawasi will become the site of a humanitarian disaster the likes of which we haven't seen in the Strip.

Yarden Michaeli and Avi Scharf report that the entire population of the Gaza Strip, 2.3 million people, is supposed to evacuate into an area of 16 square kilometers (6.2 square miles), about the size of Ben Gurion International Airport. All of Gaza in the area of the airport—just imagine.

Amira Hass calculated that if only 1 million people go to Al-Mawasi, the population density there will be 62,500 people per square kilometer. There is nothing in Al-Mawasi: no infrastructure, no water, no electricity, no homes. Only sand and more sand, to absorb the blood, the sewage and the epidemics. The thought of this is not only bloodcurdling, it also shows the level of dehumanization Israel has reached in its planning.

Blood will be spilled in Al-Mawasi, as it has been spilled recently in Rafah, the penultimate safe haven offered by Israel. The Shin Bet security service will come up with some beat officer affiliated with Hamas who has to be eliminated by dropping a one-ton bomb on the new tent camp. Twenty bystanders, most of them children, will be killed. The military correspondents will tell us, their eyes shining, about the wonderful work the IDF is doing in liquidating the top command of Hamas. Total victory is near; Israelis will be sated once again.

But even through this force-feeding, the Israeli public must wake up, and with it the Biden administration. This is an emergency more dire than any other during this war. The Americans must block the invasion of Rafah with actions, not words. Only they can stop Israel.

The conscientious sector of the Israeli public seeks sources of information other than the "cakes for soldiers" stations here that call themselves news channels. Watch pictures of Rafah on any foreign network—you won't see anything in Israel—and you'll understand why it can't be evacuated. Imagine Al-Mawasi with the 2 million displaced people, and you'll understand the war crimes that are rampant here.

On Saturday, the body of 6-year-old Hind Hamada—or Rajab, in some news outlets—was found. The girl had become famous all over the world after the moments of terror she and her family experienced on January 29 in the face of Israeli tanks—moments that were recorded in a phone call with the Palestinian Red Crescent, until her aunt's screams of terror stopped. Seven members of the family were killed; only the fate of little Hind had remained a mystery.

Hind was found dead in her aunt's burned car at a gas station in Khan Yunis. She had been wounded, covered by the seven bodies of her relatives, and she bled to death before she could extricate herself from the vehicle. Hind and her family had responded to Israel's "humanitarian" call to evacuate. Anyone who wants thousands more Hinds should invade Rafah, whose population will be evacuated to Al-Mawasi.

With the 'Perfect' Hostage Rescue Operation, Israel's Dehumanization of Palestinians in Gaza Reached a New Low

February 14

Just like the good old days, Israel once again worships its army. The raid that released Louis Norberto Har and Fernando Marman sparked a crescendo of joy coupled with a resurgence of national pride. The video clips "permitted for publication" took us back to the time when the army was like a Hollywood production, and everyone competed to see who could heap the most praise on the Yaman counterterror unit and on the Shin Bet security service. It was a perfect operation, said all the intelligence experts—with zero casualties.

It was indeed an impressive operation and cause for joy, but it wasn't perfect, and it certainly wasn't "zero casualties." The fact that at least 74 Palestinians, including women and children, were killed during the operation was hardly mentioned in Israel. Perhaps those deaths were inevitable. Perhaps even if the number of Palestinian deaths were seven times greater it wouldn't have dampened the celebration. Two very sympathetic Israeli-Argentinians were released, and all the rest doesn't matter.

The images I saw from the hospitals in Rafah on the day of the rescue were among the most horrific I have seen in this war. Children ripped to shreds, convulsing, looking helplessly upon their deaths. The horror. There is no need to go into the moral dilemma of whether the release of two hostages justifies the deaths of 74 people—that question is superfluous in such a cruel war—in order to point to Israel's complete disregard for collateral deaths. On the day of the operation, Israel killed 133 people across Gaza, most of them, as is the norm in this war, innocent civilians, among them many children.

We were all happy that they were freed, and the operation in itself was moral and fully justified. But the disregard for the deaths of dozens of people as if they were not human is an outrage. Release more and more hostages, as many as possible. Marvel, rejoice and be proud—but at least mention the terrible price paid by Gazans for this just operation. The children ripped to shreds played no part in seizing the hostages. They have been destined to pay the cruel price for what Hamas did. Alongside our joy, one cannot help but think of them and their fate. An operation cannot be perfect if that is its price.

The disregard for 74 people killed in a just and righteous operation should surprise no one. The dehumanization of Gazans in this war has sunk to a level we have not known before—even after decades of dehumanizing Palestinians under occupation.

The disgraceful lack of coverage of Gaza's suffering by most of the Israeli media will be eternally remembered in disgrace, at least I hope so. As a result, Palestinians are seen by most Israelis as nonhuman and even non-animal. In Israel, the more than 28,000 Gazan fatalities are considered a mere number, nothing more. The uprooting and displacement of millions of people moved from place to place as if they were a flock of sheep and the unbelievable, brazen portrayal of this as a "humanitarian measure" have dehumanized Gazans even further. If one believes them to be human beings, then surely people cannot be treated like this. You can't abuse people for so long if you believe they are human.

Prime Minister Benjamin Netanyahu is not the most tempestuous politician in his government—even the International Court of Justice in The Hague failed to come up with a single genocidal statement by him (unlike the case with President Herzog). However, he expressed this dehumanization in a particularly picturesque way when he compared Israel's war against Hamas to a glass cup that we had already broken; now, he said, the fragments remain and we are treading on them until nothing remains.

Netanyahu was speaking about Hamas, but, after all, everyone knows that Gaza is Hamas. We broke Gaza's glass, now we tread on its fragments until they turn into grains of sand, air, nothing—human dust, subhuman dust.

Palestinian Teens Are Writing Wills, and for Good Reason

February 17

Abdel Rahman Hamad wrote a last will and testament. A long text with detailed instructions, in his scrupulous handwriting. More and more Palestinian teenagers in the occupied West Bank are writing wills these days, and with even greater intensity in the wake of the events in the Gaza Strip. Hamad requested to be buried as quickly as possible, and asked his family to use a good shot of him as his profile photo in the social networks and to add a prayer verse next to it and, above all, not to mourn his death.

"Do not place me in a freezer," he wrote, "bury me immediately. Lay me on my bed, cover me with blankets and take me to burial. When you lower me into the grave, remain behind me.

But don't be sad. Remember only the beautiful memories of me and don't mourn for me. I don't want anyone to be sad." Hamad wrote the will last July 18 and gave it to a friend for safekeeping. A photo of the text is stored in the bereaved father's cell phone.

Iyad Hadad, a field researcher for the Israeli human rights organization B'Tselem, translates and reads it for us. Suddenly he chokes up, before bursting into heartrending tears that don't stop. We've never seen Hadad cry. He's been dealing with human rights in the territories since 1986, first for the Palestinian organization Al Haq, and for the past 24 years for B'Tselem. He's seen everything, investigates every case of killing and other crimes of the occupation throughout the Ramallah area, and now he's weeping profusely. The last will and testament of someone who was not yet 18 has made him break down. The face of the dead boy's father, Abdel Rahim, is grief-stricken, but his eyes remain dry. An oppressive silence falls upon the room.

On January 29, we traveled to the village of Al-Mazra'a a-Sharqiya to investigate the circumstances of the killing of Tawfic Abdeljabbar, an American teenager, who was shot to death by Israeli soldiers or settlers—or both. On the way there we passed through the town of Silwad. When we got to Al-Mazra'a a-Sharqiya, we were notified that another teenager had been killed, this one in Silwad, shortly after we left it. This week we went back to Silwad.

Perched on a hill, it's a well-to-do, relatively developed town of about 6,000 residents, northeast of Ramallah. There is intense construction going on here, such as we haven't seen in other towns and villages. It's also a militant place, which the Israel Defense Forces frequently raids, provoking the residents, whose town is close to Highway 60, the West Bank's main artery, on which settlers travel and stones are thrown. In the past five years, Silwad has lost seven of its sons; Hamas leader Khaled Meshal was born here in 1956 and grew up in the town.

This past Sunday would have been Abdel Rahman Hamad's 18th birthday. He didn't celebrate it—he'd already been dead for two weeks. This week, on a street where splendid marble mansions are being built, next to the Al Huriya residential tower, a truck unloaded construction materials into the yard of one of those mansions. Across the road, two Palestinian pennants stick up from the ground, and there are two circles made from broken pieces of marble, on one of which the name of Abdel Rahman Hamad has been inscribed in pencil. Garbage flutters around the improvised memorial. This is where the teenager was killed.

It was a Monday, and Abdel Rahman was on his way home from school. On social media it was announced that the Israeli army, which had invaded the town a little after 8 a.m., had begun to pull out. But on the street Abdel Rahman was walking along, apparently by himself, there were still two Israeli armored vehicles: a police jeep and an army car. The street is parallel to the avenue with the homes under construction, on the slope of the hill, and afterward it emerged that between the skeletons of the mansions, all of them belonging to the extended Qassam family, a few more youths were hiding. They were tracking the departing security forces and waiting for an opportunity to throw stones at them.

Suddenly the door of one of the parked vehicles opened. A soldier or a Border Policeman stuck his body out and fired a single shot, as precise as it was lethal, straight into Abdel Rahman's stomach. The distance between the sniper and his victim was about 150 meters, and the youth higher up the street than the shooter. Immediately afterward, the door of the armored vehicle was shut and both vehicles sped away. They shot, they killed, they fled.

They aborted the life of a youth and destroyed the life of a family, though it's unlikely that this was something they considered for even a second. Even if Abdel Rahman threw a stone or (as the police claim) a Molotov cocktail, there is no way he could have endangered the lives of the soldiers and Border Police in the least. At that distance he didn't have a chance of hitting the armored vehicles. Nonetheless, why not terminate the life of a youth if you can? After all, no one will take an interest in it afterward, apart from the shattered family.

As all this was happening, an eyewitness, whose identity is in the possession of Hadad, the field researcher, was seated on the balcony of his home, opposite the two security vehicles, observing the events. He had just exchanged messages with his wife, who resides in Jordan. She asked him how he was doing, and he had informed her that an invasion by the Israeli army was underway and that the soldiers had blanketed the center of the town with tear gas. The view in Silwad is that the encroachment by the IDF and the Border Police that day was no more than a demonstration of strength orchestrated by the new area commander of the Shin Bet security service, codenamed "Omri."

In any event, the man's wife asked him to film the events for her, and he did so. The footage he took through the top of an olive tree in the yard shows an amazingly quiet and tranquil street, with no stones and no Molotov cocktails flying through the air. Suddenly, the silence is broken by the sound of a shot from the direction of one of the armored vehicles. Immediately afterward, paramedics, who came from an ambulance that was parked nearby, are seen running toward the victim, as the two Israeli vehicles pull out fast in the opposite direction. The heroes had done their day's work—time to go.

The driver of the Palestinian ambulance, which had been waiting at the end of the street, the usual practice when the security forces invade, saw Abdel Rahman fall to the ground. He and his team rushed him to the urgent-care service in the local clinic. The youth was in critical condition. The bullet entered his hip and exited from the chest—he was apparently bending over when he was hit. Attempts to revive him were unavailing.

The IDF Spokesperson's Unit referred *Haaretz* to the Border Police. A spokesman for the Israel Police (under which the Border Police serve) this week stated in response to *Haaretz*'s request for comment: "During activity by the security forces, the suspect threw a Molotov cocktail at the fighters and endangered their lives. In response a fighter shot at him and neutralized the danger."

Abdel Rahman was the firstborn son of Abdel Rahim, 44, and his wife, Inam Ayad, 42. He was student in the 12th grade, in the science track. His ambition was to study medicine, so he worked hard ahead of the matriculation exams not only to gain admission to medical school, but also with the hope of obtaining a scholarship. Photographs show him speaking at school assemblies and holiday celebrations. Tall and good-looking, he stood out among his peers. He played on the Silwad soccer team, but in recent months devoted all his time to his studies, as he also did on the last night of his life.

On the morning of January 29, as his father was about to leave for work (in construction) in the nearby village of Ein Sinya, he noticed that his son was still asleep. He decided not to wake him, as he knew that Abdel Rahman had studied late into the night. His father left the house at 6:30 a.m., and the youth's mother woke him up about an hour later and drove him to school in her car. At 11:30 she called her husband to say that the army had invaded Silwad. She asked him to call their younger son, 15-year-old Sliman, who works in construction in the town, to check that he was all right. They didn't worry about Abdel Rahman, knowing he was in school. Sliman was fine, the security forces hadn't been to the place where he worked.

At 12, Abdel Rahim called his wife. "What's happening?" he asked, and was told that the center of the town was covered by a cloud of tear gas that was penetrating homes. As long as the kids are fine, the father thought. At 12:30, as he was having a late breakfast with the workers, he received an anonymous phone call, which disconnected without anyone saying anything. A few minutes later, his brother called and told him to get back home quickly. Why? "Ubeida was wounded"—using Abdel Rahman's nickname. The father says he went into shock.

"I didn't know what to do," he recalls. "I was totally confused. My hand went to Ubeida's phone number and I called him." A Palestinian ambulance driver answered. He asked how his son was, and the driver replied, "He's all right. I'll update you soon."

Distraught, Abdel Rahim waited a minute or two and called again. This time the driver said, "We're hoping he will be all right." Abdel Rahman was already dead, but his father didn't know that yet, and was certain that his son would now be rushed from the Silwad clinic to the Governmental Hospital in Ramallah. He asked the driver to pick him up on the way—his place of work is on the main road to Ramallah. A moment later his brother called and said again: "Come back to town, and fast."

By now he understood that his son was dead. Still in a daze, he went to the first clinic, where he was told that his son was at the hospital. When he arrived there, he stepped out of the car and fainted, collapsing on the ground. He remembers nothing of the minutes that followed.

Photos of the dead youth hang on the wall of the elegant living room. One of the images is made up of portraits of the three members of the family who have been killed by Israeli troops over the years: Abdel Rahman in the center, flanked by his two dead uncles. His uncle Jihad Iyad, his mother's brother, was killed by Israeli soldiers in 1998, when he was 17; the other uncle, his father's brother, Mohammed Hamad, was killed by soldiers in 2004, at the age of 21. Abdel Rahman didn't know either of them. His father adds in a whisper that his own uncle as well was killed, in 1989, and once more an oppressive silence descends upon the room.

The World Must Force Peace on Israel

February 18

Now is the time for the United States, and in its wake the international community, to make a decision: Will the endless cycle of violence between Israel and the Palestinians continue, or are we going to try to put a stop to it? Will the United States continue to arm Israel and then bemoan the excessive use of these armaments, or is it finally prepared to take real steps, for the first time in its history, to change reality? And above all, will the cruelest Israeli attack on Gaza become the most pointless of all, or will the opportunity that came in its aftermath not be missed, for a change?

There is no point in appealing to Israel. The current government, and the one that is likely to replace it, does not and never will have the intention, courage or ability to generate change. When the prime minister responds to American talks about establishing a Palestinian state with words indicating that he "objects to coerced moves," or that "an agreement will only be reached through negotiations," all one can do is both laugh and cry.

Laugh, because over the years Prime Minister Benjamin Netanyahu has done all he can to foil negotiations; cry, because Israel is the one employing coercion—the nature of its policy toward the Palestinians is coercion carried out in one big unilateral, violent, aggressive and arrogant move. All of a sudden, Israel is against acts of coercion? Irony hides its head in shame.

It is therefore pointless to expect the current Israeli government to change its character. To expect a government led by Benny Gantz, Gadi Eisenkot or Yair Lapid to do so is also painfully futile. None of them believe in the existence of a Palestinian state that is equal in its sovereign status and rights to Israel. The three of them together and each one separately will at most, on a really good day, agree to the establishment of a Bantustan on part of the land. A genuine solution will not be found here. It's best to leave Israel to wallow in its refusal.

But the world cannot afford to let this opportunity pass. This is the world that will soon have to reconstruct, with its funds, the ruins of the Gaza Strip, until the next time Israel demolishes it. It is the world whose stability is undermined as long as the occupation persists, and is further undermined every time Israel embarks on another war. This is the world that agrees that the occupation is bad for it, but has never lifted a finger to bring it to an end. Now an opportunity to do so has cropped up. Israel's weakness and dependence following this war must be exploited, for Israel's benefit as well.

Enough with words. Enough with the futile rounds of talks held by US secretary of state Antony Blinken and the barbed words uttered by President Joe Biden. They lead nowhere. The last Zionist president, perhaps the last one to care about what is happening in the world, must take action. One could, as a prelude, learn something from the amazingly simple and true words of European Union foreign policy chief Josep Borrell, who said: "Well, if you believe that too many people are being killed, maybe you should provide less arms [to Israel]."

However, the issue is not just ending the war but mainly what will happen when it's over. If it depended on Israel, under any government, we would return to the warm bosom of apartheid and to living by the sword. The world cannot accept this any longer and cannot leave the choice to Israel. Israel has spoken: No. The time has come for a Dayton Accords–like solution. It was a forced and imperfect agreement reached in Bosnia-Herzegovina that put an end to one of the cruelest wars, and in contrast to all predictions, it has held for 29 years. The agreement was imposed by coercion.

A Palestinian state may no longer be a viable solution because of the hundreds of thousands of settlers who ruined the chances for establishing one. But a world determined to find a solution must pose a clear choice for Israel: sanctions, or an end to the occupation; territories, or weapons; settlements, or international support; a democratic state, or a Jewish one; apartheid, or an end to Zionism. When the world stands firm, posing these options in such a manner, Israel will have to decide. Now is the time to force Israel to make the most fateful decision of its life.

Israel Is Blaming Everyone but Itself for Its Own Disgrace

February 22

There are not many countries so desperate for national honor and pride as much as Israel. Whether it's the Olympics, Eurovision or the backgammon world championship, every Israeli victory evokes "national pride." Every medal in the Taekwondo Championship in Albania "brings honor." A gold medal in the rhythmic gymnastics group hoop competition puts it on the world map; the

European RSX Surfboards Championship lifts its status among the nations. A former Israeli representing Luxembourg at this year's Eurovision? "Blue and White Pride."

It's unlikely that there is any other country in whose eyes such minor achievements are considered so important. It's as if someone somewhere in the world feels better about Kazakhstan because one of its athletes once won a figure skating competition. In Israel, this is considered a national event meriting a call from the president.

This childish longing for recognition might be touching, even moving—a young country making its way—if not for Israel's forfeit of its honor in the important issues. Deducting its achievements in sports and Eurovision, Israel is a country without honor. Perhaps it imagines that Eden Golan performing in Malmö will cover up what is happening in Khan Yunis. But, of course, this is a false hope.

It's hard to believe that a country so anxious over its honor acts like it doesn't care about its international standing. The war in the Gaza Strip has brought Israel's status to an unprecedented low, but Israel has closed its eyes and mind yet again in a childish way, hoping that if it ignores the reality it can ignore the disgrace. It does nothing to improve its standing and dignity and regain a little pride.

It's hard to think of other countries whose conduct has brought it to The Hague twice in the space of a few weeks on the charge of genocide, and for deliberations about what is clearly an illegal occupation. And Israel? It thinks the spit in its face is rain. It blames the damned judge, antisemitism, the world's hypocrisy and wickedness. It will take no part in challenging the accusations against it. They aren't even a matter of interest. All the world's important television networks broadcast the court sessions in The Hague this week, while only Israel ignored it. Not interesting, not important. If we close our eyes, they won't see us. If we ignore The Hague, The Hague will go away.

But The Hague lives and breathes, and its proceedings should have caused great embarrassment and shame for Israel. After the world saw Gaza, saw and cringed—there is no human being who does not react like that—The Hague hearings followed. Incisive, grounded and serious about the charge of genocide, and even more so about the occupation. But Israel ignores it.

Israel will invade Rafah, even if it means that its standing in the world's eyes falls further. It won't participate in The Hague's deliberations on the occupation. This will only show it has no line of defense. Israel has given up the remnants of its dignity. It doesn't care about being an ostracized, marginalized country (if the whole world is against us, it doesn't matter how we behave), as long as it doesn't result in any practical measures being taken against it.

But beyond the US weapons airlift, the UN Security Council veto and the absence of sanctions so far, the country, just like a person, has an important asset in its good name. Israel gave that up. Perhaps it has despaired of the world, maybe it has discovered that it can get along without its good name. This is certainly not among the factors it considers before and after every war.

It was not too many years ago that the same world was in love with the State of Israel, when it acted as a member of the family of nations. The world may be cynical and only love power, as Israel tells itself, but there is also justice, international law and moral considerations, civil society and public opinion, and they are important—at least as much as the "honorable" third place in Eurovision 2023.

Israel Has No Real Alternative to Netanyahu

February 25

Once again it has been proved that there is no real substitute, no genuine alternative and no true opposition to Benjamin Netanyahu.

The behavior by the centrist parties throughout the war, including the results of two important votes in the Knesset last week, clearly prove that on the state's fundamental issues which define Israel's character—the occupation, the war and, incredibly, democracy—there are no significant differences among the right, the center and the Zionist left. On these issues we are a state with one voice, one outlook, one opinion: Together we will win.

These things are particularly astonishing in light of the raucous political struggle now raging between the camps. Everyone speaks of a division, a rift, a chasm, when in fact no real differences of opinion exist.

One could think that Israel during war would be a different country were Benny Gantz, Gadi Eisenkot or Yair Lapid to lead it. Absolutely not. Their personal conduct would surely be more upright and humble, but the results would be remarkably similar. Here is the evidence.

In a result that would not shame a Belarusian election—99–9—the Knesset supported a government resolution opposing "unilateral" recognition of a Palestinian state. Tempers flared, and hands were raised in overwhelming support of Israeli rejectionism.

The state, whose occupation and settlement policy are the mother of unilateralism, scoffs at the entire world and unites unanimously against a unilateral measure that is ostensibly accepted by half its lawmakers. What a disgrace, albeit not a surprise.

No less predictable was the near-unanimity in the vote to oust MK Ofer Cassif [for expressing support for South Africa's case against Israel at The Hague]. It doesn't have to do with the Palestinians and the territories but, rather, with democracy, the issue that has stirred the country above all others over the past year.

Israel was divided between democracy's guardians and its destroyers, and in the first test of democracy, it united nearly entirely behind an anti-democratic measure of unparalleled danger. Most of those who fought against the government coup, almost all of those shrieking for democracy, either raised their hand in favor of removing a lawmaker for his opinions and his worldview or fled from the vote in cowardice.

The coup has already won, and this time not only with the votes of the right but also with the votes of Yesh Atid, the National Unity Party and even the Labor Party. The wretched fleeing from the vote by Benny Gantz, Gadi Eisenkot, Yair Lapid, Merav Michaeli and their colleagues was a badge of shame for ones purporting to fight for democracy.

They should have voted no, loud and clear. After all, they know that had the measure succeeded—it was defeated by four votes—it would lead to the removal of all of the Arab lawmakers. And yet they ran away. Another shame, another disgrace for which there is no pardon.

Finally, the behavior in the war: The left and the center supported all of Israel's wars, the just war and the criminal wars, in the beginning. But in the past they soon came to their senses, and there was opposition to every previous war.

Israel's most brutal and most futile war does not have a single voice of opposition in the Knesset, not even after more than four months and almost 30,000 Palestinian deaths, besides the Arab MKs.

Parts of those not on the right support the war from within the government, and another part supports it from the outside, and everyone in the choir sings the same song, conducted by the right. The whole world is calling for an end to the war, and in the Knesset there is not a single Zionist MK who will do so. Democracy? Opposition? Alternative? Not here, not now.

Only the loathing for Netanyahu reminds us that there still remains a coalition and an opposition, but this loathing is mainly personal. He is a liar, he is a hedonist, he is corrupt and thinks only of himself. He forsook the hostages, he sold his soul to the Kahanist right and legitimized it, and perhaps he was always there. All of this is very true and infuriating. But it is not a proposal for an alternative.

March

Gaza's Night of Death and Hunger

March 3

It was a night of death and hunger. When it ended, at least 112 people had been killed and another 760 were injured. Israel tried to deny responsibility—the trucks hit them—but there is no denying its responsibility for what is happening now in the Gaza Strip: Israel is the occupying force there.

Not only that: Dr. Mohammed Salha, the acting director of Gaza City's Al-Awda Hospital, told the Associated Press that of the 176 wounded brought to the facility, 142 had gunshot wounds and the other 34 showed injuries from a stampede. A physician at the city's Shifa Hospital said that most of those treated there had gunshot wounds.

Trucks, as far as is known, don't shoot. And the claim that Hamas security guards were the ones who fired such an insane amount of ammunition into the crowd is as credible as the initial claim that it was Palestinians who fatally shot the Palestinian American journalist Shireen Abu Akleh in Jenin in 2022.

Nor do the edited videos distributed by the IDF Spokesperson's Unit show people being hit by the trucks. In the videos, people flee for their lives like insects—black dots running around that reflect with marvelous precision the attitude directed at them and their lives—but none of the insects are being run over.

At 11:30 p.m., on Instagram, hundreds of people are seen gathering around bonfires in an attempt to relieve the winter chill. They are waiting for trucks that might arrive at the location where aid distribution has been carried out in recent days. At around 4 a.m., a convoy of trucks from Egypt that passed the Israeli checkpoint makes its way north on Al-Rashid Street. The Israel Defense Forces says there were 30 trucks; an eyewitness told the BBC there were 18.

At about 4:45 a.m., the convoy of trucks was surrounded by crowds of people as they approached the Nabulsi rotary. The IDF videos show four trucks surrounded by people as well as people lying on the road. Army vehicles are parked on the side. Al Jazeera showed a video filmed partly at the back of the convoy in which bursts of gunfire can be heard and people can be seen crawling on the trucks or sheltering behind them. Eyewitnesses said the shooting came from the direction of the Israeli vehicles. One witness, Mahmoud Awadeyah, said the Israelis prevented any access to the wounded.

Even if it is proved that it was IDF soldiers who shot at this horrifying assembly and who killed and wounded hundreds of starving people, no one in Israel will be upset by it. It's a war, you know; October 7, remember. The minimal compassion for the Palestinians stopped completely in Israel on October 7 and has shown no signs of life ever since. It's in a coma. We only feel compassion for ourselves, our soldiers and our hostages, and everyone else can just explode for all we care.

And explode they do: the Gazans literally and the world from anger. The danger of being a pariah is closer than ever: Israel has never been denounced, been renounced and provoked such hatred as it has today. You can shrug your shoulders, but soon every Israeli will feel it.

What else needs to happen? The spokesman for the World Health Organization, Christian Lindmeier, said Friday that a 10th child was officially registered in a Gaza hospital as having starved to death. What else needs to happen for Israelis to wake up from their complacency and activate their moral sensors about what has been happening since October 7? Time, which stopped in Israel that day, has moved on. For nearly five months,

Gaza's toll of dead, wounded, hungry and sick has been soaring. It turns out that even the deaths of 30,000 people, two-thirds of them women and children, do not satisfy the appetite for revenge.

If the night of death and hunger, the night when body bags replaced the bags of food on the trucks and when blood mixed with flour, did not inspire resistance to the war in Israel, nothing will make Israel stop, if only to think about its actions and their cost: if not the horrific price that the nonhuman Gazans are paying, then at least the price that Israel will pay. From here on, we shall only whisper in vain: Enough.

After 150 Days of Death and Destruction in Gaza, Israel Is Neither Stronger Nor Safer

March 7

With the war now having passed the 150-day mark, all Israelis should ask themselves honestly: Are we better off now than on October 6, 2023? Are we stronger? Safer? Do we have greater deterrence? Are we more popular? Prouder of ourselves? Are we more united? Better in any way? The incredible thing is that the answer to all these questions is unequivocally no.

These 150 days have been cruel and difficult and have done nothing to benefit Israel and will do nothing for it, neither in the short nor long term. On the contrary, Hamas has come out stronger. Thousands of its fighters have been killed, but it has become the hero of the Arab world. Still, most Israelis want at least 150 days more of the same; there has been zero public opposition to the war, even after five months of death and destruction on an unprecedented scale, after Israel has become an outcast, hated across the world, bloodied and economically damaged.

There isn't one area in which the country is better off after these dark last few months—the darkest in its history. Israel is now a lot less safe than it was before the war; it faces the risk of a regional escalation, global sanctions and the loss of American support. It is also a lot less democratic—the harm wreaked by the war on Israel's democratic institutions is greater even than that of the judicial coup—and the damages piling up will remain after the IDF withdraws from Gaza.

As for Israel's international status, this country has never been such a pariah; even our all-but-guaranteed ties with the United States have deteriorated to a low we have never experienced before. The daily toll of fallen soldiers, the fact that most of the hostages have yet to be released, that tens of thousands of Israelis have been internally displaced, that half the country is a danger zone. The West Bank is threatening to explode, and nothing can hide the bottomless hate that we have managed to sow in Gaza, the West Bank and the Arab world.

And no improvement can be seen on the horizon as long as Israel refuses stubbornly to every proposition for a fundamental change. Still, Israelis want more of the same, like a gambler who has lost all his money but is still convinced that one more bet will win him the jackpot.

With 100 Palestinian deaths every day, Israelis seem convinced that 30,000 more deaths will turn Gaza into a paradise, or at least a safe place. It's difficult to recall such blindness, even in Israel. Such a state of moral obtuseness is also difficult to recall. Let them go hungry and without water, let them choke, let them die—even the left and the media have adopted this way of thinking. Led with their eyes covered, no one stops to ask where we are going. The main thing is to push forward with the war because Hamas wants it to stop and we are here to show them what's what.

We have a duty to draw up a balance sheet—"What has Israel gotten out of the war?"—and then ask ourselves courageously: Should we have gone to war? Set aside the slogans about how no country would have overlooked such a cruel attack on its people, and a country's right to protect itself, and what would people have wanted Israel to do. After 150 days in which there is nothing to enter into the benefits column on this balance sheet, just heavy costs, we can start to doubt its wisdom from Israel's perspective.

We have said nothing yet of the shocking price paid by Gaza

and its residents who, under the shadow of war, are suffering greater abuse than ever before.

Most Israelis—those for whom the plight of the Palestinians is of little interest and those who are even pleased by it, and there are many Israelis like that—need to ask themselves: Other than joy at Gaza's calamity, what else have we gotten out of this war? Look at the results. Things will only get worse. Is that what you really want?

Israeli Soldiers Shot Two Brothers to Death, a Third Is Wounded and a Fourth Is Arrested

March 8

Human hunting. There's no other way to describe what Israel Defense Forces soldiers were doing last Thursday at the separation barrier in the southern West Bank. Spotting a young man climbing over the wall on a rope ladder, with others awaiting their turn, snipers opened fire at them from an ambush, hitting two of them in the back, one after the other. They fell to the ground on top of each other, bloodied.

The soldiers could have easily arrested the men, called out, fired warning shots in the air or ignored them and allowed them to return home, as they often do in such situations. But this time the preference was apparently to shoot with the intent to kill, to gun down young men whose only sin was to sneak into Israel to find a way to provide for their family, to pick an edible sort of thistle called akkoub in the rocky soil and return home safely.

The two men who were shot were brothers who had permits to work in Israel, as does their father; everyone in the family speaks excellent Hebrew. But since October 7, Palestinians have been barred from entering Israel to work. All together three brothers and a friend set out for the akkoub fields, some of which in fact belong to their family—the security barrier has in essence annexed part of their village's lands to Israel—but they became killing fields.

THE KILLING OF GAZA

And with a vengeance: two brothers killed, a third wounded slightly when the bullet missed him and he was miraculously saved, and a fourth taken into custody. His grieving family still does not know his whereabouts, and he probably doesn't even know that two of his brothers were killed. Israel isn't even considering releasing this fourth brother, who attempted to climb over the wall with other family members after the incident to see what happened. Not so much as an iota of humanity or compassion has been shown by the authorities toward this doubly bereaved family. No compassion or humanity for Palestinians are to be shown here—and that's an order.

Dura is a small city southwest of Hebron. Most of the access roads leading to it, as in virtually all the cities and villages of the West Bank, have been blocked by the army since the war in Gaza erupted. The main route into Dura these days is via the congested streets of Hebron. For our part, while making our way there, we saw a phenomenon we had never witnessed before: resistance at its finest.

The road leading to Dura from the south had been blocked by the army with the usual ramparts of earth and boulders. A local initiative brought about the removal of the ramparts, and a few young people, wearing quasi-military garb and equipped with walkie-talkies, were directing traffic for a fee of 10 shekels (about $2.80) per car, for a round trip. Driving on this improvised toll road is difficult and demanding, it's a rocky route, but hey, we saved an hour by circumventing Hebron.

We were told about this rather amusing new toll road by our escort, Basel Adra, a field researcher for the Israeli human rights organization B'Tselem and a co-director of the film *No Other Land*, which won the Berlinale Documentary Film Award at the international film festival in the German capital last month. Adra had returned directly from the red carpet in Berlin to his home in one of the hamlets in Masafer Yatta, an enclave in the South Hebron Hills—which is the subject of his award-winning film. It's evident that he feels more comfortable here than in the glitter and spotlights.

You have to head west across Dura to get to the small village of Deir al-Asal, whose homes are a few hundred meters from the separation barrier and whose residents usually make a living from work in Israel. Four days after their calamity, members of the Shawamra family are still sitting in front of the residence of their extended family, a five-story stone structure. The bereaved father, Suleiman Shawamra, and the wounded survivor son are dressed in splendid camel-skin desert robes. The family has 150 dunams (37.5 acres) of olive trees on the other side of the wall, which they are given access to once a year for the harvest. This year there is a war in the Gaza Strip, so there was no olive harvest in the Hebron Hills. You try and figure out why.

There are eight remaining siblings in the family. Suleiman, 62, has worked in Israel all his life, mainly in restaurants in Netivot and Jerusalem. He relates that, as a youth, he basically grew up in Moshav Ahuzam, near Kiryat Gat, where he worked in the fields and became friendly with his employers, the Suissa family. "We slept in the same place together," he says longingly.

Last week he decided to send three of his sons to the hills across the cement security barrier and the fence next to it, to gather akkoub, a particularly in-demand ingredient in the Palestinian kitchen, in order to sell it and earn a bit of money. For five months the family has had no source of income. "I sent them," he says, perhaps accusing himself. "I told them: 'Go and make some money.' They didn't want to go. They have wives and children at home and they were afraid. I told them: 'There's no danger. There are no Jews there. You are not going to the city, you are going out to fields. There are only Bedouin there.' My sons also worked in restaurants in Israel since they were 18. Until recently they lived on Hayarkon Street in Tel Aviv and worked at a branch of Tiv Ta'am [a supermarket chain]. We felt no racism and no hatred between us; we grew up together with the Jews."

Early last week they set out: Nur a-Din, 30, the father of a baby boy not yet a year old; Nazem a-Din, 29, the father of a 5-month-old daughter; and Salah a-Din, 24, who married half a year ago. Nur a-Din is sitting with us now—he was spared when the bullet missed his head. Nazem and Salah were killed. Their unmarried 27-year-old brother, Muhi a-Din, 27, was the one who climbed over the wall after the incident and was arrested.

Last Thursday afternoon the three brothers made their way back from the hills. Their akkoub harvest was meager; each of them held a bag containing two or three kilos of not completely ripe plants. The men got to the Israeli side of the barrier at around 4 o'clock. A Palestinian observer standing nearby signaled to them that there were no soldiers and that they could climb over safely.

Nazem a-Din was first up the rope ladder. As he started to climb, three bullets were suddenly fired at him, out of nowhere. He tumbled off the ladder and fell onto his friend and fellow villager, Mohammed Imru, 21, who was standing below waiting for his turn. Instead Mohammed found himself on the ground with Nazem a-Din on top, covered in his blood. Mohammed, who is here with us now, relates that he went into a state of shock; his jittery demeanor and speech show that he's still affected by what he witnessed.

Salah a-Din rushed to the aid of his dying brother. Six bullets slammed into him. He fell on the fence of the patrol road abutting the wall, his arm severed from the force of his fall.

As Nur a-Din bent over to try to help his brothers, a bullet whistled by and grazed his head. He was lightly wounded, but his head is still bandaged. His mental state appears to be dire. During our visit he held his head in his hands and stared at the floor, his body trembling. He says he remembers fainting at the sight of his two fatally wounded brothers.

A military vehicle pulled up and took the two of them, dead or dying at that point, to the nearest checkpoint, Negohot, where a Palestinian ambulance rushed them to the hospital in Dura. The family is certain that if they had been taken to Soroka Medical Center, in Be'er Sheva, the life of Salah a-Din, who died four hours later from loss of blood, would have been saved.

In the meantime, Mohammed, the shocked friend, was handcuffed and blindfolded by the soldiers. He recalls that two soldiers, one a woman, approached and asked, "How is it that you're still alive?" Mohammed lay there, in shackles, for around three hours, he says, and was then taken to an army base, where soldiers occasionally jolted him with a Taser. At 3 a.m. he was released at Negohot. One of his brothers came to pick him up.

The IDF Spokesperson's Unit this week stated, in response to a query from *Haaretz*: "A few months ago, following the outbreak of the Swords of Iron War, and in the wake of the security situation, the rules of engagement were updated in the area of the security barrier and the Judea and Samaria boundary line, with the aim of preventing terrorist activity and infiltration, and in order to thwart the unauthorized crossing of the barrier, other than via the official points of passage. It should be emphasized that approaching the security barrier and the boundary line is forbidden and endangers one's life.

"In the case mentioned, a number of illegally present [Palestinians] tried to cross over the security barrier near the village of Beit Awwa in [the territory of the] Judea Brigade. IDF troops who were on active duty in the area tried to prevent them from crossing by acting in various ways. When the suspects failed to heed the actions, the forces fired at them, and hits were observed. The circumstances of the case are being clarified.

"The [other] suspect was taken into custody, and we do not know of allegations about how he was treated. If complaints are received in this regard, they will be examined according to the regular procedure."

"We grew up in Israel," Suleiman says now. "If our friends there hear what happened to my sons, they will cry. I am ashamed to phone them. Even if there is a war going on, there needs to be a law of human beings. How can you even kill a cat that way? I'm asking you: Put the soldiers on trial. You're a democratic country. My children didn't do anything. Three kilos of akkoub in their hands. Help us. We don't know who to turn to. I worked at Ilan's Corner restaurant in Netivot—everyone knows me."

Muhi a-Din, the fourth brother, tried to tell the soldiers who arrested him that he had a permit to work in Israel—but to no avail, as all such authorizations have been suspended. The family hasn't heard a thing from him since. "Look at our faces," the father says, sadly. "Do you see hatred?"

When Israel Becomes Like Hamas

March 10

Terrible news: Another 27 captives have died in the tunnels of evil; some of illnesses and injuries that went untreated, others from beatings and the horrific conditions in which they were held. For months they have been kept in cages, blindfolded and handcuffed, 24 hours a day. Some are old, many are manual laborers. One was paralyzed, and even when the death rattle began, witnesses reported, he received no medical care.

Representatives of the International Committee of the Red Cross have not been allowed to visit them even once, and their captors have not released their names, so that their families could be informed. The latter know nothing about their fate; perhaps they have lost hope. Their exact number is unknown; their captors provide no information about them. There are an estimated 1,000 to 1,500 detainees, if not more. Of these, 27 have died, and they will not be the last to die in their cages.

No one demonstrates for their release; the world shows no interest in them. They are held in inhumane conditions and their fate is considered inconsequential. They are the captives from Gaza who have been held by Israel since the war began. Some are innocent, some are brutal terrorists. Hagar Shezaf, who uncovered the deaths of so many detainees, reported that most of them are held by the army at the Sde Teiman military base, where soldiers regularly beat and abuse them. Hundreds are Gazans who had worked in Israel with permits and were arrested on October 7 without any cause, and have been held in cages ever since.

On Monday, October 9, two days after the massacre, I saw one such person in the yard of a community center in Sderot that had been turned into a military post: a very old man, who sat on a stool in the yard where anyone could see him the whole day, zip tie handcuffs around his wrists and a blindfold over his eyes. I will never forget the sight. He was a laborer who was arrested; he may be in restraints still, or perhaps he died.

The news about this massacre in prison aroused no interest in Israel. Once, the ground would shake when one detainee died in jail; now 27 have died—most, if not all, because of Israel—and there's nothing. Every death in custody raises the suspicion of foul play; the death of 27 detainees raises the suspicion of a deliberate policy. No one, of course, will be prosecuted for their deaths. It is doubtful anyone will even investigate their causes.

This report should also have raised concern in Israel for the fate of its own captives. What will the Hamas jailers think and do when they hear how their comrades and compatriots are treated? The families of the hostages should have been the first to cry out against the treatment of the Palestinian captives, at least out of concern for the fate of their loved ones, if not out of the knowledge that a state that treats captives in such a way loses moral basis for its demands that its own captives in enemy hands be treated humanely.

Israelis should have been shocked for other reasons as well. There is no democracy when dozens of detainees die in custody. There is no democracy when the state holds people for 75 days without bringing them before a judge and withholds medical care from the sick and injured even when they are dying. Only the most benighted of regimes keep people restrained and blindfolded for months, and Israel is beginning to resemble them at an alarming rate. There is also no democracy that does any of this without transparency, including releasing information on the number, identity and the condition of the detainees in its custody.

How convenient it is to be shocked by the cruelty of Hamas, to present its actions to the entire world and to call its people monsters. None of this gives Israel the right to act similarly. When I said in an interview a few months ago that Israel's treatment of Palestinian captives is no better than Hamas's treatment of ours, and perhaps even worse, I was denounced and fired from the most enlightened current affairs program on Israeli television. After Shezaf's report, the picture is even clearer: We have become like Hamas.

Israeli Leftists, Shake Off the Shock of October 7 and Open Your Eyes to Gaza

March 13

Dear friends and former friends: It's time to sober up from the sobering up.

It was baseless to begin with, but now, nearly half a year after your "eyes were opened," it's time to return to reality. It's time to go back to seeing the whole picture, to reactivate the conscience and the moral compass that were shut off and stored away on October 7, and to see what has happened since then to us and, yes, to the Palestinians.

It's time to remove the blindfolds you put on, not wanting to see and not wanting to know what we're doing to Gaza, because you said that Gaza deserves it and its catastrophes no longer interest you.

You were angry, you felt humiliated, you were stunned, you were terrified, you were shocked and you grieved on October 7. This was fully justified. It was a huge shock for everyone.

But the conclusions you derived from this shock were not just mistaken, they were the opposite of the conclusions that should have been drawn from the disaster.

You don't come after people in their sorrow, certainly not Zionist leftists whose sorrow is their art, but it's time to shake off the shock and wake up. You thought that what happened on October 7 justifies anything? Well, it doesn't. You thought that now Hamas must be destroyed at all costs? Well, no. It's not just about justice, but about recognizing the limits of force.

It's not that you are evil and sadistic, or racist and messianic, like the right. You only thought that October 7 suddenly proved what the right always said: that there is no partner because the Palestinians are savages.

Five months should be enough for you to get over not only your gut reaction, but also your conclusions. October 7 needn't have changed any of your moral principles or your humanity. But it turned them inside out, which is a serious cause for concern about the steadfastness of your moral principles.

Hamas's vicious, barbaric attack on Israel does not change the basic situation in which we live: of a people that has been harassing and tyrannizing another people in different ways and at varying intensities for over a century now.

Gaza didn't change on October 7. It was one of the most miserable places on the planet before October 7 and became even more miserable after it.

Israel's responsibility for the fate of Gaza and its guilt did not change on that terrible day. It is not the only guilty party and does not bear full responsibility, but it has a decisive role in Gaza's fate.

The left cannot evade this responsibility and guilt. After the shock and anger and sorrow, it's time now to sober up from the sobering up and to look not only at what was done to us, as the Israeli media commands us to do day and night, but also at what we are doing to Gaza, and to the West Bank, since October 7.

No, our catastrophe does not make up for that, nothing in the world can make up for that. The right is celebrating Palestinian suffering, reveling in it and wanting more, while the left looks away and keeps dreadfully silent. It is still "sobering up." It's time to stop that.

What the whole world sees and understands should also be understood by at least part of what was once the camp of conscience and humanity. We won't go into the Zionist left's part in the occupation and apartheid, or dwell on its hypocrisy.

But how can an entire people avert its eyes from the horrors it is committing in its backyard, with no camp remaining that will cry out against them? How can such a brutal war go on and on without any opposition within Israeli society?

The Zionist left, which always wants to feel good about itself and consider itself enlightened, democratic and liberal, needs to remember that one day it will ask itself, or be asked by others: Where were you when it all happened? Where? You were still sobering up? It's time for that to end, because it's already getting late. Very late.

Every Person Killed in Gaza Has a Name

March 20

A pretty woman has her picture taken with others in her family. She rests her head on her hand, gazes softly at the camera, a wisp of a smile on her face, aware of her beauty. The woman on her right, possibly her sister, makes the "V for victory" sign with her fingers, and the smile of the third woman, possibly their mother, is restrained. The picture was taken at some kind of graduation ceremony.

It was the last graduation ceremony. The woman in the front of the picture is Jannat Iyad Abu Zbeada. She dreamed of teaching at Gaza University. Earlier this month her face looked out from the front page of the *New York Times*. She was 21 years old. In an initiative to which it is impossible to remain indifferent, the newspaper presented some of the faces behind the numbers, some of the stories behind the dead, some of the people behind the terrorists.

"Their stories offer a snapshot of the vast human loss—about 1 in every 73 of Gaza's 2.2 million people."

As portraits of our hostages and our dead accompany us in the media, in social media, on the streets, as their stories are being told nonstop for about half a year now, it is necessary to have a look at the other, even darker side of the reality as well, the side we refuse to respect, to acknowledge, to feel or observe.

Heba Jourany was a physiotherapist who dreamed of visiting Ireland. Youssef Salama had served as the minister of religious affairs in the Palestinian Authority. Jeries Sayegh belonged to the

Greek Orthodox minority; decades ago he had worked as a bank accountant in Israel. He died, according to *The Times*, from an undiagnosed health crisis after the fighting prevented him from reaching a hospital.

Farajallah Tarazi was also a member of the Greek Orthodox minority and had "studied aviation engineering in Egypt and worked for airlines in Libya and Uganda before returning to Gaza and managing an aid program for the United Nations. He lived near the sea and swam often when the weather was warm. He sheltered with other Christians in a church during the war and died after clashes prevented him from reaching a hospital after his gallbladder ruptured."

Sayel al-Hinnawi, 22, was a law student who initiated a campaign with the slogan "We want to live" aimed against the Hamas regime in Gaza. Osama al-Haddad raised pigeons and goats. Belal Abu Samaan was a gym teacher at the American International School in Gaza. Faida al-Krunz had 15 grandchildren and was about to leave Gaza for the first time in her life for a visit to Turkey. She had already packed her suitcase and had tucked olive oil and za'atar into it.

Mahmoud Elian was Lubna's father. He had bought his 14-year-old daughter a violin. She studied at a conservatory and dreamed of becoming a violinist.

Dr. Abdallah Shehada was a surgeon and had directed the Abu Yousef al-Najjar Hospital in Rafah until his retirement. Ahmed Abu Shaeera, 39, was a garage mechanic. He had left Gaza only once, for the World Cup in Qatar. Salah Abo Harbed was photographed in an amazing parkour stunt on the Gaza seashore and had taught circus arts to children at the Free Gaza Circus Center. Hedaya Hamad was a mental health nurse.

Yousef Abu Moussa was a 7-year-old with a mop of curls, whose mother called him "medallion" and whose father dreamed he would be a doctor like himself. Farah Alkhatib was 12 years old; her twin sister, Marah, survived the bombardment. Her baby sister, who was born during the war, was named after her. Youmna Shaqalih was 4 months old. Her mother was killed in another bombardment. Nada Abdulhadi was 10 when she died. Her 8-year-old sister, Leen, was found dead, trapped among the ruins, four days later.

Siwar and Selena al-Raiss were 3 years old and 21 months old, respectively. The elder sister loved Kinder chocolates; the younger loved to play with a toy Jeep with a picture of a duck on it. In their photo, the girls are seen playing with what appear to be Duplo blocks.

April

Four Black Dots in Khan Yunis, Gaza

April 7

Four friends set out. They walk on a road of leveled sand where homes once stood. They walk with determination; from above they don't look scared. Occasionally they pick up the pace a bit. The road has been furrowed by tank treads. Where are they going? We shall never know. Rubble escorts them on either side of the road.

Their hands are bare, they are unarmed. Here was the Al-Sika neighborhood of Khan Yunis, now just ruins. The man on the far right is talking, gesturing broadly with his arms. What are they talking about? That, too, we shall never know.

Suddenly, from the sky, two bursts of fire in rapid succession and then a cloud of sand and smoke rises above the four. When the smoke clears, we discover the sight of the two mutilated bodies.

The drone continues to film. Like a phoenix, one of the four rises from the inferno and moves away. He tries to flee for his life, but fails. The drone refuses to leave him alone; the drone operator, his or her hand on the joystick, does not relent. The man runs, and the drone camera pans up. Now the man is a tiny black dot, running in terror. No face, arms or legs, just a black dot fleeing desperately for its life.

Zoom out and immediately afterward zoom in, almost a close-up. Now you can see him clearly. Stumbling, he carries a piece of clothing or carpet in one hand. Once more, from the sky, a missile and fire and pillars of smoke. Another successful hit.

The white smoke slowly dissipates, the camera pans left. The second survivor limps and then falls to his knees on the sand, crawling, and then lies down with the last of his strength. These are also his last seconds. The Israeli military does not leave wounded behind.

As he crawls, the fourth missile hits. Another mushroom cloud of smoke, through which another body can be seen. The camera pulls back, like at the end of a movie.

The four bodies lie on the sand, like four crushed insects, surrounded by black ash. What were they thinking when they went unknowingly to their deaths? What were they dreaming about that might have come the next day? What did they leave behind?

Al Jazeera broadcast the video Thursday; Israel yawned Friday. The "General Staff's Fact Finding and Assessment Mechanism," the latest fashion in the field of cover-ups, is examining the incident. That will presumably be the end of it. After all, the Israel Defense Forces does not shoot unarmed people, certainly not intentionally.

"Khan Younis [*sic*] is an active combat zone that underwent significant civilian evacuation. IDF troops have experienced many encounters with terrorists who were disguised in civilian clothing, accessing weaponry hidden within civilian infrastructure," the IDF said on its English-language X account.

The soldiers who shot through the flickering screen in front of them wanted their mandatory military service to be "meaningful," and they got it. What could be more meaningful than killing fleeing figures with remote guided missiles?

They will carry their memories and experiences from the war with them; perhaps one day they will regret it, perhaps not. Perhaps their victims were Hamas fighters—the drone operators presumably will never know. Perhaps they were innocent civilians who went out searching for food for their hungry family. The rumblings of their stomachs could not be heard over the buzzing of the drone. Even if it is proved that the four were looking for food and were members of Gaza's imaginary Salvation Army, no one's conscience will be pricked.

After all, the incident took place beyond the dark mountains of Israeli awareness, perhaps on the India-Pakistan border. People are alive one moment and dead the next; what's the big deal? *C'est la guerre.*

In Six Months in Gaza, Israel's Worst-Ever War Achieved Nothing but Death and Destruction

April 10

Sunday is the six-month anniversary, and it seems this won't be the war's last six-month milestone; no one in Israel has any idea how to end the worst war in its history, whose costs are piling up at an alarming rate and whose benefits are negligible, nonexistent in fact. That is why we must muster the courage to say, after six months of calamities, that it would have been better had it not broken out.

No, no. Israel did have a choice: Don't go to war. If these are its results, it would have been better to show restraint, to punish those who should have been punished for the horrors of October 7 and move on.

Everyone would have benefited, apart from Israel's masculine and military ego, which always imposes disproportionate repayment and punishment, whatever the price may be. This is a supremely childish and foolish policy. Scariest of all is the fear that Israel will behave this way vis-à-vis Iran.

Not even the most advanced ground-penetrating radar could burrow into the ruins of Gaza and its graves to find a single benefit Israel has gained from the war. The unprecedented mountains of damage, by contrast, are visible to the naked eye.

It has all been said before, to no effect, but worst of all is the damage to Israel's moral reputation and, as a result, its global standing. This is near irreversible. It will take years for Russia to recover its position after Ukraine; Israel, similarly, will have to work for years to recover its position after Gaza. But Israel is not Russia; it is much more vulnerable.

Set aside all the stories about antisemitism abroad; only some are true. Anyone who sees what Israel is doing in Gaza could be expected to hate and despise it. But never mind the world; look at what has happened to us: We were always indifferent to the Palestinians' suffering, but now we have set new monstrous records for this indifference.

Limbs are routinely amputated at the Sde Teiman detention facility, and there's no reaction. There are 17,000 children in Gaza who have been orphaned or separated from their parents—and nothing. Israel's physicians aren't protesting over Sde Teiman; neither are its social workers over the starving children and those who have died or been killed. We have become as monsters. Not only in our actions, but above all in our apathy.

Once there were Israelis who were shocked and who called for action. Nearly all of them are gone. Only one righteous doctor in Sde Teiman wrote a letter. It is not known whether he continues cooperating with the evil there.

October 7, six months ago on Sunday, destroyed Israelis' conscience. The agenda now is all-Israeli: There is no one else but us. Only our disasters, our suffering, our sacrifices—and everything else can burn for all we care.

However, when the largest and most advanced medical center in Gaza went up in flames, so did Israel's soul, which was problematic even before. At the end of this war, Gaza will be destroyed and killed, and we will discover a different face staring at us in the mirror. The world will treat us accordingly, just as we would expect it to treat any evil state acting this way.

More and more Israelis are beginning to understand, daring to speak and to sober up from their post–October 7 "sobering-up." The calls for an unconditional ceasefire are growing, even from the pages of *Haaretz*, but they are too late and too hesitant. Bloodthirstiness and sadism have come out of the closet in the past six months and are considered politically correct in Israel.

The next six months of the war could be even worse than the

first. An invasion of Rafah could make the mass killing we've done so far look like a movie trailer.

If so, Israel's northern border will also boil; Iran will also roil. It's better not to go into the completely realistic horror scenarios. Israel will continue collecting the bodies of its hostages, as it did this weekend; the West Bank will join the clients of the war; and, for the first time in its history, Israel will stand alone in the face of all this.

It's better to stop here. Stop with the rather realistic apocalyptic descriptions and stop the war. The first six months was enough for us: More than enough; we're in over our heads.

If Iran Attacks Israel, the Blame Lies on Israel's Irresponsible Decision-Makers

April 12

Gen. Mohammad Reza Zahedi was killed April 1 in a strike on the Iranian consulate in Damascus. Two weeks later, Israel is anxiously bracing for what's next. Judging by the US warning, the Iranian attack is already making its way here, and it could even arrive in the hours between the writing of these lines and their publication.

After a few days of the usual marveling over the amazing targeted-killing capabilities demonstrated in the Syrian capital— what brilliant intelligence forces, what precise weapons—the time to pay the price is approaching, and the cost this time may be unbearably heavy. In any case, it will exceed the value of the killing, which may have been justified but, like all of Israel's targeted killings, was unnecessary, pointless and, this time, probably also dangerous.

Zahedi was a military man; his elimination, like all of Israel's targeted killings, was meant to send a message of deterrence and to reduce the military capabilities of the other side—Iran, in this case. Is there even a single officer in the Israeli military whose killing would significantly affect Israel's military capabilities? There is not, and there never will be.

Why is it that we always tend to believe that in Hamas, Hezbollah or Iran are officers whose elimination would improve our national security? Israel killed Zahedi because the opportunity to kill him arose. And when that kind of opportunity knocks, no one in the top brass ever resists the sweet temptation to execute another brilliant James Bond mission. What will happen afterward?

The fact that nothing has ever happened before is good enough for us. We have never paid a price for these killings. For several years now, Israel has provoked Iran constantly, in Lebanon, in Syria and also on Iranian soil, and has not paid any price. It would be foolish to believe that the rope Israel has stretched will not break. That moment may have come.

Even such a measured and sober military analyst as Amos Harel wrote in *Haaretz* Friday that the killing of Zahedi and that of members of Ismail Haniyeh's family in Gaza on April 10 were carried out without sufficient consideration of the consequences. Harel reported that the relevant Israeli officials apparently did not discuss the implications of the acts at all. It takes an insane amount of arrogance to think that Iran will never react to these provocations.

Anyone who embarks on such a dangerous adventure as killing a Quds Force commander in Lebanon, without first debating the consequences, is a dangerous and irresponsible person for whose actions we will all pay the price. Harel says the assassination in Damascus was carried out following pressure from the military. The political leadership, which approved the operation—Prime Minister Benjamin Netanyahu, to be explicit—bears all the responsibility and the blame for the results, of course.

This must be said, loud and clear: If a war with Iran is ignited this week, or if Iran launches a serious attack on Israel, the responsibility will lie with those who approved the assassination in Damascus.

This is already the second targeted killing of Iranians since the war in Gaza began. Where Iran is concerned, there are no questions of morality or justice, only of wisdom. To provoke Iran at this time—while the Israel Defense Forces is slogging away and bleeding in Gaza, Israel's border with Lebanon is burning, and the West Bank is threatening to do so as well—is a dangerous act that cannot be ignored.

It was clear on the day of the strike in Damascus, while Israelis were winking at each other and drooling over the reports. It is doubly clear now, on the verge of an Iranian attack. It's hard to believe that even after it Israel will begin to demonstrate restraint and reason: The Israeli counterattack will follow immediately, and there we are, at war with the most dangerous and powerful enemy Israel has ever faced.

Is this what the masterminds, the people who issued the orders, the people who carried out the assassination in Damascus, wanted? Is this what we Israelis want? Is this really what we need right now, war with Iran?

Just don't say, again, that there was no choice. There was a choice: not to kill. Even if it is deserved, even if it is permitted and even if it is possible. The person who sent the assassins put Israel at risk of war with Iran.

Israel's Right-Wing Can Never Seem to Get Enough Death and Destruction

April 21

"Dardaleh!" is Israel's new battle cry. "Dardaleh"—Hebrew slang for a weak kick in soccer—is the latest expression of the right's unquenchable thirst for blood and destruction.

"Dardaleh!" Itamar Ben-Gvir tweeted in connection to Friday's strike near Isfahan, expressing his disappointment at the scope of the death and destruction that Israel sowed, and was quoted throughout the world.

It's never enough for the right. It's always dardaleh. The Israeli attack that fully satisfies its lust has not been born. You will never hear the right say: "Enough. We killed and destroyed enough." It will always want more. It is always only the "dunes" that are bombed in Gaza, and even now, when the Strip is in ruins, it's not enough for the right. It wants Rafah. Not Rafah as a military goal, but as a place whose upright condition illustrates the military's dardaleh-ness.

When the army destroys Rafah, and all its refugees are scattered to the winds, this, too, will be a dardaleh operation, which will be followed immediately by the demand to return to the northern Strip and begin the destruction all over again. Otherwise, this will be considered a dardaleh war. "In Gaza we were a herd of elephants that left ruins behind it," Brig. Gen. Dado Bar Kalifa boasted in an interview with Ynet on Friday. To the right, even this herd of trampling elephants is dardaleh.

A word whose origin is unclear, that pretends to be Yiddish but is not, that is mainly used in soccer, has become the truest expression of the right's desire to strike, kill, punish, avenge. Israel kills seven people in an Iranian diplomatic compound in Damascus, including two generals. Iran responds with a fierce attack, but the damage is minimal thanks to the defense systems, and Israel cannot resist. It absolutely must respond.

For the first time in a long while it does so with praiseworthy restraint, but the Ben-Gvirs don't see it this way. As in Gaza, they only want to see more and more Palestinian blood being shed, and they also want to see blood in Iran.

The fact that a harsher Israeli response would have sparked a regional war not only fails to dissuade them—it excites them. Just give them a regional war, preferably against everyone. They're foaming at the mouth; all they want is more. They want Gog and Magog, Armageddon.

When Ben-Gvir tweeted "Dardaleh!" he meant that he wanted a big war with Iran, an all-out war that sparks the imagination, the kind that would bring about the final solution he dreams about.

All the rest—the terrible price that Israel will pay, the blood, the world—is overshadowed by this desire to see as much death and destruction as possible. This is the right's true aspiration.

Ben-Gvir knows that a larger operation would have required Iran to respond, and then Israel would have no choice but to retaliate in its usual manner, and then we are at war with Iran, a nation of 90 million people with an enormous military. This is what the father of the dardaleh theory wants.

It's doubtful there has ever been so much thirst for blood and war in Israel, certainly not so visibly or from a partner in the government. The right has always wanted much more—more territory, more force—but it never lusted for war.

Ben-Gvir knows that in writing "Dardaleh!" he is serving his ever-growing base. They want another war. A war with Arabs and Muslims is the best, bro. Watch Channel 14 news and see the "talent" whose eyes are all but popping out of their sockets in their zeal for war.

We will strike and ravage, ruin and plunder. First we take the Palestinians; then we take the Persians. No one can stop us; we can do it all alone. There is no world, no diplomacy; only force, everything by force, without limit.

The irony is that these people who are so disappointed by the dardaleh are themselves quite the dardaleh. If Israel is attacked, at least some of them will be the last to pay the price—such as Ben-Gvir himself, a paper general who distributes guns to the masses and wants a big war, in which he will take no part, of course. Ben-Gvir the dardaleh.

Palestinian Released from Israeli Prison Describes Beatings, Sexual Abuse and Torture

April 28

There is no resemblance between the young man who sat with us this week for hours in his backyard, and the video of his release from prison last week. In the clip, the same young man—bearded, unkempt, pale and gaunt—is seen as barely able to walk; now he's well groomed and sports a crimson jacket with a checkered handkerchief tucked into its pocket. For 192 days, he was forced to remain in the same clothes in prison—maybe that accounts for his extreme elegance now.

Neither is there any resemblance between what he relates in a never-ending cascade of words that's hard to staunch—more and more shocking accounts, one after the other, backed up by dates, physical exemplifications and names—and what we knew until now about what's been happening in Israeli detention facilities since the start of the war. Since his release, on Monday of last week, he hasn't slept at night for fear of being arrested again. And seeing a dog in the street terrifies him.

The testimony of Amer Abu Halil—from the town of Dura, near Hebron, who was active in Hamas—about what is going on in Ketziot Prison in the Negev is even more shocking than the grim account reported in this column a month ago, of another prisoner, Munther Amira, aged 53, who was incarcerated in Ofer Prison. Amira likened his prison to Guantanamo; Abu Halil calls his prison Abu Ghraib, evoking the notorious facility in Saddam Hussein's Iraq, and later used by the Allies following Saddam's overthrow.

Among candidates for US sanctions, Israel's Prison Service should be next on the list. This is apparently the realm where all the sadistic instincts of the minister of national security, Itamar Ben-Gvir, find their outlet.

We were accompanied on the visit to Abu Halil's home in Dura this week by two field researchers of B'Tselem, the Israeli human rights organization: Manal al-Ja'bari and Basel al-Adrah. Abu Halil, who's 30, is married to 27-year-old Bushra and is the father of 8-month-old Tawfiq, who was born while his father was in prison. Abu Halil met him for the first time last week, though it's still emotionally difficult for him to hold the infant in his arms.

Abu Halil is a graduate in communications from Al-Quds University in Abu Dis, adjacent to Jerusalem, where he was active in the school's Hamas branch, and he is a former spokesperson for the Palestinian cellular communications company Jawwal.

Since his first arrest, in 2019, he's spent a cumulative period of 47 months in Israeli imprisonment, much of it in "administrative detention"—in which the detainee is not brought to trial. The Palestinian Authority also wanted to take him into custody at one time, but he didn't report for the interrogation. Like some of his brothers, Amer is active in Hamas, but he's not a "senior figure in Hamas," he says in his few prison-Hebrew words.

The brothers: Umar, 35, lives in Qatar; Imru, 27, who is suffering from cancer, is incarcerated in Ofer Prison for his activity in Hamas and has spent seven years imprisoned in Israel and 16 months in a Palestinian facility; 23-year-old Amar is sitting with us in a white robe and a kaffiyeh—the imam of the mosque in Dura, he hopes soon to hold the same position in a mosque in North Carolina, which he would like to emigrate to. Not since 2013 have all the brothers—Amer, Amar, Imru and Umar—sat together for a holiday meal. Someone was always in custody.

On one occasion, Amer Abu Halil was summoned to an interrogation by the Shin Bet security service, through a call to his father: "Why haven't you been praying in the mosque lately?" the Shin Bet agent asked him. "Your quiet is suspicious." "When I'm quiet you suspect me, and when I'm not quiet—the same," he told his interrogator. That's how they "sat on" him, as the term goes.

He was in and out of interrogation rooms up until December 4, 2022, when his home was raided in the dead of the night, he was again arrested, and again he was sent into administrative detention with no trial. This time it was for four months, which was extended twice, each time for an additional four months. Abu Halil was slated to be released in November 2023. But then the war broke out and the prison underwent a radical change. The terms of all the Hamas prisoners who were scheduled for release—Abu Halil among them—were extended automatically and sweepingly.

In his latest term, he worked as a cook in the prison's Hamas wing. On the Thursday before the war broke out, he thought of preparing falafel for the wing's 60 inmates, but then decided to postpone the falafel until Saturday. On Friday he delivered the sermon in the afternoon prayers and talked about hope.

On Saturday he awoke at 6 a.m. to prepare the falafel. Inmates there were no longer allowed to prepare their own food or deliver sermons. Not long afterward, Channel 13 broadcast images of

Hamas pickup trucks driving through Sderot, and a barrage of rockets fired from Gaza fell in the area of the prison, which is north of Jerusalem, in the West Bank. "Allahu akbar"—"God is greatest"—the prisoners said accordingly, as a blessing. They hid under their beds from the rockets; for a moment they thought Israel had been conquered.

Around midday, the prison guards arrived and impounded all the televisions and radios and the cell phones that had been smuggled in. The next morning they didn't open the cell doors. The shackling, beating and abuse began on October 9. On October 15, large forces entered the prison and confiscated all personal items in the cells, including watches and even the ring Abu Halil wore that had belonged to his late father. That marked the start of 192 days during which he was unable to change clothes. His cell, which was meant to hold 5 inmates, now held 20, afterward 15 and more recently 10. Most of them slept on the floor.

On October 26, large forces of the Prison Service's Keter unit, a tactical intervention unit, accompanied by dogs, one of them unleashed, stormed into the prison. The wardens and the dogs went on a rampage, attacking the inmates whose screams left the whole prison in a state of terror, Abu Halil recalls. The walls were soon covered with inmates' blood. "You are Hamas, you are ISIS, you raped, murdered, abducted, and now your time has come," said one warden to the prisoners. The blows that followed were brutal; the inmates were shackled.

The beatings became a daily affair. Occasionally the guards demanded of prisoners that they kiss an Israeli flag and declaim, "Am Yisrael chai!"— "The people of Israel live!" They were also ordered to curse the prophet Mohammed. The usual call to prayer in the cells was prohibited. The prisoners were afraid to utter any word starting with the sound "h" lest the guards suspect they had said "Hamas."

On October 29, the supply of running water to the cells was halted, except between 2 p.m. and 3:30 p.m. And each cell was permitted only one bottle for storing water for an entire day. That was to be shared by 10 inmates, including for use in the toilet inside the cell. The doors of the toilet were ripped off by the guards; the inmates covered themselves with a blanket when they relieved themselves. To avoid a stench in the cell, they tried to contain themselves until water was available.

During the hour and a half when there was running water, the prisoners allocated five minutes in the toilet to each cellmate. With no cleaning supplies, they cleaned the toilet and the floor with the bit of shampoo they were given, using their bare hands. There was no electricity at all. Lunch consisted of a small cup of yogurt, two small, half-cooked sausages and seven slices of bread. In the evening they received a small bowl of rice. Sometimes the guards delivered the food by throwing it on the floor.

On October 29, the inmates of Abu Halil's cell requested a squeegee to wash the floor. The response to that was to send the terrifying Keter unit into their cell. "Now you will be like dogs," the guards ordered. The prisoners' hands were cuffed behind their back. Even before they were shackled, they were ordered to move only with their upper body bent over. They were led to the kitchen, where they were stripped and forced to lie one on top of the other, a pile of 10 naked prisoners. Abu Halil was the last. There, they were beaten with clubs and spat on.

A guard then started to stuff carrots into the anus of Abu Halil and other prisoners. Sitting at home now, reciting his story, Abu Halil lowers his gaze and the flow of words slows down. He's embarrassed to talk about this. Afterward, he continues, dogs hunched over them and attacked them. They were then allowed to put on their underwear before being led back to their cell, where they found their clothes thrown into a heap.

The loudspeaker in the room wasn't silent for a second, with curses of Hamas leader Yahya Sinwar or a sound check in the middle of the night to the tune of "Get up, you pigs!" to deprive the prisoners of sleep. The Druze guards cursed and abused in Arabic. They underwent checks with a metal detector while naked, and the device was also used to deliver blows to their testicles. During a security check on November 2 they were made to chant "Am Yisrael am hazak" ("The people of Israel is a strong people"), a variation on a theme. Dogs urinated on their thin mattresses, leaving an awful smell. One prisoner, Othman Assi from Salfit, in the central West Bank, pleaded for more gentle treatment: "I am disabled." The guards told him, "Here no one is disabled," but agreed to remove his handcuffs.

Yet the worst was still to come.

November 5. It was a Sunday afternoon, he recalls. The administration decided to move the Hamas prisoners from Block 5 to Block 6. The inmates of cells 10, 11 and 12 were ordered to come out with hands bound behind their back and the usual hunched-over walk. Five guards, whose names Abu Halil provides, took them to the kitchen. Again they were stripped. This time they were kicked in the testicles. The guards would lunge at them and kick, lunge and kick, again and again. Nonstop brutality for 25 minutes. "We are Bruce Lee," the guards proclaimed. They shook them and shoved them around like balls from one corner of the room to the other, then moved them to their new cells in Block 6.

Guards claimed that they had heard Abu Halil saying a prayer on behalf of Gaza. In the evening the Keter unit entered his cell and began beating everyone, including 51-year-old Ibrahim al-Zir from Bethlehem, who is still in prison. One of his eyes was almost torn out from the blows. The prisoners were then forced to lie on the floor as the guards stepped on them. Abu Halil lost consciousness. Two days later came another round of blows and he passed out again. "This is your second Nakba," the guards said, referring to the catastrophe experienced by Palestinians at the time of Israel's founding. One of the guards struck Abu Halil on the head with a helmet.

Between November 15 and 18 they were beaten three times a day. On November 18, the guards asked which of them was Hamas, and no one replied. The blows weren't long in coming. Afterward they were asked, "Who here is Bassam?" Again, no one replied, because none of them was named Bassam—and again the Keter unit was called in. They came that evening. Abu Halil says that this time he passed out before being beaten, from sheer fright.

Around this time, Tair Abu Asab, a 38-year-old prisoner, died in Ketziot Prison. It's suspected that he was beaten to death by guards for refusing to bow his head as ordered. Nineteen guards were detained for questioning on suspicion of having attacked Abu Asab. They were all released without any charges.

In reply to a request for comment, a Prison Service spokesperson sent *Haaretz* the following statement this week: "The Prison Authority is one of [Israel's] security organizations, and it operates in accordance with the law, under the strict supervision of many oversight authorities. All prisoners are held in accord with the law and with strict protection of their basic rights and under the supervision of a professional and trained corrections staff.

"We are not familiar with the claims described [in your article], and to the best of our knowledge, they are not correct. Nonetheless, every prisoner and detainee has the right to complain via the accepted channels, and their claims will be examined. The organization operates according to a clear policy of zero tolerance of any action that violates the values of the Prison Service.

"With regard to the death of the prisoner, you should be in touch with the unit for the investigation of prison officers."

May

Let Israel's Leaders Get Arrested for War Crimes

May 5

All decent Israelis must ask themselves the following questions: Is their country committing war crimes in Gaza? If so, how should they be stopped? How should the culprits be punished? Who can punish them? Is it reasonable for crimes to go unprosecuted and criminals to be exculpated?

One may, of course, reply in the negative to the first question—Israel is not committing any war crimes in Gaza—thereby rendering the rest of the questions superfluous.

But how can one answer in the negative in the face of the facts and the situation in Gaza? About 35,000 people killed and another 10,000 missing, about two-thirds of them innocent civilians, according to the Israel Defense Forces; among the dead are around 13,000 children, nearly 400 medical workers and more than 200 journalists; 70 percent of homes have been destroyed or damaged; 30 percent of children suffer from acute malnutrition; 2 people in 10,000 die each day from starvation and disease. (All figures are from the United Nations and international organizations.)

Is it possible that these horrific figures came to be without the commission of war crimes? There are wars whose cause is just and whose means are criminal; the justice of the war does not justify its crimes. Killing and destruction, starvation and displacement on this scale could not have occurred without the commission of war crimes. Individuals are responsible for them, and they must be brought to justice.

Israeli hasbara, or public diplomacy, does not try to deny the reality in Gaza. It only makes the claim of antisemitism: Why pick on us? What about Sudan and Yemen? The logic doesn't hold: A driver who is stopped for speeding won't get off by arguing that he's not the only one. The crimes and the criminals remain. Israel will never prosecute anyone for these offenses. It never has, neither for its wars nor its occupation. On a good day, it will prosecute a soldier who stole some Palestinian's credit card.

But the human sense of justice wants to see criminals brought to justice and prevented from committing crimes in the future. By this logic, we can only hope that the International Criminal Court in The Hague will do its job.

Every Israeli patriot and everyone who cares about the good of the state should wish for this. This is the only way that Israel's moral standard, according to which it is permitted everything, will change. It is not easy to hope for the arrest of the heads of your state and your army, and even more difficult to admit it publicly, but is there any other way to stop them?

The killing and destruction in Gaza have gotten Israel in way over its head. It is the worst catastrophe the state has ever faced. Someone led it there—no, not antisemitism, but rather its leaders and military officers. If not for them, it wouldn't have turned so quickly after October 7 from a cherished country that inspired compassion into a pariah state.

Someone must stand trial for this. Just as many Israelis want Benjamin Netanyahu to be punished for the corruption of which he is accused, so should they wish for him and the perpetrators subordinate to him to be punished for much more serious crimes, the crimes of Gaza.

They cannot be allowed to go unpunished. Neither is it possible to blame only Hamas, even if it has a part in the crimes. We are the ones who killed, starved, displaced and destroyed on such a massive scale. Someone must be brought to justice for this.

Netanyahu is the head, of course. The picture of him imprisoned in The Hague together with the defense minister and the IDF chief of staff is the stuff of nightmares to every Israeli. And yet, it is probably warranted.

It is highly unlikely, however. The pressure being exerted on the court by Israel and the United States is enormous (and wrong). But scare tactics can be important. If the officials actually refrain from traveling abroad in the next few years, if they actually live in fear of what may come, we can be sure that in the next war, they'll think twice before sending the military on campaigns of death and destruction of such insane proportions. We can find a little comfort in that, at least.

What About the Palestinian Hostages?

May 16

Dr. Adnan al-Bursh was the head of the orthopedic wing at Shifa Hospital in Gaza City. During the war, he had to wander from one hospital to the next, as they were all destroyed by the IDF. He has not been back to his home in Jabalya since the start of the war, and last December all trace of him disappeared. Recently, it transpired that he had died in an Israeli jail, apparently due to the torture of beatings during interrogation.

The last people to see him were other doctors and detainees who have been released. They told *Haaretz* correspondents Jack Khoury and Bar Peleg that they had barely recognized him. "It was clear he had been through hell, torture, humiliation and sleep deprivation. He wasn't the person we knew; he was a shadow of himself."

A photo of him published after his death showed an elegant man. A photo from during the war showed his hospital gown covered in blood. He had a wife, Jasmine, and they had six children. He studied medicine in Romania and did a residency in the United Kingdom. The rapper Tamer Nafar wrote a beautiful lament for him. (*Haaretz*, May 6.)

A doctor, a hospital ward director, was beaten and tortured to death in an Israeli jail. That did not set off alarms here. Nearly all his physician colleagues, including heads of the medical establishment and those who take part in the horrific torture ongoing at Sde Teiman base and in Israeli prisons, did not say a word. A department director was beaten to death.

So what? After all, almost 500 doctors and medical staffers have been killed in the war and their fate failed to arouse any attention. So why should al-Bursh's death attract any attention? Because he was a department director? No war crime committed by Israel in Gaza has aroused any feelings here in Israel, with the exception of the joy felt by the bloodthirsty right-wing.

On top of the doctor's death came another heinous act: the response of the authorities. The Shin Bet was silent as usual. Ex–Shin Bet officers are now star commentators on television, asked to show us the way, to give us their opinion, but the Shin Bet never talks about those it has interrogated and tortured. The IDF shirked responsibility; the doctor was only "processed" at an army detention facility and was immediately transferred to the Shin Bet interrogation facility in Kishon, and from there to Ofer Prison, which is under the charge of the Israel Prison Service. The IPS response was pure audacity: "The service does not address the circumstances of the deaths of detainees who are not Israeli citizens."

A man dies in prison, yet the Israel Prison Service does not think it should report the circumstances of his death to the public because he was not a citizen of the state. In other words, the lives of those who are not citizens have no value in Israeli prisons. We should remember this when an Israeli is arrested in Cyprus for rape, or in Peru for drugs, and we are outraged by the conditions of his detention. We remember this even more poignantly when we complain to the world, and rightly so, about the fate of our hostages.

How can people identify with the pain felt by Israelis over the fate of the hostages, when these same Israelis turn out to be cold-hearted and indifferent to the fate of the other side's hostages?

Why isn't there a single banner in Tel Aviv's "Hostage Square" calling for an investigation into the killing of the doctor from Gaza? Is his blood less red than the blood of the Israeli hostages who died? Why should the whole world take an interest and work only for our hostages, and not for the Palestinian hostages, whose conditions of imprisonment and whose deaths in Israeli prisons should horrify everyone?

At Last, Justice; but Will Israelis Start Waking Up?

May 23

At last, justice; the very earliest signs of the beginning of a late, partial justice, yet still a measure of justice.

There is no joy in your prime minister and your country's defense minister about to become wanted all over the world, but it is impossible not to feel some satisfaction about the beginning of some doing of justice.

In Israelis' wallowing and victimhood, in endless self-righteous panels on TV, in cries about an antisemitic world and the injustice of bundling Israel with Hamas, there's one fundamental, fateful question missing: Did Israel commit war crimes in Gaza? No one dares deal with this critical, key question: Were there, or were there not, crimes?

If war crimes were committed, mass killing and starvation, as suggested by the courageous prosecutor Karim Khan (in whose appointment Israel was involved behind the scenes, having found his predecessor suspect), then there are criminals responsible for them. And if there are war criminals, it is the world's duty to being them to justice. They must be declared wanted and arrested.

If Hamas committed war crimes—and there seems no argument about this—then its criminals must be brought to justice. And if Israel committed war crimes—and there seems no argument about this in the world, except in suicidal, self-deceiving Israel—those responsible for them must also be brought to justice.

Bundling them does not imply moral symmetry or legal equivalency. Even if Israel and Hamas were accused separately, Israel would have raised a ruckus against the court.

The only argument heard now in Israel is that the judge is a son of a bitch. The only means suggested preventing his harsh sentence is by causing harm to the International Criminal Court in The Hague.

To convince friendly nations not to uphold its rulings, to impose sanctions (!) on its judges—this is how every criminal thinks, but a state has no right to think that way. The two international courts, in which Israel and Israelis are standing trials, deserve the state's respect, not its contempt. Contempt of court by Israel will only add to the list of accusations and suspicions against it.

Better for Israel, at this difficult moment, to look inward, at long last, to see its own portrait. Better it blamed itself for something, anything, rather than blame the entire world. How did *we* come to this? That should be the question, rather than how did *they* come to this?

When will we finally take responsibility for anything, for something done in our name? The 106 MKs who've signed the petition against the ICC and the zero MKs who've signed the nonexistent petition against Israeli war crimes are a sad reflection on the country: united against doing justice, united in an eternal sense of victimhood, no right and no left, a heavenly choir. If Israel is one day convicted of war crimes, it must be remembered that 106 MKs voted to whitewash those of Benjamin Netanyahu and Yoav Gallant.

The Gaza Strip is in ruins, its residents killed, wounded, orphaned, starved, destitute, though most of them were innocent. This is clearly a war crime. Starvation is viewed by everybody in Israel as a legitimate means, to be supported or opposed, as is intentional mass killing. How could anybody make the case that there was no starvation or intentional mass killing?

The day after the ICC, Israel must regroup for an introspective national reckoning, something it has never done before. Every

Israeli must ask themselves: How have we come to this? It is not enough to blame Netanyahu, the main culprit; neither is it enough to whitewash this with evasive arguments about hasbara, faulty legal counsel and extreme remarks from Israeli officials.

The issue runs far deeper: For 57 years, Israel has been maintaining a regime of wrongdoing and evil, and now, at last, the world is waking up and starting to act against it. Will it also be able to wake up at least some Israelis from their heedless, twisted sense of justice?

Obeying the ICJ Order Is Israel's Last Opportunity to Save Itself from Becoming a Pariah State

May 26

Israel has only one way out; it won't choose it. The only way to avoid tumbling into the abyss whose edges we now skirt is to say yes to Friday's ruling by the International Court of Justice.

This is how a state governed by laws must behave. This is how a state that aspires to be a legitimate member of the family of nations should behave. Prime Minister Benjamin Netanyahu should have already promised compliance on Friday evening. The gates of hell that threaten to open on Israel would remain closed, at least briefly. An Israel that obeys the court will be a state that is ruled by laws and that must be respected.

By saying yes, he would not only have saved it from further pointless bloodshed in Rafah, he also would have stopped the international snowball that is barreling toward the state. Ending the fighting in Rafah and the entire war is Israel's last possible chance to regain its prewar international standing. It's not much, but it's much more than it has today.

If Israel decides to ignore the order—a near certainty—it will be declaring itself a pariah state. Recovery from this situation will take years and extract an intolerable price, some of it personal, from every Israeli.

But as always, Israel is searching for ways to ignore the order and to recruit Washington into undermining international law. It is hard to imagine any greater folly. We must hope, of course, for America and for Israel, that this time the United States will draw the line on its willingness to defy the entire world, and international law, for the sake of its wayward protégé state.

One step from the abyss, there are two urgent measures that Israel must take: ending the war and replacing its government. The world's top two courts ordered it to do exactly that. The chief prosecutor of the International Criminal Court requested international arrest warrants for Israel's prime minister and defense minister, and the International Court of Justice ordered an end to the fighting in Rafah.

If arrest warrants are issued for Netanyahu and Defense Minister Yoav Gallant, they will have to replace the government if they want to survive. Ending the fighting in Rafah will bring an end to the whole war and also the release of the hostages. Israel will not comply with either ruling. They are too logical, correct and just for it.

Since the hasty withdrawal from Sinai in 1956, Israel has never acceded to the will of the international community, as if the world and its decisions have nothing to do with it. Invulnerable and protected by America, the Bible and a certain nuclear research center in Dimona, it has always acted as if it had license to scoff at the whole world. That ended the day it invaded Gaza in such a brutal, unchecked manner.

Judge Nawaf Salam, the president of the ICJ, barely finished reading out the verdict when Israel intensified its attacks on Rafah, a city from which almost 1 million people have fled for the beaches and in which just one eight-bed hospital remains.

Salam was still reading the ruling when, for the first time in years, Sufyan Abu Zaydeh, a former minister of prisoners' affairs in the Palestinian Authority, who fled from Gaza to Cairo, called me: Eight members of his family were killed Wednesday in Jabalya.

Marwa, his niece, was the only one who was not asleep when the missile tore into her family's home. She saw it all, like in a horror movie, she told her uncle in the Egyptian capital. The missile killed his other niece, Iman; in her arms was her 7-month-old daughter, who was also killed. Her 4-year-old son was thrown into the neighbors' apartment and killed. She also saw how the missile tore apart the bodies of her 4-year-old twins, Isr and Asr, and severed the arm of her son Nasser, 7. Marwa's mother and brother were also killed before her eyes by the missile. She lost her husband at the beginning of the war. He was killed during the funeral of his niece.

This is what the International Court of Justice demanded an end to Friday. This is Israel's last chance.

June

Biden Wants Peace, but Israel Wants War

June 2

When Benjamin Netanyahu rejects the US president's proposal from Friday night—actually, he's already done that—Israel, and not just the International Criminal Court in The Hague, will be compelled to declare him a war criminal. A negative response to Joe Biden's proposal, the best offer in town, the last chance for saving the hostages, will constitute a war crime.

Saying no to Biden means saying yes to more futile, wholesale bloodshed, of Israeli soldiers and, more so, of Gaza's inhabitants; yes to the death of the last of the hostages in Hamas captivity; yes to genocide; yes to war in the north; yes to declaring Israel a pariah state. If Netanyahu says no to Biden—nothing could be more certain—he will be saying yes to all of the above. And someone affirming all of the above should be condemned as a war criminal by his own country, unless we are all war criminals.

Between Friday and Saturday nights, one could still have taken pleasure in the delusion that Netanyahu would say yes and that the war would end. The US president's offer, ostensibly an offer made by Netanyahu, was a work of art in its composition, a judicious diplomatic plan for exiting the disaster zone of Israeli-Palestinian relations. There will never be a better plan. It heralds the last chance for Israel to abandon this war and cut its losses.

But every Saturday comes to an end, with warmongers emerging from their Shabbat lairs. With his choice of presenting his plan during the evening prime time for secular Israelis, Friday night, Biden afforded us a glimmer of hope, one that vanished as soon as it appeared, with the appearance of three stars in Israel's skies, heralding the end of Shabbat and the continuation of the war.

Biden means well. Israel has nefarious intentions. Biden wants peace, but Israel wants war. Even Hamas, at this point, wants peace more than Israel does. Throughout this war, I refused to believe that Netanyahu was driven entirely by his own political fate.

The Netanyahu I knew, I believed, had other considerations. In saying no to Biden, he is erasing the last vestiges of statesmanlike demeanor he had assumed, if any still remain, the aura of relative moderation and mainly what we believed for years: that when deploying the army and embarking on war, he was the most cautious and measured prime minister Israel has ever had.

The October 7 war cracked this belief from its outset. Continuing the war now will end this perception for good. Continuing the war not only bolsters suspicions regarding Netanyahu's motives, it also bolsters suspicions regarding his partners and extortionists on the right: Genocide is what they're after. There is no other way of describing their lust for revenge and blood, always insatiable.

But one doesn't have to wait for their words. Leaflets dispersed on Saturday by the IDF in Beit Hanoun, calling on refugees who had returned to their destroyed homes to again evacuate them, are the true Israeli response to President Biden's plan to end the war. They also illustrate what the war will look like from now on: an endless cycle of death and destruction. After Rafah we go back to the beginning, to the northern Gaza Strip, like in a game of Monopoly, but with cruelty, and from there southward to Rafah, through the ruins of Jabalya, and so on, in blood-soaked mud.

The army's printing presses will not stop printing leaflets, and the refugee Palestinians will be moved like cattle in a slaughter-house, until no stone is left standing in Gaza, or "wood scraps for a fire or coal for a stove, a place with no bread, fire, water, only with handfuls of ashes," in the words of the poet Moshe Tabenkin.

Biden wanted to put an end to all this. He's wanted to for a long time. He wants to but doesn't do a thing. To his plan presented on Friday he should have added one resolute sentence: If Israel rejects this plan, the US will immediately stop providing it with arms. Right away. Only thus can this nightmare be ended, a horror with no end in sight for now.

Why Did Israel Conceal Hundreds of Gazans' Deaths in "Perfect" Hostage Rescue Operation?

June 12

Can a society exist without a conscience? Can a state continue to function after its removal? Is the conscience a vital organ, like the heart or the brain, or is it like the spleen or the gallbladder, which you can live without?

Perhaps it's like the thyroid: You can live without it, as long as you take a replacement for the hormone. These questions should be asked by every Israeli now, after the country underwent a total "consciencectomy" on October 7, 2023. Israel has been without a conscience ever since. For now, it appears to be alive.

The process that Israel has undergone in the past several months can only be described as a separation from its conscience. It had been sick for years; now it is dead. There are a myriad explanations and justifications, but the question remains, in all its force: How can a society continue to endure over time without a conscience?

On the night of October 7, with all the atrocities that the day brought, Israel said to itself: We are done with conscience. From now on, it is only us, there is no one else. From now on, there is only force, nothing else. For us there are no dead children in their thousands, or their dead mothers; no total destruction or starvation; no expulsion of destitute people or the inflicting of total terror.

Nothing interests Israel anymore other than its sacrifice, the punishment it was subjected to, its suffering and courage. Recent days have provided definitive proof of this. Subsequently, there is no more room for questions about its moral sense. It's gone.

The euphoria that erupted in Israel after the rescue last Saturday of the four hostages was justified, human, sweeping and very moving. The blindness that accompanied it attested to the demise of the national conscience.

On the day of the rescue operation alone, according to the Hamas-run Gaza health ministry, 274 people died in the Nuseirat refugee camp and another 698 were injured. The images of convoys of ambulances, private cars and donkey carts carrying hundreds of wounded people and corpses to the completely overwhelmed hospital in Deir al-Balah were among the most difficult of the war.

Israel chose to conceal them, to erase their memory, to deny their existence, as though, if they are hidden and ignored, they did not happen.

Israel wrapped itself in joy; this whole week, songs of praise—for the bold operation, which was indeed bold, for the bravery of the rescuing soldiers, who were indeed courageous, for the officer who was killed and for whom the operation will be named—have been on constant repeat, and with not a word about what else happened in Nuseirat in the course of the operation.

When Daphna Liel of Channel 12 news describes the operation as "perfect," what does she mean? That 300 deaths are perfection? And if 1,000 people had been killed, would Liel still think that the operation was perfect? Would tens of thousands of dead bodies have crossed Liel's line of perfection? What number would have been crossing the line for Israelis? Would 1,000 bombs dropped on Nuseirat have raised questions? It is very doubtful.

When the commander of the Border Police, Maj. Gen. Itzhak Brik—the hero of the hour, whose forces rescued the hostages—says they carried out a "surgical" operation and were driven by "values," what is he referring to? What would killing people in a manner not driven by values look like? Are 300 dead people a "surgical" operation? What would genocidal killing look like?

When no one says differently or corrects such statements, when no one expresses reservations or even adds an asterisk so as not to mar the joy of the masses on the country's beaches, something is very sick here.

Obviously the moving rescue should have been celebrated. Israelis deserve a moment of joy in the hell they've been living in for months, which isn't over yet. But one cannot, must not, ignore the price paid by Palestinians, even if there are people who believe that the price was unavoidable or even entirely justified.

A society that ignores so blatantly the price paid by tens of thousands of people, with their lives, bodies, souls and property, for the rescue of four of its hostages and for a moment of joy for its members, is a society that is missing something vital. It is a society that has lost its conscience.

Afterword

Two hours ago, the streets of Tel Aviv were again filled with the call of air-raid sirens. It was a surprise. It's been seven months since the war began, three months have passed since I wrote the introductory lines to this book, which I opened with a description of the first round of rocket fire, on the morning of October 7, and again rockets are being launched at Tel Aviv. If any further proof were required of the hopelessness of this Gaza war, of its endless complications, the eight rockets fired two hours ago from east of Rafah, and which landed in the northern and eastern suburbs of Tel Aviv, should have provided it. It is a war without purpose or benefit, without victories or victors. One of the world's best-armed, most technologically advanced and well-trained armies has been unable to destroy Hamas, an organization that is short on financial means, armaments, personnel and technology, not even after 233 days of fierce combat and the partial conquest of the Strip. Another 233 blood-filled days like this are unlikely to change anything.

Israel's situation has worsened beyond description as a result of this war, while the standing of Hamas has soared to a level it's never before known. Its fighters, both those who have fallen and those still alive, are heroes in the Arab world, as well as in certain circles in the Western world, notwithstanding the crimes they carried out on October 7. Even if the organization paid a heavy price in the damage sustained by its forces, the damage suffered by Israel is far worse.

Israel has become a pariah state, more so than at any time in the past. Its balance sheet reflects only heavy losses, some of them irreversible, and includes no obvious accomplishments. It did not destroy or incapacitate Hamas, of course; neither has it succeeded in freeing the majority of hostages being held by Hamas, which is the Israelis' greatest desire. It would be difficult to overstate the significance of this issue in terms of the impact it has on the connection Israelis feel toward the state, or about the latter's responsibility to its citizens at a time of need.

Many Israelis feel betrayed. The shadow of the hostages' fate, and the inability and even lack of desire on the part of the government and the army to effect their release, hover over Israeli society and will continue to do so, like a black cloud, for years to come.

From the global perspective, Israel is even more of an outcast than it was on October 6. Economically, socially, and in terms of its leadership and its security, it is weaker than before, its security is more threatened, on all fronts, than ever before, and its army was revealed at its weakest and most incompetent, both on October 7, and after it, too. The only accomplishments the army can point to consist mainly of an insane number of deaths among Palestinians and the sowing of a level of destruction no less incomprehensible.

During these months of war, Israelis have begun again to ask whether their country will still exist in another 50 years, a question that is not asked about any other country. Many Israelis—it's difficult to estimate their numbers—see no future for themselves here, and certainly not for their children. A life lived by the sword has become intolerable for many of them.

Two international tribunals are currently considering hearing cases involving charges against Israel. This is unprecedented. The International Court of Justice is examining the question of whether Israel is carrying out genocide in Gaza, while at the International Criminal Court, prosecutor Karim A. A. Khan has requested the issuance of international arrest warrants against not only three Hamas leaders, but also against Israel's prime minister, Benjamin Netanyahu, and its defense minister, Yoav Gallant.

University campuses in the US and Europe have been roiled this spring by anti-Israel demonstrations, and the BDS movement has chalked up unprecedented victories in the form of boycotts that are only growing and spreading. Israelis are beginning to feel the world's ostracism in a growing number of fields. Many airlines did not resume their flights to Israel (following the initial weeks of the war), and boycotts are becoming more prevalent in academia, the economy, culture and the arts. Israel is being punished for its deeds, perhaps for the first time in its history.

All this, however, is dwarfed by the price paid by Gaza and its residents. At the time I wrote the introduction to this book, 25,000 deaths were being reported in Gaza. Now, as I write this afterword, the death toll had exceeded 36,000, and according to the World Health Organization, the situation there was "beyond catastrophic." Nearly a million Gazans have been made refugees three times over, most recently being forced to flee Rafah, the city of refuge earlier declared such by Israel, for the village of Al-Mawasi. There, they can look forward neither to safety nor to basic human services—but to little more than sand.

Refugees who have remained in Rafah have been exposed to intense Israeli attacks. It's unlikely that anyone who is not personally in Gaza today, at the start of summer 2024, is truly able to imagine the life of a refugee there. It is no better than hell—a hell created by humans, Israelis in this case.

Two days ago, my cell phone rang. This was around the same time that the president of the International Court of Justice, Nawaf Salam, was reading out the ruling of the court on the motion filed by South Africa, joined by other nations, calling for an order to halt the Israeli invasion of Rafah. On the phone was a friend from the past, Sufyan Abu Zaydeh, who was once the minister of prisoner affairs in the Palestinian Authority, a resident of Jabalya refugee camp in Gaza, who fled to Cairo at the start of the war.

After we exchanged a few sentences of polite greeting—we hadn't spoken for a number of years—Sufyan told me how eight members of his extended family had been wiped out a day earlier when an Israeli missile hit their home in Jabalya. He struggled to find the words to describe the horrific news, and so he sent me instead a long text message, which I am offering here verbatim:

How can one heal this rupture? Marwa, my beloved niece, was the only one still not asleep when a missile penetrated the window of one of the rooms and shredded to pieces the bodies of the members of an entire family. She saw it all, as if she were watching a horror movie. The missile exploded as it made a direct hit on the body of Iman, the daughter of my second sister, who held her 7-month-old daughter, turning the two of them into slabs of meat. Iman's son, Sami, who was not yet 4—his small body was sent flying toward the neighbor's house.

Marwa had not lost consciousness, saw how the rocket ripped through the bodies of the twins, Isr and Asr, before it hit her 7-year-old son, Nasser, whom God spared when he had the rocket suffice with just cutting off his left hand.

Marwa, whom I so loved, saw how her brother, Abdul Rahman, my beloved nephew, had his body ripped into by the missile: He was still alive when he reached the hospital, where he offered up his soul to the Creator. In the other room was my sister, Umm Salah, who had taught generations of children at the UNRWA [United Nations Relief and Works Agency] school in Jabalya camp, and her husband, my cousin Abu Salah, and [their child] Adam, my beloved nephew, age 12, whose small body was unable to withstand the force of the explosion, and he, too, was blown to bits. Umm Salah ... did not survive the cursed explosion, and whatever the missile did not do to her directly was completed by her being buried beneath the ruins of the house. Abu Salah, God should give him salvation, came out with only a few broken bones.

Will the world believe that such a combination of disasters could befall a single Palestinian woman, all of 32 years old? Marwa had lost her husband at the start of the war, when he was bombed by a plane while he was in the cemetery. He had been there to bury his niece, who had been murdered a short time earlier, and he ended up being buried himself at the same place.

Now she has lost her twin children, she has lost her mother, who had embraced her and provided salve for some of her pain after her husband's death, she has lost her foot and had her son lose a hand, she has lost her sister Iman and her two children, she has lost Abdul Rahman and Adam, both of whom were torn into pieces before her eyes.

Yesterday, when she told me in detail, what had happened, she recounted how when her son Nasser was taken to the hospital, she begged the doctors not to bury him by accident. He told her, "I am not dead, I'm alive. Don't bury me, I only fell." O God, O God, how can this sadness be made to go away, and how can one possibly heal this rupture?

Sufyan Abu Zaydeh was one of the prominent people of peace belonging to the Fatah movement during the era of the Oslo Accords. Prior to that, he had been imprisoned for some years in an Israeli prison for involvement in terror crimes. After his release, he did a doctorate at the University of Exeter, in the United Kingdom, on the subject of Israeli policy on the Jerusalem question. He speaks Hebrew fluently, has many Israeli friends, and during the Oslo period, he would appear frequently in the Israeli media, when Palestinians were still interviewed in the local press.

Now Abu Zaydeh is a refugee in Cairo, and has just suffered the destruction of part of his family, and he asks: "How can this sadness be made to go away, and how is it possible to heal this rupture?" His question can only remain hanging in the air, unanswered.

Here, apparently, there are no more words.

Tel Aviv, May 25, 2024

Acknowledgments

This book would not have come into existence were it not for two important organizations: *Haaretz*, the newspaper that is my second home, and Verso Books, my regular publisher.

I have been writing for *Haaretz* for 42 years, 36 of which I have spent covering the occupation of the Gaza Strip and the West Bank. Such work would not have been possible at any other media outlet in Israel—and it's by no means clear that there are many papers in the world that would have allowed it. To write about the crimes committed by your country and your army; to see as human beings those whom many of your countrymen view as enemies; and to describe life and death among another people, who live under the boot of conquest of your own state—these are subjects that are easy neither to digest nor to publish. In an Israel that has undergone brainwashing of a sort, they are close to impossible. *Haaretz* allowed me to do just that. It has supported me over all of these years—stubbornly, steadily and with trust—even when that support came with a heavy price.

Hence, my initial gratitude is to the publisher of *Haaretz*, Amos Schocken; its editor-in-chief, Aluf Benn; the editor of its opinion pages, Alon Idan; and to the rest of my colleagues, the editors and writers of *Haaretz*. They stood by me, even when they didn't always agree with my positions, and they made this journalistic endeavor possible. A special thanks goes to the translators at *Haaretz*, one of the only newspapers in the world that comes out daily in two languages, Hebrew and English. A special thanks to David B. Green, who, in addition to editing a large portion of my columns in *Haaretz*, also translated the introduction and the afterword of this book, and to Ralph Mandel, who translated nearly all of the columns when they original appeared in the paper.

Verso Books encouraged me to bring out my first collection of columns, *The Punishment of Gaza*, in 2014, and it was Verso that initiated publication of this book. My thanks to editorial director Leo Hollis, my editor there, and to all the people at Verso who participated in the creation of this book.

I would not be able to carry out my journalistic work without the help of Israel's dedicated, brave and professional human rights organizations. In particular, I owe a debt of gratitude to B'Tselem—the Israeli Information Center for Human Rights in the Occupied Territories, whose field researchers have accompanied me for years with limitless dedication. A big thanks also to photographer Alex Levac, winner of the Israel Prize for Photography, who for years has been at my side on my expeditions into the occupied territories with his sensitive camera and gaze.

A final thanks goes to Catrin Ormestad, a journalist in the past, and a novelist in the present, my partner and my love. We met in Gaza and together we set off on an exciting and fascinating journey that has continued for 18 years—which is roughly the amount of time that Israel's siege of Gaza has been in place. That may be one of the only good things that has emerged from Gaza during these cursed years. Without Catrin, her support or her wise counsel, this book would not exist.